Writing Deafness

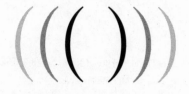

Writing Deafness

THE HEARING LINE IN

NINETEENTH-CENTURY

AMERICAN LITERATURE

CHRISTOPHER KRENTZ

The University of North Carolina Press

Chapel Hill

The paper in this book meets the guidelines for permanence and durability
of the Committee on Production Guidelines for Book Longevity of the
Council on Library Resources.

Library of Congress Cataloging-in-Publication Data

Krentz, Christopher.

Writing deafness : the hearing line in nineteenth-century American
literature / Christopher Krentz.

p. cm.

Includes bibliographical references and index.

ISBN 978-0-8078-3118-2 (cloth: alk. paper)

ISBN 978-0-8078-5810-3 (pbk.: alk. paper)

1. Deaf—United States—History—19th century. 2. Deaf, Writings of the,
American. 3. Deaf authors. 4. American literature—19th century—History
and criticism. I. Title.

HV2545.K74 2007

810.9'3527209034—dc22   2006039794

Portions of this work appeared earlier, in somewhat different form,
in "Exploring the 'Hearing Line': Deafness, Laughter, and Mark Twain," in
Disability Studies: Enabling the Humanities, ed. Sharon L. Snyder, Brenda
Jo Brueggemann, and Rosemarie Garland-Thomson (New York: Modern
Language Association, 2002), and in *A Mighty Change: An Anthology of
Deaf American Writing 1816–1864* (Washington, D.C.: Gallaudet University
Press, 2000). Reprinted here with permission of the publishers.

cloth   11 10 09 08 07   5 4 3 2 1

paper   11 10 09 08 07   5 4 3 2 1

For my parents

(((CONTENTS)))

(((ILLUSTRATIONS)))

(((ACKNOWLEDGMENTS)))

Writing Deafness has roots in my personal experience. I am late deafened; my hearing has gradually faded since I was nine years old. As I was growing up, literature provided me with a welcoming place. While spoken conversation was sometimes difficult for me to follow, and films and television programs typically were not captioned, reading offered a way for me easily to comprehend what was being said (on a literal level, anyway). After college, I found my way to the deaf community and began to learn American Sign Language, interact with deaf signers, and proudly identify myself as deaf. When I went to graduate school at the University of Virginia and reread classic works of American literature, I found I experienced them in a new way.

Many friends, teachers, and institutions have shaped this book, and it is a pleasure to thank them even if I cannot acknowledge them all here by name. This project started as my dissertation. Eric Lott and Stephen Railton believed in it from the very beginning and offered invaluable encouragement, guidance, and insight as it gradually took shape. When I began writing, I was part of a group lobbying for the establishment of an American Sign Language (ASL) program, and that spirit of activism probably animates these pages. Ellen Contini-Morava, Lisa J. Berke, and John Bonvillian made especially good co-agitators in the cause, as did a lively cadre of deaf and hearing students.

I am indebted to Michael Olson and Ulf Hedberg at the Gallaudet University Archives and to David Halberg and Winfield McChord Jr. at the American School for the Deaf for their affable and essential assistance. They not only enabled me to find the information I was seeking, but also told good stories along the way. The library staffs at Yale, Harvard, the University of Virginia, the University of Chicago, the American Antiquarian Society, and the Portsmouth Athenæum helped me to locate additional archival materials.

A portion of chapter 5 appeared in Sharon L. Snyder, Brenda Jo Brueggemann, and Rosemarie Garland-Thomson, eds., *Disability Studies: Enabling the Humanities* (Modern Language Association,

2002). Very early versions of segments of chapters 1 and 4 were published in my anthology, *A Mighty Change: An Anthology of Deaf American Writing 1816–1864* (Gallaudet University Press, 2000). Thanks are due to the publishers for permission to reprint this material and to Rosemarie Garland-Thomson and John Vickrey Van Cleve for their editorial guidance.

A number of people generously read the entire manuscript or individual chapters and offered helpful suggestions and advice: Stephen Arata, Alison Booth, Arlene Clift-Pellow, Stephen Cushman, Jessica Feldman, Rita Felski, Susan Fraiman, Jahan Ramazani, Lisa Woolfork, and especially Douglas Baynton, Brenda Jo Brueggemann, Ellen Contini-Morava, and Lennard J. Davis. Their comments have greatly improved the book, although I know I have not answered all their penetrating questions. Jennifer Wicke was a generous source of advice, and Eric Schramm helped to prepare the manuscript. Sian Hunter and Ron Maner at the University of North Carolina Press provided immense support in bringing the book to completion. I am also grateful to the University of Virginia for a Sesquicentennial Associateship and small grants that enabled me to focus on writing.

This study also would not have been possible without Gallaudet University, the world's premier college for deaf people. Inspired by the 1988 Deaf President Now movement and the school's charismatic deaf president, I. King Jordan, at age twenty-three I sought a staff position there. During four wonderful years at Gallaudet, I discovered how rich deaf experience can be. Jean Lindquist Bergey initially made me feel welcome. Stephen Ryan, Lorraine Flores, and Angela Farrand were my first ASL teachers, serving as models of patience and encouragement as I tried to learn a radically new language. Bernard Bragg, Clayton Valli, and Gilbert Eastman introduced me to the grace and beauty of ASL poetry and storytelling, while Jack Gannon and Vic Van Cleve interested me in deaf history. Mary Anne Pugin traveled with me to visit alumni chapters in thirty-three states and Canada, giving me a fun and fascinating tour of deaf America. Lynda Carter, Kubby Rashid, and Anne Marie Baer also taught me much and remain good friends.

Others have kept me going along the way. My students at the University of Virginia have helped me to develop my ideas, as have the gifted and witty instructors in the U.Va. ASL program. Greg Propp, sign language interpreter par excellence, has added to my joy in teaching. Ben Bahan, Dirksen Bauman, Carol Padden, Kristen Harmon, and others in the small field of Deaf Studies have offered indispensable encouragement. The Disability Studies in the Humanities and Deaf Academics e-mail discussion lists have given me supportive communities of scholars who are interested in similar topics; my work would have been far more challenging without them. My college roommates Patrick Clyde, John Comeau, Elbert Ocañas, and Andrew Silbiger kept me laughing with their messages from afar. Friends in my deaf game night group and at Charlottesville signing suppers have provided many fun get-togethers, while I have gained happiness and companionship from the women I have been lucky enough to date.

Finally, I wish to thank my family. My siblings Peter, Michael, Elizabeth, Susie, and Matthew have, each in their own way, added much to my life and kept me both confident and humble. I cannot begin to say what I owe my parents, Edgar and Marion Krentz, to whom this book is lovingly dedicated.

Writing Deafness

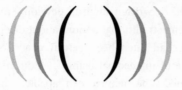

Introduction

The instruction of deaf mutes has now become so general,
that it has almost ceased to excite the amazement which was at
first felt, on seeing those who were deemed beyond the pale of intellectual
beings, addressing themselves to others, in intelligible language, often in
signs and gestures far more expressive than words. The prejudice . . .
is vanishing before the demonstrative evidence given, even in
our country, that they possess minds not less susceptible of
cultivation than those of other men, and often far
above the ordinary level.
American Annals of Education (1834)

We are not beasts, for all our deafness! We are MEN!
John Jacobus Flournoy (1858)

It is as though we dread to acknowledge the complex,
pluralistic nature of our society, and as a result we find
ourselves stumbling upon our true national identity under
circumstances in which we least expect to do so.
Ralph Ellison (1986)

During the nineteenth century, deaf people became much more visible in the United States. With the rise of deaf education, they began to come together, learn written English, develop American Sign Language, and challenge traditional notions about deafness. Whereas before deaf people had often been perceived as isolated individuals "beyond the pale of intellectual beings" ("Education" 2), now they increasingly seemed to be members of a capable, cohesive group. They not only fascinated hearing people who saw them in public, but also started to publish essays, poetry, and fiction, making an impression on the nation's consciousness. No surprise, then, that hearing authors like Herman Melville and Mark Twain began to include deaf references in their work, for, as Toni Morrison puts it, "National literatures . . . do seem to end up describing and inscribing what is really on the national mind" (*Playing* 14). Such writing by hearing and deaf Americans forms a compelling discourse over what it means to be deaf or to hear, a revealing aspect of American literature and identity formation that has generally been overlooked.

This study examines how nineteenth-century American writers treat what I call the hearing line, that invisible boundary separating deaf and hearing people. I deliberately echo W. E. B. Du Bois's color line, for one argument of this book is that the history of deaf Americans contains some striking parallels to that of African Americans and other minorities, and I frequently draw upon theoretical work on race and culture to explain how Americans negotiated deafness.[1] Scholars have begun to recover the history of deaf education and the American deaf community[2] and, more generally, have made strides in considering disability and physical difference in the project of American self-making.[3] However, the way deafness figures into national literature and identity has not been adequately explored.[4] By considering the complexities surrounding the literary emergence of deaf people in nineteenth-century America more carefully, we will find that the meanings of deafness and its conceptual opposite, "hearingness," were at least as unstable as other identity categories, and something that Americans repeatedly felt constrained to test, probe, and attempt to demarcate. These negotiations with the hearing line have significant implications for our understanding of our founding literature, of the minority experience in the United States, of the nation's history and culture, of the production of American identity, and of nineteenth-century thought about such central topics as language, humanity, intelligence, religion, disability, normality, and passing.

To get at these matters, *Writing Deafness* adopts a contrapuntal approach. First, this study calls attention to an overlooked literary corpus: writing by deaf Americans, who, like other minorities in the nineteenth century, turned to writing to demonstrate their reason and humanity to the American public. It also offers fresh perspectives on canonical authors like Washington Irving, James Fenimore Cooper, Melville, and Twain, whose work often has a surprising amount to say about deafness and hearingness. By putting deaf and hearing authors into conversation with each other, my project strives to deepen our appreciation of both. As Edward Said has noted, "It is more rewarding —and more difficult—to think concretely and sympathetically, contra-puntally, about others than only about 'us'" (*Culture* 336). This study attempts just such a method. In the process, I strive to illuminate ways that deafness parallels, intersects with, or differs from other, more recognized identity categories, such as race, gender, class, and sexual orientation. I seek some idea of the ways that people in nineteenth-century America experienced their deafness or hearingness, a topic that goes to the heart of how Americans grappled with difference and defined themselves.

Some readers might think that deafness is a rather marginal concern, of interest only to a few people. When I described this project to a senior professor of American literature, he looked thoughtfully into space for a moment, then admitted that he could not think of a single example of deafness in canonical writing. His reaction typifies a general sentiment: critics rarely consider deafness, and when it does arise they often perceive it as tangential or even antithetical to both "American" and "literature."[5] However, one insight of some recent scholarship is that the margin can illuminate the center. I aim, in Rosemarie Garland-Thomson's words, to "probe the peripheral so as to view the whole in a fresh way" (*Extraordinary* 6).

Yet more to the point, deafness was not quite a minor concern in nineteenth-century America. It was a site of fascination. Hearing Americans often viewed deaf people as mysterious, captivating figures, wondering how they thought, what they experienced, and seeing them as a way to explore what it means to be human. To them, educated deaf people were exciting examples of progress who destabilized long-held assumptions. Public exhibitions of deaf students routinely attracted hundreds of spectators, including notables such as presidents James Monroe and John Quincy Adams. Many other prominent influential leaders and thinkers during the period had contact with deaf individuals. When the deaf educator Laurent Clerc visited Congress in 1820, Speaker of the House Henry Clay declared a half-hour recess so congressmen could meet him. Clay later visited a school for deaf students, as did Monroe, Andrew Jackson, the artist John Trumbull, General William Tecumseh Sherman, and Rutherford B. Hayes. Charles Willson Peale painted Clerc and his family, while John Carlin, a deaf artist, painted the son of Jefferson Davis. Carlin also developed friendships with William H. Seward, Horace Greeley, and the wife of President Franklin Pierce. Samuel Morse and Alexander Graham Bell were married to deaf women. Bell's invention of the telephone ironically resulted from his efforts to create a device that would make speech visible to deaf people. Thomas Edison became quite deaf himself. Horace Mann wrote on deaf education, while Samuel Gridley Howe spent years teaching Laura Bridgman, a deaf-blind woman. During the Civil War, Laura Redden Searing, a deaf journalist, interviewed congressmen, generals, and soldiers by writing back and forth with them. Searing also maintained a long correspondence with General Ulysses S. Grant. Moreover, writers such as the Hartford Wits, Lydia Huntley Sigourney, William Cullen Bryant, and Mark Twain personally interacted with deaf people. At the end of the century, Helen Keller attracted national notice. Such a partial listing suggests the many ways that deaf Americans began to engage the national psyche. This new attention became especially apparent in 1864, when Congress authorized the first college in the world for deaf people and President Lincoln signed the bill into law. The new National Deaf-Mute College (now Gallaudet University) gave recognition and opportunity to a group long confined to the social margins. Located in Washington, D.C., just a mile from the U.S. Capitol, the college symbolized how deaf Americans had begun to move from the outermost regions of society toward the center of the nation's consciousness.

As deaf people became more prominent in society, they also became more evident in the national literature. The hearing line appears not only in writing by nineteenth-century deaf authors like Clerc and John J. Flournoy, but also in our most familiar classics. From Ishmael calling a whale deaf to his discussion of a deaf "weaver-god" in *Moby-Dick* (1851), from Jim trying to communicate with his deaf daughter 'Lizabeth to the duke acting deaf in *Huckleberry Finn* (1885), the hearing line shows up again and again. It resides in Ellen Craft's feigning deafness as she escapes from slavery in *Running a Thousand Miles for Freedom* (1860), in Melville's mysterious deaf stranger at the beginning of *The Confidence-Man* (1857), in Sigourney's sentimental poems about deaf children, and in the deaf boy protagonist of Ambrose Bierce's horrific tale "Chickamauga" (1889).

Without the hearing line, in the twentieth century we would have no fiction like Carson McCullers's *The Heart Is a Lonely Hunter* (1940), Flannery O'Connor's "The Life You Save May be Your Own" (1953), or Ken Kesey's *One Flew over the Cuckoo's Nest* (1962); no plays like Elmer Harris's *Johnny Belinda* (1940), William Gibson's *The Miracle Worker* (1959), or Mark Medoff's *Children of a Lesser God* (1982), all of which became films; no performances of Beethoven's music or of the Who's rock opera *Tommy* (1969); no *Seinfeld* episodes with deaf characters; no National Theatre of the Deaf stage productions; and no videos of deaf artists performing stories and poetry in elegant American Sign Language. Such imaginative works reveal another frequently unacknowledged element of what Ralph Ellison calls "the complex, pluralistic nature of our society" (*Going* 125).

More generally, we could say that the hearing line resides behind every speech act, every moment of silence, every gesture, and every form of human communication, whether physical deafness is present or not. In terms put forward by Eve Kosofsky Sedgwick, this study employs both a "minoritizing" and a "universal" view of difference, one which simultaneously recognizes a specific minority population (deaf Americans) while seeing issues surrounding deafness and hearingness as having "continuing, determinative importance in the lives of people across the spectrum of [identities]" (1). The discourse over the hearing line pertains to all people and is ultimately as pervasive as discourses about race, gender, sexuality, class, and disability. In the United States, it was during the nineteenth century, as deaf Americans collectively emerged into society, that the significance of this hearing line began creatively to be tested and explored.

ON BINARIES AND REALITY

Some readers may resist my metaphor of the hearing line, and with good reason. First, it seems to create yet another reductive binary opposition, parceling human beings into two opposing categories and ignoring the complexities therein. As the essayist Nancy Mairs points out, "Binary thinking is merely a habit of mind, and despite the comfort of order and familiarity it offers, it doesn't apprehend reality, which is, let's face it, a frightful jumble" (13). Yet even while acknowledging this complexity, Mairs often invokes a neat dichotomy—disabled and nondisabled—to describe people. It seems humans have the need to classify and label, even if those generalizations are often not accurate.

Nineteenth-century Americans routinely employed categorical language about auditory status that masked a more complicated truth. Early in the century, the preferred term for people who did not hear was "Deaf and Dumb"; toward midcentury, "deaf-mute" became widespread; and later in the century, as oralist educators insisted that all deaf people possessed the ability to speak, simply "deaf" became prevalent. Occasionally authors distinguished these groups from people "who hear and speak," but usually hearingness was left unremarked, an omnipresent norm. The reality was much more chaotic. Today we know that most so-called "deaf" people have some residual hearing (only about 10 percent of deaf people hear nothing at all). While some deaf people were born deaf, many others lost their hearing later, after they had heard sound and learned spoken English. Some "Deaf and Dumb" people could use their voices effectively. Nineteenth-century writers periodically employed liminal terms like "semi-mute" or "semi-deaf" in attempt to rectify such inaccuracies, with limited success; as frequently happens with identity labels, there is often a gap between the nomenclature and the reality. Moreover, some "hearing" people had progressive hearing loss, were tone deaf, experienced temporary deafness, or had a hearing loss on certain frequencies. When we recall that some deaf people successfully passed as hearing, and that a few hearing people signed as fluently as their deaf counterparts, we further see how the division of humans into "deaf" and "hearing" obscured a wide assortment of identities that was quite variable and fluid. The binary does not do justice to this more unstable reality, and yet in the nineteenth century, as today, absolute labels were routinely employed. I turn to the hearing line not to reify fantasies of absolute division, but because it usefully expresses how many nineteenth-century Americans thought about deafness.

As a concept, the hearing line complicates theory on identity formation by drawing from both essentialist and constructivist notions of difference. One significant undertaking in recent literary criticism has been the deconstruction of secure, independent notions of the self. Post-structuralist scholars have focused on how one's identity depends on culture, often maintaining that classifications like race, gender, and sexuality have no inherent biological basis. Yet deafness and hearingness do of course have an essential component, what David Mitchell has called the "hard kernel" of physical difference "that cannot be deconstructed away" ("Narrative" 17). During the nineteenth century, some hearing people, like Edward Miner Gallaudet, signed well and supported deaf causes, attaining special stature in the deaf community. However, they were never considered "deaf." Similarly, gifted deaf lipreaders who associated with hearing people, like Alexander Graham Bell's wife, Mabel Hubbard Bell, were never "hearing." The biological difference always remained. Because audition is invisible—because deaf and hearing people look the same, after all—the manifestation of the hearing line often comes as a surprise. It appears unexpectedly through behavior, when a person does or does not react to sound or communicates in a specific manner. As we will see, so incongruous does the hearing line sometimes seem that people occasionally suspect that it is not real. It serves as a recalcitrant reminder of the consequence of corporeal variation to who we are. At the same time, its significance is always socially inflected, varying with historical moment, culture, discourse, and context. As soon as it appears explicit, the hearing line fades; as soon as it appears not to exist, it inevitably reemerges. It must perpetually be retested and reimagined. Endlessly elusive, the hearing line reveals a complex and shifting relationship between physical difference, cultural fabrication, and identity, which has implications for larger contemporary debates in the humanities over the formation of the self.

Readers may also object that the hearing line unfairly mimics the color line, a metaphor that plays such a dominant role in America's past. For while this study aims to place auditory status alongside gender, race, ethnicity, and sexuality—alongside the broad array of identity categories—it most often, and most specifically, compares deaf Americans to African Americans. These two groups are of course not mutually exclusive. However, during the nineteenth century, deaf authors and public figures were invariably white (and predominantly male), the closest to the hegemonic norm in American society. They faced fewer obstacles than their black deaf peers. In every southern state except Maryland and Kentucky, it remained illegal to teach a slave—hearing or deaf—to read and write until after the Civil War.[6] Information on education of black deaf people in the North during the nineteenth century is difficult to locate. In 1834, the *American Annals of Education* reported that "in the Northern institutions, colored pupils are received as well as white; but . . . a very small number are yet under instruction" ("Education" 15). Most black deaf people seem to have gone without education and participated only tangentially if at all in the emerging white deaf community.[7]

Critics could rightfully point out many obvious and crucial differences between white deaf Americans and hearing African Americans. After all, blacks made up a significant portion of the U.S. population, while deaf people were relatively few in number. While blacks could trace their ethnic roots to a specific continent, deaf people had no geographical homeland. Although deaf Americans encountered severe prejudice and ostracism, they did not have to endure anything like the crime of chattel slavery, were not forcibly separated from their families, and were not the victims of lynch mobs. Despite the public fascination with deaf people, their struggles were not nearly as prominent as those of blacks in American culture as a whole, and they were not at the center of a devastating civil war. In addition, African Americans, for all their unique oral forms, could communicate directly through vocal speech with white people, while deaf people often struggled to make themselves understood to hearing people who did not know sign language. Furthermore, while African Americans pass on their cultural identity through family, from generation to generation, deaf people seldom do so. Although at least 30 percent of deafness is genetic, less than 5 percent of deaf children have deaf parents (Mitchell and Karchmer 157). As a result, most deaf children enter families that have little understanding of their situation, an experience more akin to that of gay people than blacks.[8] There is danger that, in comparing white deaf people with hearing African Americans, such important differences will be elided and this project will be seen as trying to co-opt the hard-won history of the color line.[9]

Accordingly, *Writing Deafness* strives to acknowledge critical distinctions while calling attention to some intriguing parallels that can enrich our understanding of both groups, and of minority experience in nineteenth-century America in general.[10] Both African Americans and deaf people have been deemed inferior, savage, and less than fully human; both have been denied full participation in society; both have been linked with evil; and, most important for this study, during the nineteenth century both groups employed similar strategies to gain recognition of their intelligence and humanity and to achieve a measure of social justice. These parallels allow me to use and modify African American theories to approach deafness, even as I seek to heed crucial differences.

One does not have to look far to find evidence of the historical derogation of black and deaf people. In the Greco-Roman and Judeo-Christian traditions, black and deaf people often are presented as lesser, deficient, or immoral. For example, in Plato's *Phaedrus*, Socrates uses a figure of both blackness and deafness to describe one of the parts of the soul, "badness": "The other is crooked of frame, a massive jumble of a creature, with thick short neck, snub nose, black skin, and gray eyes; hot-blooded, consorting with wantonness and vainglory; shaggy of ear, deaf, and hard to control with whip and goad" (qtd. in Gates, *Signifying* 237). People often saw blackness as a sign of malevolence, disorder, and lewdness versus the purity and grace of whiteness; in the same way, they frequently perceived deafness as the antithesis of the intelligence, awareness, and spirituality of hearing. Regardless of the Declaration of Independence's assertion that "all men are created equal," in 1776 few Americans truly subscribed to this egalitarian vision. As Michael McCarthy has pointed out, the view of black people as biologically subordinate, reinforced by a belief in the natural supremacy of whites, justified the use of African Americans as slaves. In 1823, William Faux reported to his British countrymen that "contempt of the poor blacks, or niggers, as they are there called, seems the national sin of America" (9). In the same way, society often viewed deaf people as lesser creatures bearing an unfortunate curse. This attitude goes back at least as far as Aristotle, who was credited with saying that people born deaf were incapable of reason, a statement that contributed to a long line of thinking that equated deafness with stupidity and insanity.[11] According to Katherine Jankowski, in the first decades of the republic this association led many states to legislate that deaf people could not be held responsible for criminal acts (20). The very word "deaf" contains these negative implications; it has its roots in the Indo-European base *dheubh*, which denotes confusion, stupefaction, and dizziness.

Such perceptions gave credence to the view that neither African Americans nor deaf Americans were worth educating. Although many people did not have access to schooling in the first decades of the republic, for deaf or black individuals education was extremely rare. At the time of the 1790 census, more than 90 percent of the black people in the United States were enslaved and all but a few illiterate. While they did not have to contend with slavery, most congenital deaf people also had no schooling. It is true that some African Americans, such as Benjamin Bannaker, managed to educate themselves, while some deaf children from wealthy families, like the Bollings of Virginia, were able to attend schools for deaf students in Europe. But for the most part, black or deaf individuals in early America were uneducated and could not read or write, and lived ostracized (in very different ways) from society.

If African Americans and deaf people frequently lived in oppressive circumstances, at the outset of the nineteenth century several broad but influential cultural forces held out the prospect of change. The spread of humanism, together with the founding democratic ideals of the nation, contributed to a view that all people had worth and deserved opportunity to pursue liberty and happiness. Religion was also a dominant force, inspiring Quakers and evangelical Protestants to campaign for the abolition of slavery (of course, it also provided proponents with strong arguments to justify slavery). In addition, as Douglas Baynton has demonstrated, during the Second Great Awakening religion made ministers wish to convert and civilize purportedly savage groups, including Native Americans, blacks, and deaf people. Going along with these trends, many nineteenth-century Americans had a desire to see "progress," especially social progress, where the nation as a whole would grow stronger, more just, and more successful.

Developments in Europe also had an impact, causing some Americans to think that their nation lagged behind in its treatment of blacks and deaf people. In 1807, the British Parliament voted to abolish trade in slaves, giving new encouragement to abolitionists everywhere. Britain emancipated slaves in its colonies in 1838, while France followed suit ten years later. Such actions made at least some Americans feel the United States was less progressive than European countries. Similarly, in the eighteenth century deaf education began to take hold in the Old World. Since the Renaissance, various priests and philosophers in Europe had experimented with educating individual deaf people, chipping away at the old notion that deaf people were ineducable. In France in the 1760s, the Abbé de l'Epée, a supporter of sign language, founded the Royal Institute for the Deaf, which contributed to the rise of a vibrant deaf community in Paris. By the conclusion of the eighteenth century, at least eighteen schools for deaf students had opened in Europe, including institutions in Amsterdam, Edinburgh, Madrid, Malta, Munich, Paris, Prague, Rome, and Zurich. With slavery still firmly entrenched in the American South, and no schools for deaf people at all, some observers could understandably perceive the United States as less civilized than their European counterparts. Almost all white, hearing Americans in the nineteenth century still firmly believed the biological paradigm that they were inherently superior to black or deaf individuals, but some thinkers began to express the conviction that, with charity and education, such "lesser" people could be brought up closer to their level. They argued that freeing slaves and educating blacks and deaf people was the Christian, moral, and patriotic thing to do.

In this climate, with its mixture of subjugation and opportunity, during the nineteenth century African Americans and deaf Americans took a more active role in shaping their fate. As we will see, both groups turned to writing to demonstrate their reason and humanity to a skeptical public. In addition, both employed public speeches and exhibitions to challenge widespread assumptions about deafness and blackness, and both forged partnerships with white, hearing advocates to work toward their goals. As the century unfolded, each group began to come together and empower themselves. Outside of the South, the maturation of free black communities, the rise of abolitionism, and the opening of African Free Schools helped blacks to form a stronger, more educated collective consciousness, much as the establishment of schools and associations of deaf people lead to the emergence of a distinctive deaf American "we." They were further united linguistically. While some members of both groups became literate in standard English, most also used original modes of communication (American Sign Language and black vernacular English), linguistic systems that bonded them together and expressed their communal identity apart from the majority. The founding of publications by and for black and deaf people signaled this developing consciousness further. Moreover, in some places blacks and deaf people established their own churches, clubs, civic organizations, and artistic groups. Brought together by their common languages, experiences, and values, not to mention their shared subjection, they regularly came to present a more positive version of their identities to the world.

As the meanings of blackness and deafness became increasingly unhinged in the United States, African Americans and deaf people occasionally found themselves torn between a desire to assimilate with mainstream society and a desire to preserve their unique sense of self apart from it. Tellingly, at various times members of both groups argued that blacks and deaf people should relocate to places where they could escape prejudice and manage their own affairs. This separatism contrasted with advances in civil rights and recognition of black and deaf people's capabilities, including the emancipation of slaves and the establishment of federally chartered colleges for deaf Americans and African Americans in Washington, D.C. The National Deaf-Mute College opened in 1864, three years before one of the nation's first colleges for African Americans, Howard, another indication of how the odysseys of African Americans and deaf people resemble each other.[12]

In the latter decades of the century blacks and deaf people saw some of their hard-won gains recede. Freed blacks had to endure racial hatred, bigotry, and systematic segregation; in the South, as many as one thousand African Americans were lynched during the 1890s. With the advent of "oralism"—an insistence that deaf people communicate only by speaking and lipreading, and not through sign language—culturally deaf Americans found their language of signs under attack, their job opportunities diminished, and their right to marry each other increasingly proscribed. Intermixed with these developments was a growing uneasiness over the increasing diversity in culture and languages in the United States. New theories of evolution and the rise of the eugenics movement led many white, hearing Americans to see black and deaf people as unfit, which was another way of expressing the classic notion that they were biologically inferior. Such attitudes were often tragically self-fulfilling: discriminated against and denied opportunity, black Americans and deaf people were less successful in society than their white, hearing peers. As this all-too-brief overview suggests, the dynamics of the color and hearing lines are not unconnected.

The historical parallels I have sketched out above have implications for this study, for they enable me to draw upon theories of African American experience and literature to understand how nineteenth-century Americans responded to deafness. *Writing Deafness* employs not only Du Bois's concepts of the color line and double consciousness, but also criticism on racial passing and blackface minstrelsy. The work of Henry Louis Gates and others on the paradoxes of African American authors trying to represent themselves in standard English, a language in which blackness is often a mark of evil and emptiness, helps to elucidate the similar challenges with which deaf American writers struggled. In the same way, Toni Morrison's concept of an Africanist presence in the founding literature of the United States allows me to discern a similar "deaf presence," made up not just of deaf characters, but also of depictions of silence, sound, and deaf-related metaphors. Just as the Africanist presence helps to construct whiteness, so the deaf presence participates in the formation of hearingness, another aspect of the invisible but prevalent norm in nineteenth-century American culture. Because the subject here is not race but deafness as a metaphor and reality, my study in turn modifies and transforms these theories, bringing to light new issues such as the role of vocal speech, the biological family, and deaf racial minorities that are not usually discussed in race politics.

While I most often use theories related to African Americans, I also employ postcolonial, disability, gender, and class readings to explore the hearing line and to call attention to the ways that the hearing line revises our understanding of these approaches. For example, I discuss how the establishment of residential schools for deaf students in some ways resembles a colonizing enterprise. Yet even as such schools segregated deaf people and taught them the dominant ideology, they also empowered deaf students by bringing them together, revealing how in certain situations colonization can have benefits and showing new aspects of concepts such as hybridity and affiliation. My study also illuminates disability issues. While deaf Americans who use sign language resemble an ethnic group or linguistic minority, they also have links to blind, lame, or other disabled people who differ from the majority because of genes, illness, or accident. Nineteenth-century deaf people were the first disabled American group to receive special education, the first to organize in a widespread way, the first to contest lack of access, prejudice, and pathological views of their difference, and as such pioneered the beginnings of disability activism in the United States, a contribution that has not received sufficient acknowledgment from scholars in disability studies. Standing at the juncture of minority culture and disability, deaf Americans offer insight into both phenomena while remaining distinctly unique. With regard to gender, *Writing Deafness* points out that most nineteenth-century deaf leaders were men, while hearing authors who chose to write sentimental or horrifying representations of deaf people almost always depicted deaf women (or children). Class, too, shows up in this analysis, as the majority of deaf writers were educated and of a higher class than the average deaf American citizen, while Melville and others sometimes depicted deaf beggars. Through such examples, we see how the hearing line is gendered, reflects race and class, and revises our understanding of postcolonial and disability approaches. In this way, I aim not only to build on prior frameworks, but also to generalize new theoretical as well as political knowledge.

As my overview indicates, binary oppositions like the color line and hearing line express and sustain a system of power relations. Such divisions are never equal. In a well-known analysis, Sedgwick explains how oppositional categories that seem natural and equivalent (heterosexual/homosexual in her case, but by extension male/female, white/black, and similar dichotomies) actually exist in a dominant-subordinate relationship, where the first group is esteemed and the second degraded. However, the first group achieves its superiority only by repeatedly shunning the second group, an ongoing division that must be continually enforced. As a result, the first group paradoxically depends on the second group for its dominance and identity, which puts the supposed supremacy of the first group in perpetual danger. Sedgwick concludes, "The question of priority between the supposed central and the supposed marginal category of each dyad is irresolvably unstable, an instability caused by the fact that term B is constituted as at once internal and external to term A" (9–10). This instability characterizes both the color and hearing lines. Hearingness depends on deafness for its valued position, much as whiteness depends on blackness; deafness and blackness simultaneously validate and threaten their categorical opposites. Furthermore, just as whiteness both excludes and contains blackness, hearingness both shuns and incorporates deafness, creating a paradoxical situation where meanings constantly shift and the categories operate as simultaneously distinct from and inherent to each other.

Yet if binaries like the color and hearing lines are frequently oppressive, they can also be affirmative for the marginalized group. Boundaries are drawn and tested from both sides. Wsevolod S. Isajiw's words about ethnicity could be applied to both African Americans and deaf people: "Ethnicity is a matter of double boundary, a boundary from within, maintained by the socialization process, and a boundary from without established by the process of intergroup relations" (122). Determining who is "us" and who is "them" seems central to identity formation and to every culture. As they came together in the nineteenth century, African Americans and deaf people sometimes expressed what we would today call black or deaf pride, as they celebrated their group's capabilities, cherished their cultural differences (such as slave songs and sign language), and formed their own social organizations and values. Their very ostracism from society nurtured elements of these positive collective identities. While the daunting prejudice and obstacles facing them sometimes caused them to wish that their blackness or deafness would be removed, they also tended to value their unique identities and fight to have them respected. Boundaries such as the color and hearing lines, however unstable, shape both individual and group identity, and make social action possible. As Tobin Siebers observes, "There can be no political community without a serious conception of borders" (*Subject* 132). Depending on the circumstances, the border of the hearing line can be desirable as well as degrading.

As nineteenth-century Americans explored and sought to identify differences between deaf and hearing people, they sometimes tried to eradicate the hearing line and find common ground. Starting in 1817, the whole enterprise of deaf education, motivated as it was by some hearing people's desire to rescue deaf people's souls by teaching them the Gospel and, later, to convert them into assimilated American citizens,[13] has at its base the desire to make the differences between deaf and hearing people recede. At public demonstrations, deaf people frequently emphasized their shared humanity with their hearing counterparts. Efforts to transgress the hearing line and pass as the other (hearing people as deaf, or deaf people as hearing) further tested the possibility of the hearing line being erased.

Alternatively oppressive and protective, imposing and diaphanous, the hearing line proved resistant to easy comprehension. During the nineteenth century, an important way that Americans investigated and attempted to resolve these contradictions was through the written word.

WRITING THE HEARING LINE

Literature has the power not only to buttress and affirm the hearing line, but also to offer opportunities for its effacement. Because reading and writing are basically silent and visual acts—what Lennard J. Davis has called "the deafened moment" (*Enforcing* 100–101)—they offer a meeting ground of sorts between deaf and hearing people, a place where differences may recede and binaries may be transcended. The

(((INTRODUCTION)))

literature of the period does show inspiring moments of exchange, where both groups succeeded in appreciating each other and moving closer together. Yet moments of mutual understanding are elusive. In stories, novels, and poetry,[14] nineteenth-century hearing authors often romanticize or demonize deafness, alternatively presenting it as a mark of purity and defectiveness, of innocence and corruption, of inferiority, superiority, savagery, naturalness, reassuring sameness and threatening difference, comedy, pathos, and terror. In their published work, deaf writers occasionally replicate these meanings, but more often contest them. Together, this literature forms a discourse over the hearing line that indicates the importance writing can have in group identity formation. It is not just that literature functions, in Frederic Jameson's phrase, as "a symbolic meditation on the destiny of community" (70). Writing has the ability to shape and share cultural identity and to produce relationships between groups. Through writing, people can support or subvert power arrangements, not to mention concepts of reality and order. How authors wrote deafness and hearingness had a great deal to do with the destiny of deaf people in the United States, and this aspect of our nation's literature deserves more recognition.

In the chapters that follow I tell my story in roughly chronological fashion, although I occasionally interrupt this method to bring together similar themes. Chapter 1 examines the emergence of the American deaf community during the first part of the nineteenth century; through writing, deaf authors were able to find a voice in public discourse without speaking vocally at all, with which they could demonstrate their intelligence and humanity. However, because written English could not communicate their language of signs, they often struggled to convey their full identities. In chapters 2 and 3 I introduce the idea of a deaf presence in literature by hearing authors, whether directly through deaf characters or more metaphysically through metaphors and portrayals of silence, sound, and gesture. These hearing writers portray deafness with commingled desire and dread, an ambivalence that often amounts to abjection, as Julia Kristeva has described it, and they use this deaf presence to shore up their own identities as hearing, speaking people. Returning to deaf authors, in chapter 4 I look at how, at midcentury, they contended with a growing double consciousness, sometimes replicating dominant images of inferiority and sometimes challenging them. During a remarkable written debate in the 1850s, deaf people argued over a proposal to emigrate west to form a state of their own where they could escape prejudice and find wholeness, a debate that has parallels to nationalist movements in colonial situations. The final chapter looks at literary episodes of passing across the hearing line, of deaf people acting hearing or hearing people acting deaf, which comically both reify and question the differences between deaf and hearing people. In the epilogue, I consider how the nineteenth-century debates over the hearing line continue to this day: debates about genetic engineering and "curing" deafness, separatism versus assimilation, the value of sign language versus speech, and related topics show that the meaning of deafness and hearingness is still contested, with implications for us all.

In the process, I attempt to answer several key questions that frame this project. How did the emergence of the deaf community in the nineteenth century show up in American literature? How do hearing authors imagine deafness and deaf people? How do deaf characters spark moments of enlightenment in poetry and fiction? In what ways does deafness metaphorically show up in such texts? What cultural "work" does this deaf presence do? What happens when deaf people try to write themselves into national discourse? When does awareness of auditory status add depth to English, and when does it weaken it? How does ideology shape the minds, imaginations, and behaviors of hearing and deaf people? How are literary hearingness and literary deafness produced? I am, of course, rewriting many of the questions that Toni Morrison poses about the "Africanist presence" in our national literature, another indication of the parallels between the color and hearing lines and nineteenth-century authors' attempts to reconcile themselves to them.

Like Morrison, I can imagine a number of reasons why some readers might resist or disregard my project. They may charge that such scholarship further fragments an already fragmented field, giving rise to yet another oppressed special interest group demanding attention. To which I respond that, paradoxically, to achieve universality, we must first acknowledge and appreciate the particular. If we fail to see how deafness informs our great canonical literature, we impoverish it and diminish its relevance. Similarly, if we ignore emergent minority voices, including deaf authors, we reduce the complexity of our literary heritage. Another issue might be the whole topic of deafness and disability, which still causes discomfort, leading to a sort of willed indifference to subjects people would rather not think about. I hope that this book, like other work in deaf and disability studies, will help to reduce such sentiments by demonstrating how provocative and beneficial such lines of inquiry can be and how they apply to us all. Finally, because I am myself late deafened and a literary scholar, I am susceptible to the accusation that this inquiry arises out of self-interest, that it stands to benefit me personally. This claim is true: I have already profited tremendously from this project. More than anything else, this study has made me feel excitement and pride at the achievement of our deaf and hearing American authors. While I do sometimes point out instances of ignorance or prejudice, I also find moments of great empathy and courage. Their written efforts deserve to be recognized, explored, and celebrated, not bypassed.

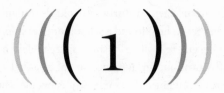

I Write What You Speak

WRITING AND THE EMERGENCE
OF THE AMERICAN DEAF COMMUNITY,
1816–1835

Why then are we Deaf and Dumb? I do not know,
as you do not know . . . why there are among the
human kind, white, black, red and yellow men.
Laurent Clerc (1818)

One of the advantages of a text-based society
is that individual voices and minority opinions can
be more easily heard, if they are permitted access.
Lennard J. Davis (1995)

In the fall of 1816, a group of civic leaders in Philadelphia assembled to see what most of them had never before encountered: an educated deaf person. Laurent Clerc, a thirty-year-old deaf man, had recently arrived from France to help found a school for deaf students in America. After a colleague read aloud a short speech Clerc had written in favor of deaf education, an audience member asked Clerc how he knew whether he thought in the same way as people who could hear. The question was interpreted into sign language and Clerc moved to a chalkboard to reply. "I can express my own ideas by writing," he wrote, "and as what I write is what you speak, I can judge that I possess the same faculties of mind as you do."[1] Clerc's answer indicates how he saw writing not only as evidence of his intelligence, but also as an effective means for him to communicate with hearing people who did not know sign language. Suddenly deaf people in the United States had a voice in national discourse.

To say a "deaf and dumb" person has a voice may seem paradoxical, but as Carol Padden and Tom Humphries remind us, "voice" has dual meaning; it may signify not just talking with the mouth, tongue, and larynx, but also *"being heard,"* no matter what the mode of communication (*Inside* 58).[2] As deaf Americans came together as a group in the early nineteenth century, they made themselves heard not so much through their vivid sign language as through their writing in English. To be sure, their signing often made a tremendous impression on hearing spectators, but because few hearing Americans understood the language, it stopped short of serving as a public voice for deaf people. However, the emergence of print culture opened up the possibility of direct communication with the larger populace that did not know sign language. In the silent, visual space of the text, they found a place where the differences between hearingness and deafness appeared to recede and the hearing line could potentially be effaced.

In this way, deaf people resemble and are somewhat representative of other disempowered groups who took advantage of a growing text-based culture in antebellum America to try to write themselves out of their marginalized status. With the advent of penny newspapers, a profusion of reform literature, and a dramatic rise in the amount of fiction and poetry, Americans increasingly perceived reality through the written word. While William Apess wrote essays in which he at-

(((I WRITE WHAT YOU SPEAK)))

tacked white attitudes toward Native Americans, Frederick Douglass eloquently criticized slavery in his autobiography, and Margaret Fuller published a spirited denunciation of society's treatment of women, early deaf authors like Laurent Clerc and John Burnet argued for the just treatment of deaf Americans, adding to a potent literature of resistance to the hegemonic norm. The words of these writers found an audience of readers, which slowly but undeniably began to affect the way society perceived their respective groups. In the terms of Henry Louis Gates, these authors' writing served as the "visible indication of reason" ("*Race*" 8), demonstrating their intellectual abilities and feelings to a public that commonly viewed them as inferior. In addition, writing "created some version of solidarity for marginalized groups," helping to reinforce their shared experiences and goals (Davis, *Enforcing* 66). At the same time, as Jill Lepore has pointed out, English literacy helped to Americanize "othered" people, to begin to unite a racially, ethnically, and linguistically diverse nation (5). By breaking out of their silenced state, deaf people and other marginalized groups began to achieve a measure of political power and move closer to the center of American society.

Yet deaf authors differed from these counterparts because they did not speak vocally to the public at all, testing whether writing could truly serve as a complete substitution for speech. Since ancient times, people believed that the ability to speak vocally is what makes one human. As George Steiner puts it, "That articulate speech should be the line dividing man from the myriad forms of animate being, that speech should define man's singular eminence above the silence of the plant and the grunt of the beast . . . is classic doctrine well before Aristotle" (36). This view contributed to the oppression and exclusion of deaf people from society for centuries, casting them as inferior beings without language;[3] the etymological root of "language," *langue*, is Latin for "tongue" (Bauman 242). With writing, deaf authors attempted to disprove such prejudiced notions and attest to their humanity without speaking vocally. Minorities who could hear and speak also found a public voice through writing, but their situation was different. Gates goes so far as to assert that "black people could become speaking subjects only by inscribing their voices in the written word" (*Signifying* 130), maintaining that, ironically, only through the silent act of writing could African Americans be heard in a society that privileged writing as proof of rationality. However, he perhaps overstates the case, as fugitive slave orators like Douglass and William Wells Brown were definitely heard in public; their vocal speeches played a crucial role in the abolitionist movement. Clearly written English allowed disadvantaged groups to gain a more effective voice in public discourse, but no other group depended on it to circumvent the long-held belief that vocal speech signified humanity. Could it alone provide the common language that Hegel, in his master-slave dialectic, argued is necessary for individuals to achieve reciprocity and recognize each other as persons (Gibson 29)? Deaf authors in nineteenth-century America offer an illuminating test of these issues, demonstrating both the power and limitations of the written word in the quest for equal rights and respect.

For deaf people, as for many other minority or subaltern groups, writing in the dominant language was not easy or straightforward. Congenitally deaf people often struggled to express themselves in written English, which was essentially a foreign language to them. Even those who found English a congenial mode of expression had to struggle to postulate a complete self in a language freighted with negative assumptions about deafness. In English, "deaf" not only means "does not hear," but also has been associated with callousness, insensitivity, evil, insanity, and isolation; such meanings are inscribed in the language, its idioms (from "turn a deaf ear" to "dialogue of the deaf"), its metaphors, and its very etymology. Furthermore, what nineteenth-century Americans referred to as "the language of signs," and we now know as American Sign Language (ASL), is not a written language. Deaf American authors had to attempt to convey their identities without using the language in which they conversed with each other in person, the language that bound them together as a community. Just as African Americans had a vernacular tradition they used for face-to-face communication before they began to write in English, so deaf Americans had a sign tradition, and both black vernacular and sign language continued to exist alongside (or outside) their writing.[4] Through writing in Standard English, they often sought to bridge the color or hearing lines, to address white hearing people who might be ignorant, biased, or even hostile to what the African American or deaf author was trying to express. Writing was thus a different kind of speech act than using black vernacular or sign. It requires more "double vision" (to use Ashcroft, Griffiths, and Tiffin's term) on the part of the black or deaf author, where they must be much more aware of identity and difference (51). Still another barrier was that deaf people of color did not have much access to education or literacy, preventing them from representing themselves in national discourse.

Given such formidable challenges, it is no wonder that scholars in postcolonial studies have vigorously debated the possibility of oppressed people achieving a true public voice at all. In her essay "Can the Subaltern Speak?" Gayatri Spivak concludes that colonized groups cannot achieve a clear and effective voice in the larger society. Since subalterns are always heterogeneous groups, they have no autonomy, Spivak asserts. Their attempts at speech are never pure but always mixed, always weakened by the conceptual categories and structures of the dominant language in which the subaltern attempts to communicate. Yet critics like Homi Bhabha perceive such hybridity more positively, seeing in the ever-vacillating complicity with and resistance to the dominant ideology a fundamental ambivalence that contains the possibility of unsettling the colonizer's power.[5] While Spivak and Bhabha are referring to oppressed people in colonial situations, their insights directly relate to deaf Americans' efforts to enter the discourse of the dominant hearing society around them, and deaf authors, in turn, offer a compelling test case for subaltern theory.

How did deaf American authors represent themselves? What forces shaped their written voices? How did they internalize, reject, or adapt for their own ends the language that hearing people applied to them? This chapter examines the formation of a public deaf voice and the deaf community on a national level in the early nineteenth century by considering the first three published deaf writers in America: Laurent Clerc, James Nack, and John Burnet. These authors learned to write by reading works in their cultural moment and in the dominant Western literary tradition, which shaped their voices. Yet if, in writing in the language of the majority, they often replicate hearing forms and attitudes, they also occasionally appropriate English to give a sense of their own unique identities. Behind the work of each writer lies a shared sign language and communal consciousness, although the way they express this consciousness varies a great deal. In moving from

Clerc to Nack to Burnet, we can trace the evolution of early deaf American voices and discern how these writers repeated, imitated, and revised each other. Like other minorities, they used writing to break the discursive silence that the majority sometimes cited as evidence of their inferiority. Their literary production helped to define not just themselves as individuals, but also their class, as it was often called. Instead of letting hearing people fill the deaf side of the line with their own imaginings, writing allowed deaf people to gain more control over their own representation, to prove their reason and humanity, and to contest prejudice. With writing, they began to unhinge traditional assumptions about deaf identity as the antithesis of language, awareness, intelligence, goodness, and citizenship,[6] and opened up new ways for being deaf in America.

BEGINNINGS: LAURENT CLERC

By the time Laurent Clerc came to the United States from France in 1816, he already had substantial experience representing deaf people to a hearing public. Deafened as an infant, he had become a brilliant student and, later, teacher at the National Institute for the Deaf in Paris, where he regularly participated in exhibitions before crowds of inquisitive spectators, including leaders like the emperor of Austria, the members of Parliament in London, and the pope. At these events the school's hearing director, the Abbé Sicard, would lecture theatrically about his methods of instruction, and then Clerc and Jean Massieu, another gifted deaf man, would answer questions from the audience to demonstrate the effectiveness of these methods.[7] The queries were interpreted into French Sign Language and the two would write their replies in French on a chalkboard for all to see. Despite the freak-show overtones of these exhibitions, in which he was, in Lennard J. Davis's phrase, "the focal point of the clinical gaze" (*Enforcing* 56), Clerc participated in them willingly, for he saw them as educating the public about deaf people's potential. In 1816, when a young hearing minister from Connecticut named Thomas Hopkins Gallaudet asked Clerc to return to the United States with him to assist in establishing a deaf school there, Clerc quickly assented. He liked Gallaudet and was eager to help spread deaf education to other countries. During their fifty-two-day voyage across the Atlantic, Clerc tutored Gallaudet in

Laurent Clerc. (Painting by Charles Willson Peale, 1822.)
Courtesy of the American School for the Deaf.

French Sign Language while Gallaudet coached him in written English.[8] By their arrival, Clerc was ready to serve as the voice of deaf
education to America, but to do so he had to negotiate a confusing
welter of linguistic and ideological constraints.

As he and Gallaudet traveled through New England to raise funds
for the proposed school, Clerc's initial written voice was deeply hybrid, marked by the dominant concepts and rhetorical figures of the
day. He not only answered questions from audiences, but also wrote
short speeches for Gallaudet to read aloud, thereby taking Sicard's
former role. Perhaps not surprisingly, in these first addresses Clerc
replicated some of the dramatic imagery with which he had seen
Sicard impress emperors and nobility. To a group in Boston in September 1816, Clerc wrote, "Mr. Gallaudet and I are in the design of
raising those unfortunates [uneducated deaf people] from their nothingness" ("Laurent" 109). This language is reminiscent of Sicard's
habit of comparing uneducated deaf people to blocks of unchiseled
marble or statues not yet animated with life (Sicard, in turn, probably
borrowed the statue image from the French philosopher Condillac,
who used it to describe humans' awakening senses and mental understanding).[9] We see Sicard's influence more clearly when Clerc warns
that if no action is taken, deaf people "would be condemned all their
life, to the most sad vegetation" ("Laurent" 108); Sicard had employed
the same trope the year before, stating that a deaf person is "doomed
but to vegetate, when left to himself" (Ladebat xxi). Such echoes raise
the question of whether, in Spivak's terms, Clerc truly has a voice here.
Clerc goes on to assert that the new school would enable deaf people
to "pass from the class of brutes to the class of men" ("Laurent" 108).
His language of blankness and brutishness assumes a colonizing mentality, making uneducated deaf people appear subhuman, much as
contemporary representations depicted black people and Native
Americans as savages. Steeped in the dominant ideology of the time,
Clerc's words advance the Enlightenment concept that, as Gates puts
it, "the absence or presence of reason . . . delimit[s] and circum-
scribe[s] the very humanity" of people deemed different from the
norm (*Signifying* 130). Clerc presents education as the means to lift
deaf people up the great chain of being, to transform them from
obscurity and animalism into conscious, civilized members of society.

What is harder to determine is whether Clerc completely subscribed to this view or employed such rhetoric because he knew it would appeal to the sensibilities of his hearing spectators.

As Clerc was no doubt aware, these hyperbolic representations distorted reality. True, before the rise of deaf education many deaf Americans lived apart from each other, largely isolated and illiterate. Some did not know a language at all. Given such severe circumstances, we can perhaps understand how sensationalistic descriptions came about. However, as F. A. P. Barnard pointed out in 1834, "To be deaf from birth . . . is to be ignorant, not weak, stupid, or savage" (6). Before the founding of deaf schools, some deaf Americans led productive, socially connected lives. Nora Ellen Groce has shown that on Martha's Vineyard from the seventeenth to the nineteenth century, a high rate of hereditary deafness led to a vibrant community in which both deaf and hearing people used a sign language. In addition, since a small percentage of deaf children had a deaf parent, some deaf people had families that knew and understood their situation. For instance, Thomas Brown, a nineteenth-century deaf leader, had a deaf father, Nahum Brown, who signed, so Thomas grew up in an environment where he felt unstigmatized and could readily communicate. Despite not knowing how to read or write, the elder Brown was a successful farmer in New Hampshire, married a hearing neighbor, and raised a family. According to the deaf writer William Chamberlain, Nahum Brown's "shrewdness, as well as sterling honesty, were everywhere recognized and acknowledged, and many an anecdote is told of him to show his keen native humor, which found ready and intelligible pantomimic expression and was always appreciated" (*In Memoriam* 5). Far from being nothing or brutish, Brown was a respected member of his village. Nor were all deaf Americans before 1817 uneducated. A few wealthy families sent their deaf children to Europe to attend school, while other deaf people managed to educate themselves. Although he was born deaf and apparently received no formal education, John Brewster Jr. learned to write some words, could communicate via home signs and pantomime, and had a successful career as a portrait painter in early America.[10] Such accounts contradict Clerc's bleak language describing deaf Americans in 1816.

Further complicating Clerc's voice was the evangelical enthusiasm of the moment, which caused many Americans to view those who did not know the Gospel as lesser beings in need of being saved. Historically, efforts to rescue deaf people's souls were often the *raison d'être* behind attempts at deaf education. Many hearing pioneers in teaching deaf individuals were priests or clergymen, who were often among the first to reach out to disadvantaged groups.[11] Clerc, a Catholic, continued this tradition. When Sicard reluctantly agreed to allow his star teacher to accompany Gallaudet to the United States, he wrote that Clerc was "the Apostle to the Deaf-Mutes of the New World" (qtd. in Lane, *When* 203). In his public presentations, Clerc often accepted that role, suggesting that the new school would be the site not only of education and socialization for deaf people, but also of Christian conversion. Uneducated deaf people, he told a group in Boston, live "without any knowledge . . . of the benefits of God toward us all, and of a better happiness in the other world!" ("Laurent" 109). He provided living proof that deaf people could be Christians, too. Clerc stopped short of calling uneducated deaf people "long-neglected heathen," as his hearing collaborator and friend Thomas Hopkins Gallaudet did in a well-received sermon in 1824 ("Duty" 217).[12] Still, an antebellum culture that valued narratives of conversion probably encouraged him to employ stark before-and-after language. Almost a half-century before, the black slave poet Phillis Wheatley had written of how her "benighted soul" was saved by being taken from her "Pagan land," gently admonishing whites that black Christians would be in heaven too ("On Being"). In 1845, Frederick Douglass would structure his *Narrative of the Life* around similar language of conversion to illustrate the transition from the evil of slavery to Christian freedom. Such rhetoric played into the dominant mindset of the Second Great Awakening and made the case for education or abolition all the more compelling. In this context, to Clerc such appellations as "brutes" may have appeared logical.

Yet even as Clerc replicated Sicard's imagery of vegetation and nothingness in his initial addresses, he almost inadvertently mimicked it, subtly beginning to destabilize the very topos he had been reproducing. He achieved this simply by applying Sicard's model to himself. Describing himself before he was educated, he wrote to his Boston audience: "I had it is true a mind, but it did not think; I had a

(((I WRITE WHAT YOU SPEAK)))

heart, but it did not feel" ("Laurent" 108). Because Clerc is himself deaf, we get a voice very different from Sicard's. Instead of Sicard masterfully animating a lifeless statue through education, Clerc presents himself as being animated. It is, in Homi Bhabha's phrase, "almost the same, but not quite" (86), and that mimicry contains both subtle mockery (of course Clerc could think and feel before he went to school at age twelve) and a certain menace, for it punctures the authority of the dominant discourse. Simply by taking the stage himself and expressing Sicard's metaphors from a first-person perspective, Clerc implicitly reveals how flimsy they are. He goes on to say that, before education, "I believed many . . . droll and ridiculous things" ("Laurent" 108), but that is a long way from being a nothing or a brute. We see how figurative and excessive such imagery is.

In the ensuing question-and-answer sessions, Clerc appeared to break free of Sicard's influence and develop a more spontaneous, informal voice. As he had countless times in Europe, Clerc wrote directly to audiences on a chalkboard (instead of Gallaudet reading aloud what he had previously written). During these exchanges, hearing spectators probed the differences between deafness and hearingness, testing Clerc's understanding of abstract principles and sound. Rather than being intimidated by such interrogations, Clerc, the lone deaf man surrounded by staring hearing people, handled them with aplomb.

Q: What is truth?
A: It is the conformity of an action with its fact, of what we say with what we have seen, or heard, or learned.
Q: What is your idea of music . . . ?
A: I have no accurate idea of everything which relates to the sense of hearing, but if I may judge from what I have been told & what I have read, I may say that music is a concert of various sounds, emanated either from the voice or from some instrument, which form a most agreeable harmony for the persons endowed with the sense of hearing. . . .
Q: What is the difference in the manners and habits of the people of this country and those of the French people?
A: Your manners and habits seem to me to be more regular &

simple and consequently more salutary. Those of the French, though less regular & less constant, are nevertheless more elegant and polite, but you improve more and more every day and I hope you will be quite equal to them in a few years. ("Answers"; "Further answers")

Like Benjamin Franklin before him and Frederick Douglass after, Clerc consciously presents himself as an ideal example of a what a person like him could achieve in America. With his confident presence, he embodies the answer to the troubling rhetoric of brutes and nothingness. Far from appearing pitiable, he comes off as intelligent, honest, and witty, even adopting a playful tone of superiority as he counsels Americans on their manners. We can sense him drawing on his experience in Paris, with its active deaf population, sophisticated sign language, and prominent school for deaf students. Clerc's message is that educated deaf people like him resemble hearing citizens—human, intelligent, and Christian—except that they communicate through hand and eye rather than mouth and ear. He also illustrates how deaf and hearing people can begin to work out their similarities and differences through the in-between space of the written word.

In producing his initial public voice in America, Clerc seems both to have been limited by the dominant categories of the period and cleverly to have manipulated them to achieve what he wanted, the founding of deaf schools and empowerment of deaf Americans. Proving a skilled rhetorician, he created a hybrid written voice in a language he had been studying for only a year to persuade American audiences that deaf people could and should be educated. He appealed to spectators' sentiment and pity, depicting uneducated deaf people as wretched beings in need of charity (a strategy that modern telethons have used with great success); to their religious faith, telling them they would be rewarded in heaven for aiding their deaf counterparts; to their belief that reason is the hallmark of humanity; to their commitment to progress and social reform; and to their patriotism. "In Europe, each nation, however small, has an institution for the deaf and dumb," he wrote. "Will America remain the only nation which is insensible to the cry of humanity?" ("Laurent" 108). In the process, he challenged widespread notions that deaf people could not be educated, presented himself as a model of what education could accomplish, and subversively began to reveal the weakness of hyperbolic representations popularized by Sicard even as he employed them. That he was successful was demonstrated by the opening of the American Asylum for the Deaf and Dumb in Hartford in 1817, soon followed by the establishment of other schools for deaf students: the New York Institution in 1818, the Pennsylvania school in 1820, and the Kentucky school in 1823.[13] To be sure, Clerc did not achieve this alone; committed hearing advocates like Gallaudet and Mason Cogswell (a prominent Hartford surgeon and the father of a deaf girl) actually started the process and were essential partners. Furthermore, the time was ripe for such schools to be founded, as their establishment was part of a broader movement that led to the opening of new hospitals, prisons, and schools for impoverished children during the period. Still, Clerc's striking written voice directly contributed to a remarkable cultural shift where, in the space of fifty years, the United States went from having no permanent schools for deaf students to having twenty-eight, including the first college for deaf people in the world.

While Clerc's voice was undeniably effective, we could ask whether it came with a cost. Although he stopped using the Sicard-inspired language of brutishness and nothingness soon after his initial addresses, preferring gentler terms like "unfortunates" for uneducated deaf people, subsequent deaf authors often followed his early imagery, reproducing and expanding upon the missionary rhetoric. As the deaf author John Burnet noted in his *Tales of the Deaf and Dumb* (1835), "Those who have appealed to public sympathy in behalf of the deaf and dumb, have given highly colored, and, often, exaggerated pictures of their sad condition" (47). Yet even Burnet gave into rhetorical flourishes, writing that "without education, [deaf individuals] would be . . . condemned for life to a lot worse than that of the most ignorant savage" (8). As deaf authors retold the story of Gallaudet and Clerc bringing deaf education to America, they turned to increasingly grand language. Such rhetoric was still the norm in 1869, when Alphonso Johnson told a large gathering of deaf people at a convention that before the founding of the American Asylum, "hundreds of deaf-mutes were left to grow up in total ignorance, but little better than the brute, save in form, and without hope and without God in the world"

("Empire" 258). Through such examples, we can see how Clerc's initial vocabulary of blankness became the paradigm through which educated deaf Americans commonly defined and understood themselves during the nineteenth century. His voice, along with embellished descriptions by revered hearing educators like Sicard and Gallaudet, influenced their written voices, contributing to what Brenda Jo Brueggemann calls a "conversion-driven history of deaf people" centered on the effects of education (*Lend* 158). In this way, Clerc's original rhetoric contributed to the processing of history into myth, obscuring exceptions and transforming ambiguous grays into dramatic black and whites. It also may have had the pernicious effect of further stigmatizing deaf people who did not have access to education, especially deaf people of color who had to grapple with the overwhelming burden of being perceived as inferior in not one way but two.

Clerc's language may have affected hearing writers as well. In January 1817, an anonymous hearing poet published one of the earliest American literary depictions of deaf people in the *Connecticut Mirror*. Appearing just a few months before the American Asylum opened in Hartford, "The Deaf and Dumb" may have been inspired by Clerc and Gallaudet's efforts to establish their school. Yet the poet misses out completely on the exciting potential of deaf education, instead dwelling on a vision of an abject deaf "they":

> Would that my language could relate
> Their woe-fraught pangs, and cheerless state;
> And how I pity the sad fate
> > Of those who are deaf and dumb! . . .

> And while we thus deplore their lot,
> May that great God be ne'er forgot,
> To whom we owe that we are not,
> > Like them, both deaf and dumb! (Hodgson 95, 97)

It is as if Clerc's bleak language of vegetation and nothingness fed into the hearing poet's horrified imaginings of deafness, while none of his words on the promise of education got through. The poem presents an absolute hearing line, with the powerful hearing "we" on one side and the powerless deaf "they" on the other. In the carefully measured verses, the poet expresses a not too subtle distaste at the condition of deaf people and uses it to affirm the value of hearing. By naming deafness and demarcating its boundaries—what deaf people cannot do—the poem seeks to fence it off from the happy, healthy, gratefully hearing "we." While Clerc called attention to the social construction of deafness, to how society could be changed to make deaf people happier, Christian, and more productive citizens, this poet focuses on the biological aspects: deaf people are miserable and hearing people are happy based solely on their auditory status.

The debate over the hearing line in America had begun.

THE DEAF DOUBLE SELF

The new residential schools for deaf students had a profound effect on the lives and public voices of many deaf Americans. The schools enabled deaf people from around the nation to come together for the first time, albeit under hearing supervision: they now increasingly perceived themselves—and were perceived—as members of a group. The American Asylum and other schools had a somewhat paradoxical effect on deaf identity. Like other civilizing institutions of the nineteenth century, such as the African Free Schools, which date from around 1800, the new schools for deaf students sought to inculcate majority values into their charges, including written English, Christianity, and training in some trade such as farming or carpentry. At the same time, by segregating deaf people who otherwise might not have found each other, the schools contributed to the rise of a distinct and subversive group identity. As deaf students and teachers interacted, they gradually developed their own unique language—American Sign Language (ASL)—and values and traditions, features that made them resemble an ethnic group. In this way, the schools simultaneously made deaf Americans more and less of an Other, both closer to and further from the hearing norm. As deaf people negotiated these contradictions, moving between the written form of the dominant language and their own animated language of signs, they often expressed what W. E. B. Du Bois would famously call "double-consciousness," that sense of internal division and "two-ness" that seems to characterize so many groups that live in a society that views them as inferior (*Souls* 3). Like African Americans and the nation's other minorities,

The first home of the American Asylum at Hartford, 1817.
Courtesy of Gallaudet University Archives.

deaf people had to learn the precarious art of navigating between their own culture and the culture of the majority among whom they lived.

In *The Politics of Deafness* (1996), Owen Wrigley argues that deaf Americans were in effect colonized through the schools to make them more acceptable to hearing society. Drawing on the work of Michael Shapiro, Tzvetan Todorov, and Michel Foucault, Wrigley presents Gallaudet and Clerc as nineteenth-century versions of Christopher Columbus, crossing the ocean to put deaf Americans under hearing surveillance and control. He has a point. In their efforts to gather deaf people together and convert them into educated Christians, Gallaudet and Clerc were not completely unlike white Europeans regulating and "civilizing" Native Americans, Africans, and Indians. Gallaudet made this link explicit in 1824, preaching that uneducated deaf people had "a bondage more galling than that of the slave [and] . . . an ignorance more dreadful than that of the wild and untutored savage!" ("Duty" 230). His words show not just how he connected deaf people with African Americans and Native Americans, but also how he saw uneducated deaf people as in more need of white, hearing intervention. As principal of the American Asylum, Gallaudet arranged for students to attend chapel services twice daily during the week, catechism on Saturdays, and both twice on Sunday. Away from their families and under the schools' control, students led a regimented existence. Even the centralized physical design of the schools, in the words of Padden and Humphries, "was a way for the benevolent and patriarchal caretaker to exert moral principles on those who were afflicted with disability" (*Inside* 32). Students were taught sentimental language of gratitude toward their hearing teachers and supporters that often positioned deaf people as children under hearing parental guidance, a familiar trope in the discourse of colonization. The good intentions of educators like Gallaudet did not obviate the imperialistic overtones of their project. As Edward Said reminds us, "The rhetoric of power all too easily produces an illusion of benevolence when deployed in an imperial setting" (*Culture* xvii). Furthermore, deaf students under hearing supervision were sometimes susceptible to abuse. In *Inside Deaf Culture*, Padden and Humphries give the chilling example of how, shortly after the Pennsylvania Institution for the Deaf and Dumb was established in 1820, its hearing superintendent, David Sexias, was accused

Thomas Hopkins Gallaudet. (Painting ca. 1842; artist unknown.) Courtesy of the American School for the Deaf.

of sexually harassing deaf girls under his care and forced to resign. In one respect, then, we can see the new schools as colonizing institutions that sought to propagate the values of the hearing majority and created disturbing opportunities for exploitation.[14]

Yet in his eagerness to puncture what he calls "pious biographies" of Gallaudet and Clerc (44), Wrigley seems to miss precisely how much the schools empowered deaf people. He compares the rise of deaf education to the Great Confinement of those deemed unfit for society in seventeenth-century France. However, he ignores a crucial difference: while so-called deviant individuals like criminals, the unemployed, and the insane presumably did not want to be committed to institutions, deaf people usually cherished their schools. Anyone reading nineteenth-century deaf writing cannot help but be struck by the celebration of the schools that occurs in their pages. Rather than being confining, the schools in deaf narratives are almost invariably liberating, the means to a new sense of self.[15] It was not just that the schools brought deaf people closer to their hearing counterparts by allowing them to become educated and literate in English, gain the skills to earn a living, and join the nation's sizeable Christian community. It was not just that the schools enabled them to discover their own powerful language, self-worth, and communal identity apart from the hearing norm. It was the combination of these things, precisely the way the schools simultaneously lessened and reified the differences of the hearing line.

During the first decade of deaf education in America, the person to mediate these complex, imbricated effects of the schools both for deaf people and for the hearing public was Laurent Clerc. As instructor and role model, Clerc taught deaf pupils at the American Asylum who went on to become teachers, community leaders, and heads of other deaf schools. By visiting President Monroe in the White House, as well as Henry Clay and a session of Congress, and writing speeches to be read aloud to legislatures, Clerc also continued his role as the public voice of deaf education to hearing society. If in his 1816 addresses Clerc replicated dominant colonizing rhetoric while subtly beginning to destabilize it, in his writing after the American Asylum opened he provided a more authoritative voice, one that did not include mention of brutes or vegetation. Writing more from a sense of a collective

American deaf identity, he presented the ways the schools benefited deaf students by fostering their sign language and English literacy. Always keenly aware of dominant ideologies and how the public viewed deaf people, Clerc skillfully worked to develop a voice that would not overly discomfit hearing readers and listeners while eloquently calling for acceptance and appreciation of difference.

In an address he wrote to the Connecticut legislature in 1818, just one year after the American Asylum opened, Clerc called attention to the most immediate effect of the schools: how they suddenly gave deaf people a means to come together, to move from an often-isolated "I" to a strengthening "we." Because the United States was primarily an agrarian nation in the early nineteenth century, and because the majority of deaf children were born to hearing families, deaf individuals often lived far apart. The schools enabled them to come into contact. Of the forty-two students at the American Asylum, Clerc reported that only "four or six" had met other deaf people before coming to Hartford (*An address* 12). Prior to attending school, such children sometimes did not realize that there were others like themselves and they certainly had no sense of collective identity. Foucault has written of "recognition by mirror" in oppressive asylums, the process of humiliating inmates by showing them that they are not special because others have the same condition (262). However, as Padden and Humphries point out, the schools for deaf students reveal how this same mirroring process can be emancipating. By encountering deaf peers and teachers, deaf youth often recognized new possibilities for themselves; no longer alone and stigmatized, they felt part of an understanding group (*Inside* 33). In this way, the schools contributed to the objective formation of a national deaf community, fulfilling Antonio Gramsci's first stage in the history of subaltern classes. Moreover, they made deaf people more visible in society. In his address Clerc felt compelled to denounce a superstition that "the sight of the Deaf and Dumb, or conversation about them increase their number" (*An address* 3). So novel was the sight of an assembly of deaf people that some hearing Americans apparently felt threatened, and he tried to reassure them.

By bringing deaf people together, the new schools also enabled them to develop their own sign language, a language that Clerc celebrated as natural and worthy of esteem. He wrote that while "artificial speech" is "almost always . . . comparatively useless" to deaf people, sign, "as simple as nature, is capable of extending itself like her, and of attaining the farthest limits of human thought" (*An address* 6, 7). By aligning sign with nature, Clerc invokes not just the theories of the French philosopher Condillac, but also the prevailing American Romanticist attitudes of the day, which tended to celebrate the natural world. As Douglas Baynton has shown, antebellum Americans frequently saw vocal speech as arbitrary and gestures as retaining their "essential ties with their iconic origins" in nature (115). Reflecting such notions, Clerc repeatedly stressed the natural aspects of sign language, writing that "nothing can supply to [deaf people] the place of their natural language, *the language of signs*" (*An address* 6). He presented sign as the best path to knowledge for deaf students and as something that united deaf people around the globe. "This language of signs is universal," he wrote, and "ought to fix the attention of every enlightened man" involved in public education (*An address* 7). In the process, he depicts deaf people as possessing something of value that most hearing people do not have; instead of simply being deprived individuals, he casts deaf people as having special abilities that could enrich American society.

Clerc's claim that sign is universal may puzzle us today, for he knew that deaf people in different nations used sign languages that were linguistically distinct and mutually unintelligible. Today linguists understand that American Sign Language evolved slowly out of the specific communities created by the schools. Before 1817 some signed languages existed in the United States; deaf and hearing people on Martha's Vineyard used a sign language, while other deaf people, especially those from deaf families, also signed. When the American Asylum opened, some students brought their sign languages to the school, where they encountered Clerc's elegant French Sign Language. American Sign Language evolved out of this mixture of French and indigenous sign languages. As the *Encyclopedia Americana* described it in the early 1830s: "When a number of deaf mutes are brought together in a single institution, selections and combinations of their various dialects are formed; the best are gradually adopted by all; and a new and more complete form of the language is the result" ("Deaf Mutes"

25). American Sign Language differs markedly from, say, British Sign Language and Swedish Sign Language, and like these languages is difficult for adult nonsigners to learn.[16] In 1835, the deaf author John Burnet wrote that those "desiring to study the language of signs in its improved form, have looked at the mass of signs flitting before them, with as much dismay as if they were to be compelled to count and individually recognize a swarm of bees" (*Tales* 18), a sensation familiar to many beginning ASL students today.

Yet Clerc continued to state that sign is universal throughout his long career, indicating that it was a genuine belief rather than a rhetorical gambit. Like Burnet, he apparently saw sign language as existing on a continuum with pantomime and gesture, which are natural and common to all humanity. In their minds, as Baynton puts it, "the distinction . . . between the complex sign language found in their schools and the gestures and simple pantomime of which any uninstructed person was capable was a difference of degree not of kind" (113). Experienced signers used what Burnet called the "improved form" of the language, which was more condensed and arbitrary, but they could slide at will down to more gestural forms that were more universally comprehensible.[17] Clerc no doubt experienced such communication in dealing with nonsigners or foreign deaf people. For example, in 1815, when he met deaf students at the London Asylum, an oral school that emphasized speech and lipreading, he was able to converse with them through gesture, "unexpected communication that caused a most delicious sensation in them" according to a hearing observer (qtd. in Rée 198).[18] Yet it is instructive that when Clerc wanted to communicate his intelligence and have in-depth exchanges with hearing audiences, he turned not to universal gestures but to writing, which he recognized as a more precise and effective way to connect with that audience.

At any rate, Clerc clearly knew the empowering aspects of sign language, which flourished at the new schools. He taught sign to Gallaudet and other hearing instructors, while deaf students, rather than being mere passive receptacles for hearing colonization, actively shaped the growth of their language, which had a form and structure markedly different from English. In the 1830s the *Encyclopedia Americana* pointed to the language's distinct grammar and syntax: "It is worthy of remark, that the order of expression, in the sign language, is that which we term inverted—the subject before the quality, the object before the action, and generally, the thing modified before the modifier" ("Deaf Mutes" 27).[19] The writer also recognized that sign language, unlike spoken language, could communicate a group of ideas simultaneously, and that it was sometimes more rapid and efficient. As students graduated from the American Asylum, some became teachers at other schools for deaf students, gradually spreading the sign language to states across the nation. In the process, ASL became a force that united deaf Americans. Like Native Americans with their respective languages, or even African Americans with black English vernacular, nineteenth-century deaf Americans who signed became a linguistic minority, possessing a distinctive language in which their difference from the majority—their deafness—was actually the norm.[20] Writing of black slave culture, Lawrence Levine states that "slave music, slave religion, slave folk beliefs . . . created the *necessary space* between the slaves and their owners and were the means of preventing legal slavery from becoming spiritual slavery" (80, emphasis mine). Along the same lines, we could say that deaf Americans' burgeoning sign language created a necessary space for them, a space where they were more secure in their identities and less emotionally scathed by hearing people's frequent paternalism and pity.

If the new schools strengthened deaf Americans by enabling them to come together and develop their own language, they also did so by teaching them written English, which Clerc contended could bridge the gap between hearing and deaf Americans. As he told the Connecticut legislators, "We wish to instruct them, that they may converse with you by writing, in the room of speech, and know the truths and mysteries of religion" (*An address* 7). Clerc presents writing as a substitute for vocal talking, as the synapse through which deaf people could communicate directly with hearing people who did not know sign language. For all the similarities between deaf and other minority authors, writing arguably played a more important role in relations between deaf and hearing people than it did between blacks and whites, women and men, or the lower and upper classes. Members of these latter groups could at least *speak* to each other in person, but when deaf and hearing Americans came into contact after the rise of deaf education, they commonly wrote to one another unless the hearing person knew sign language. Thus when Clerc visited the U.S. Capitol, he conversed with the congressmen by writing back and forth; when a deaf man named Mestapher Chase was robbed in the 1830s, he gave testimony in court by writing; and at her wedding, a deaf woman named Mary Rose made her vow by reading the marriage covenant and signing her name on it.[21] Writing potentially moves toward transcending the deaf-hearing binary, toward the "third space" envisioned by Homi Bhabha that helps us to "elude the politics of polarity and emerge as the others of our selves" (38–39).

Yet even as he indicated the ability of written English to span differences, in his 1818 address Clerc pointed out that learning English is often a daunting task for people who are born deaf or become deaf in infancy, one that requires special pedagogical approaches. "The language of any people cannot be the mother tongue of the Deaf and Dumb, born amidst these people," he wrote. "Every spoken language is necessarily a learned language" (*An address* 10). Written English (in its literal, non-Derridean sense) represents spoken English,[22] and since deaf children cannot acquire English osmotically by listening, they need to learn it visually. The process could be compared to a hearing American trying to master a written foreign language without hearing it spoken, as Burnet suggested in 1835. He wrote, "Let the reader figure to himself a language (like the Chinese)[23] in which each idea is expressed by an arbitrary character, or, still worse, by an assemblage of arbitrary characters, in an order too, very different from that in which the words of his own language are arranged, and he will have some idea of the difficulties which attend the acquisition of a written language by the deaf and dumb" (*Tales* 26–27). In making this analogy, Burnet implicitly acknowledges that sign language has a grammar quite different from English.[24] For all its value, English resembles a foreign language to congenitally deaf people, while sign is invariably natural and almost effortless. After calling attention to these barriers, in his address Clerc goes on to give a detailed explanation of how, through sign instruction that followed "an uninterrupted line from the *known* to the *unknown*," deaf students learned English words and eventually became literate according to their abilities (*An address*

7).[25] Through sign, the foreign language of the majority could be imparted to deaf students.

As the new schools transformed the lives of growing numbers of white deaf people, they often found themselves oscillating between two different languages and views of self. One language was their own, newly evolving, natural, and visual-kinetic, while the other, a written form of the language spoken by some hearing people for centuries, seemed foreign. One had deafness at its center (a hearing person who could sign well was rare); the other commonly assumed the ability to hear. In moving between the two languages, deaf Americans often saw themselves in contradictory terms, from within but also from without. In Du Bois's memorable words, this "double-consciousness" often created a sense of internal conflict, of "two-ness . . . two souls, two thoughts, two unreconciled strivings" (*Souls* 11). Like other minorities, deaf Americans sometimes expressed a longing to escape this sense of division and "merge [the] double self into a better and truer self." They wanted to see themselves as full and sufficient human beings regardless of language or context.

For deaf authors, the challenge was to find ways to appropriate English and use it slightly differently, to give it a distinctly deaf tinge that would communicate their unique experience. Gates has written of how African American writers followed Western canonical traditions while always repeating "with a difference, a black difference, that manifests itself in specific language use" (*Signifying* xxii). Early in the twentieth century, Virginia Woolf similarly believed that the only way the true experience of women's bodies would be written was if language were changed. This idea of seizing the dominant language and altering it seems to run through all minority and postcolonial literature in English. In *The Empire Writes Back* (1989), Ashcroft, Griffiths, and Tiffin sum up the process: "Post-colonial writing abrogates the privileged centrality of 'English' by using language to signify difference while employing a sameness that allows it to be understood" (51). Sameness, but with a difference, seems to be the hallmark of minority literature in English, and deaf writing is no exception. In deaf authors' works, we can often observe a double consciousness, a vacillating tension between the hegemonic views and the more subversive ones based on sign language, which often coexist and overlap in the same text. Could deaf people accurately represent themselves to the majority in a language that was not their own?

While Clerc had given some evidence that this was possible in 1816, he provided a stronger answer when he appropriated English in a small but significant way to argue for just treatment of deaf people in his 1818 address. Going against the long tradition in English that invariably positioned "we" as hearing and "deaf" people as a voiceless, passive they, Clerc made "we" and "deaf" into markers of deaf communal identity by writing, "Why are we Deaf and Dumb?" He uses the words in a manner that had not been seen before in American discourse; they are the same words, but given a new orientation. In what we could call an early example of multiculturalism, Clerc proceeds to make deafness appear part of natural variation rather than a mark of almost unfathomable deviance:

> Every creature, every work of God, is admirably well made; but if any one appears imperfect in our eyes, it does not belong to us to criticize it. Perhaps that which we do not find right in its kind, turns to our advantage, without our being able to perceive it. . . . Let us, in thought, go into an orchard or forest. What do we see? Trees high or low, large or small, upright or crooked, fruitful or unfruitful. Let us look at the birds of the air, and at the fishes of the sea, nothing resembles another thing. . . . Why then are we Deaf and Dumb? I do not know, as you do not know why there are infirmities in your bodies, nor why there are among the human kind, white, black, red and yellow men. . . . I think our deafness proceeds from an act of Providence, I would say, from the will of God, and does it imply that the Deaf and Dumb are worse than other men? (12)

Just as he had emphasized the naturalness of sign language before, here Clerc stresses the naturalness of deafness and gives a reason for deaf people's existence; they are not an anomaly or irrationalism, not evil, but part of the natural diversity in divine creation. He even has the temerity to suggest that deaf people are equal to their hearing counterparts. Only God has the power to judge. Challenging centuries of received wisdom that routinely assumed deaf people are inferior or even malevolent beings, Clerc offers no colonizing rhetoric of brutes, none of Sicard's inanimate statues or Gallaudet's heathen, but instead argues for humble tolerance of diversity. By putting deafness alongside variation in skin color, he implicitly condemns prejudice against black people, Native Americans, and others based on race. By putting it alongside "infirmities," he makes a radical claim for the absolute value of every kind of human variation, including disability (an assertion that fits in with the goals of much disability advocacy and scholarship today). Clerc thus participates in the gradual destabilizing of white hearing hegemonic self-assurance, and contributes to the cause of other minority activists, including Apess and Douglass, in the decades ahead.

As we can see, the new schools did more than simply impose the values of one group on another. They had a complex effect, promoting new awareness and exchange on all sides. Along with enabling deaf people to become educated, Christian, and literate in English, the schools allowed them to develop their own language and communal identity, and made them more visible and likely to be heard in society. With the founding of deaf education, hearing people not only saw Clerc on stage, but also saw deaf students during regular visitor's days at the schools and in popular public exhibitions. For example, in the 1820s a hearing woman named Anne Royall reported that she joined spectators numbering "two thousand, at least" at an exhibition of deaf students in Philadelphia (qtd. in Berger 162). Without the schools, deaf Americans would have had a much more difficult time coming together and advocating for themselves. While such "asylums" were part of a larger impulse of the time to segregate and rehabilitate those deemed different from the norm, they seem distinct in that they were established through a symbiotic deaf-hearing collaboration. Just as later, in the 1840s, white abolitionists like William Lloyd Garrison would help former slaves like Frederick Douglass to find an audience and denounce slavery, so hearing reformers like Thomas Hopkins Gallaudet assisted Laurent Clerc in gaining a voice in the United States and arguing for deaf potential. Similarly, while Douglass would make an enormous impact on Garrison's abolitionist campaign, Clerc helped Gallaudet not only learn sign language and found lasting deaf education in America, but also to bring many deaf Americans into the Christian church. Such partnerships were mutually beneficial, even if the white, hearing participants frequently conveyed paternalistic attitudes, and if the black or deaf members sometimes struggled to express themselves in the majority's language or internalized dominant views.

If, as Wrigley asserts, in some ways deaf Americans were colonized by hearing people, their example also reminds us that colonization, for all its oppressive features, could have beneficial effects. As we will see in chapter 4, deaf Americans were unique in that their language and communal consciousness were typically not passed on through family, but through the schools founded with the help of hearing patrons. Unlike African Americans, Native Americans, or other ethnic peoples, deaf Americans had little sense of belonging to a group prior to hearing involvement, illustrating a singular way that a colonizing enterprise could enable new cultural forms. Their emergent sense of self was in some respects even more convoluted than that of other minorities or colonized groups, more bound up in and dependent upon the dominant society even as that society oppressed them. In *Culture and Imperialism* (1993), Said argues that one of imperialism's achievements was to bring the world closer together, making people more hybrid and interdependent: "Gone are binary oppositions. . . . Partly because of empire, all cultures are involved in one another, none is single and pure, all are hybrid, heterogenous, extraordinarily differentiated, and unmonolothic" (xxv). The schools illustrated this dynamic in an unusual new way. They helped to nourish a deaf cultural identity and simultaneously made hearing Americans more aware of themselves as hearing people. But they also promoted exchange, appreciation of difference, and a more hybrid society where the similarities and differences between deaf and hearing people, detached from stereotypes, could begin to be explored.

Laurent Clerc achieved a public voice and helped to initiate these cultural transformations without speaking vocally at all. In the 1840s, he recalled that he had given up trying to speak as a young student when an articulation teacher at the Paris school had struck him on the chin in frustration, causing him to bite his tongue ("Laurent Clerc" 103). Through writing, Clerc found a means to circumvent speech and communicate directly with thousands of hearing people, including presidents, congressmen, emperors, and the pope. He provided a model that subsequent deaf authors would emulate and extend; just as they often copied his early rhetoric of conversion, so they frequently followed his arguments for understanding and justice. Yet for all his achievements with the written word, Clerc was always aware that writing was not his best method of communication. In 1835, a young man who had begun losing his hearing while a student at Yale College, F. A. P. Barnard, wrote to Clerc with questions about deafness. To the query of whether he thought more clearly and rapidly by means of English words or by signs, Clerc responded, "By means of signs. The reason is that I have plenty of signs at my command to express whatever I think, whereas I want words to describe it" ("Letter"). Even the accomplished Clerc struggled to convey himself accurately through writing, but soon other deaf authors would join him in the quest to express deaf identity to the hearing public.

"I PITY THOSE WHO . . . PITY ME"

It is perhaps unsurprising that, after Clerc, two of the first deaf people in the United States to appear in print became deaf after learning some English. James Nack and John Burnet both lost their hearing at age eight. They were profoundly deaf and used sign language, but they had a different relationship to English than congenitally deaf people who had never heard the language spoken. As an adult Burnet wrote that although "nearly all . . . recollections of sounds have faded from [my] memory," he could remember the pronunciation of words well enough to make rhymes (*Tales* 230). If Nack and Burnet in some ways represent liminal figures, their situation was not unusual; more people lost their hearing in the nineteenth century due to high fever, meningitis, and other illnesses than is the case today. While Nack enrolled at the newly opened New York Institution shortly after he became deaf, Burnet was taught at home by his sister and did not interact with other deaf people until finding his way to the same school at age twenty-one. They exemplify the heterogeneity even among white male deaf Americans, who became deaf at different ages, had different degrees of deafness, and discovered sign language and the deaf community at different times in their lives. In 1827, while still a teenager, Nack became the first deaf American to publish a book. *The Legend of the Rock and Other Poems* created a stir in literary New York and proved that deaf people were capable of literary expression. Eight years later, Burnet published *Tales of the Deaf and Dumb*, a compendium of essays, poetry, and fiction that revised and extended Nack and Clerc's models. By adding their written voices to Laurent Clerc's, they advanced the argument for deaf people's capabilities and offered a more complex representation of deaf experience in public discourse.

While Clerc used writing to demonstrate his reason and humanity, James Nack went further, producing poetry that testified to his, and by extension deaf people's, intelligence, deep feeling, and religious piety. Written largely in the Romantic style of Lord Byron, the sixty-eight poems in *The Legend of the Rock* may strike today's readers as dated and conventional, but that conformity helped to give them their power when they first appeared. Reviewers were stunned that a deaf person could write poetry, which was often seen as one of the highest forms of civilization. The New York *Critic* praised the musical quality of Nack's verse, while another commentator wondered how Nack, as a deaf person "cut off" from society, could write so well about human emotions (Lang, *Deaf Persons* 270).

Such reactions recall the astonished reception given to the first African American to publish a book, Phillis Wheatley, over fifty years before. For all their differences, Wheatley and Nack resemble each other in the way they surprised white, hearing readers by composing substantive verse in a style esteemed by the majority. Notably, they both had patrons from the dominant group who encouraged their efforts. It is hard to determine how much influence mentors like the hearing poet William Cullen Bryant had on Nack's work, much as we do not know what kind of a role Wheatley's master had in her poetic endeavors, complicating issues of authenticity and voice once again. Still, both began to challenge widespread assumptions about their respective groups and to write black and deaf people into a position deserving respect.

Nack directly treats deafness in only a few poems, and in these he offers an intricate depiction of himself as a deaf person, one that wavers between sorrow and pride. Contrary to what one might anticipate, he does not plainly identify with other deaf people or even mention sign language in his work, presenting himself as an isolated but not weak figure among hearing people instead. These pieces, interspersed among poems that describe sound and contain spoken dialogue—which could pass as being written by a hearing person—serve as a subtle but effective counterpoint to the main ones, reminding hearing readers that Nack is different from them even as his mellifluous verse indicates that they share much in common. Although he attended the New York Institution for five years, used sign language, and interacted with deaf people, in his deaf-related poems Nack appears alone, as we see in the gloomy opening of "The Minstrel Boy":

And am I doom'd to be denied forever,
    The blessings that to all around are given?
And shall those links be reunited never
    That bound me to mankind, till they were riven
In childhood's day? Alas, how soon to sever
    From social intercourse, the doom of heaven
Was past upon me! And the hope how vain,
    That the decree may be recal'd again! (58)

Melodramatic lines, these, that work on at least two levels. First, as Nack indicates in a note, he wrote them when he felt "particularly unhappy." They reflect a moment when the sixteen-year-old poet, writing two years after he graduated from the New York Institution, felt isolated and forlorn as he sought to make his way in hearing society. Such dejection is perhaps understandable, given that he had lost his hearing and must have encountered barriers as one of the first educated deaf people in New York. At the same time, the lines call to mind an established trope in Romantic poetry, for Byron made such sorrow a popular pose for writers to adopt. Paradoxically, there is a certain potency in Byronic alienation. Nack simultaneously reifies hearing people's tendency to imagine deaf people as miserable and expresses a disenchanted moodiness very much in the vogue at the time. He manages to be both familiar and foreign to hearing readers, putting a new twist on a recognizable poetic theme.

In "The Music of Beauty," he takes another common form, the love poem, and again asserts a certain power, this time through a more affirmative deaf perspective.

To me thy lips are mute, but when I gaze
Upon thee in thy perfect loveliness,—
No trait that should not be,—no lineament
To jar with the exquisite harmony
Of Beauty's music, breathing to the eyes,
I pity those who think they pity me;
Who drink the tide that gushes from thy lips
Unconscious of its sweets, as if they were
E'en as I am—and turn their marble eyes
Upon thy loveliness, without the thrill
That maddens me with joys's delirium.

The initial assertion of not hearing, far from being lamentable, leads to a claim of increased perception: the deaf speaker sees exhilarating beauty that hearing people overlook. With "Beauty's music," he seizes what hearing people often say deaf individuals tragically miss—music —and turns it into a metaphor for the visual splendor only he can discern. The poem inverts the usual power relationship, where hearing people, not the deaf speaker, deserve pity. With works like these, Nack demonstrates that he is an emotionally complex, sensitive, and intelligent human, even if he displays familiar inner conflict over his identity.

Although Nack could be criticized for not producing more politically engaged work, he nevertheless provided a groundbreaking voice for deaf people in American literature. He decisively showed his humanity through a dominant literary form while occasionally appropriating it to begin to express his own experience, a new deaf "I" not seen before in American poetry. From our twenty-first-century perspective, we could easily wish that he had used his talents to identify more strongly with the deaf community of which he was a part, to convey some of the social, cultural, and political situation of that group. In contrast to Clerc, he did not call attention to the ways readers could change society to make it more just for deaf people, or even hint at the sign language he used with deaf peers. Still, nineteenth-century deaf Americans regarded Nack highly, often pointing to him as one of the first success stories of deaf education in the United States and evidence that deaf people were capable of serious literary and academic achievement. Just as Phillis Wheatley had no models other than white European Americans for poetry, Nack had no deaf models, and that encouraged them to believe that the only way to win a large readership would be to express themselves in a form that the majority admired.[26] Nack created a literary voice that would effectively reach hearing readers and set an example that later deaf writers could build upon.

A VISUAL PEOPLE

The first to follow was John Burnet, who modified and expanded upon Nack and Clerc's precedents to compose the most comprehensive overview of deaf Americans until that time. Although he became deaf as a child, Burnet did not discover sign language and the deaf community until he was a young adult, and he was so entranced by what he found that he resolved to spread awareness to the public. Published in 1835, his *Tales of the Deaf and Dumb* contained essays, statistics, poetry, and a short story designed to educate hearing people about the deaf community and "awaken . . . an interest on the subject in the bosoms of many" (229). Like Clerc, Burnet focuses on the social and political aspects of deafness, arguing emphatically for sign language, deaf education, and tolerance of difference. Like Nack, Burnet includes poetry on general topics and on the deaf experience. However, Burnet goes further, decrying prejudice, providing instructions for how families could begin to instruct a deaf child at home, and producing what was likely the first published fiction by a deaf American author. (Like other minority authors of the period, deaf writers usually turned to essays, lectures, autobiography, and poetry to express themselves and argue for understanding and justice.) In addition, he seeks to impart an idea of sign language through English and convey a sense of deaf people's communal spirit.

More than either of his predecessors, Burnet attacks prejudice against deaf individuals and argues for their humanity, repeatedly asserting that their difference is that they perceive the world primarily through vision. While acknowledging some progress has been made, in a hortatory essay he castigates those who still believe uneducated deaf people "display the characteristics . . . of *apes* or *monkeys*" (50). In something of a corrective to Clerc's initial language of brutes, Burnet posits that uninstructed deaf children are simply untaught and, often, treated with aversion or ignored.[27] Drawing on his experience visiting families with deaf children in the early 1830s, Burnet maintains that, because most hearing parents fail to appreciate that deaf children can obtain information visually, they tend to give up trying to communicate with them. As a result, an uninstructed deaf child can be selfish, willful, and irritable, but Burnet interprets this fact differently than most observers. "The world says it is because he is deaf; not so; IT IS BECAUSE HE WAS NEGLECTED," he asserts (14). In this way, he argues that deaf people are often hindered more by social attitudes than deafness. He notes how such prejudice can be self-justifying, writing that the same neglect that "crushed [the deaf person] to the dust, justifies her deed by pointing to the degraded condition to which she herself reduced him!" (48). Although Burnet has deaf children in mind, his words apply equally to Native Americans, African Americans, women, and other groups that antebellum society perceived as inferior or barbaric; like Clerc's, his writing contributes to the emerging body of literature against oppression. Burnet's target throughout is social attitudes; he seeks to convince hearing readers that deaf people are cognizant humans who have rich potential and communicate visually. If hearing parents just adjust their behavior by treating their deaf children kindly and attentively, and letting "*their eyes supply the place of ears*," their deaf offspring will flourish (15). Burnet takes this point further by suggesting that the stigma of deafness is largely a social fabrication. "Were the established mode of communication among men, by a language addressed, not to the *ear*, but to the *eye*, the present inferiority of the deaf would entirely vanish," he writes (47). Anticipating modern theorists, Burnet points out how deaf people's disadvantage is more a product of the environment in which they live than of any innate biological characteristic.[28] This remark is not merely fanciful. During frequent visits to the New York Institution, he experienced a place where visual communication was the norm, and he was no doubt aware of the deaf-hearing community on Martha's Vineyard, where many people signed.

Burnet and other deaf authors had to confront the fact that this visual language at the center of their community could not be directly represented through writing. "To attempt to describe a language of signs by words, or to learn such a language from books, is alike to attempt impossibilities," Burnet writes (24).[29] Sign, which is three-dimensional and moves in space, does not have a written form. In some respects, signing deaf communities resemble oral cultures, as James Paul Gee and Walter J. Ong have pointed out. While black English vernacular was a wellspring of African American consciousness and identity, sign language had a similar role in the lives of many deaf Americans. Sign constituted a parallel discursive domain that could not easily be brought into English or traditional written literary forms. As we have seen, Clerc wrote about sign, but he had an advantage: he wrote primarily for live audiences who would be able to see him in person. Before and after Thomas Hopkins Gallaudet read his words aloud, spectators could observe Clerc on the platform signing fluidly with Gallaudet or deaf students. Even if they could not understand his signs, they saw the vivid language at the heart of Clerc's identity; his written English did not need to bear the entire burden of trying to convey sign.[30] When Nack and Burnet set out to express themselves through the printed page, they dealt with a different kind of speech act, where their readers could not see them. Nack, following hearing precedents, did not try to represent sign language in his poetry, obscuring a part of his deaf identity from hearing readers even as he impressed them with his verse. However, Burnet does seek to give an idea of sign in his writing.

Throughout *Tales of the Deaf and Dumb*, Burnet breaks new ground by foregrounding deaf people's vivid sign language and its empowering role in deaf identity. We obtain a glimmer of the beauty of sign when he describes the conversation of two educated deaf signers as a "thousand changing motions through which every thought of the mind flashes and disappears" (18). In an essay directed to hearing parents of deaf children, Burnet instructs them on how to begin communicating visually. He describes the production of such signs as SAME, MILK, ALWAYS, and TRUTH, and includes a diagram of the American manual alphabet so they can learn how to spell English words on their fingers.[31] In Burnet's short story "The Orphan Mute," George, a young hearing man, uses a home sign with his adopted deaf sister Mary to convey something he has read in the newspaper: "George extended his arm towards the East, and seemed as if pointing to a distant place, then pointing to himself, he described with his finger, the tie of her bonnet, and placing his finger alternately on his ear and his lips, he finally joined his hands together" (157). Such moments may create what Bill Ashcroft calls a "metonymic juncture" in the text ("Congo" 8), reminding hearing readers who do not sign that, even though the story is in English, they do not share the language of deaf people: they are briefly removed from the assurance of understanding. However imperfect, these infusions of sign into English tend to have a potent effect on deaf representation, indicating that deaf people are full humans with a complex language of their own. Yet as Burnet himself admits, while these instances may give an approximate idea of sign, the actual original sign language, which includes facial expression and non-manual indicators, is lost. We may read the writings of Clerc, Nack, and Burnet in English, but how they signed is forever gone. We are left with the somewhat odd sense that we cannot now experience the natural sign language of these writers, the language they used when they interacted with each other in person. Their visual culture remains elusive, peeking out from behind English words, existing in a mood, a spirit that is hinted at, even described, but never quite directly conveyed.

If the first deaf American authors often deliberately or unconsciously repeated dominant literary forms and perspectives, in their writing we can regularly detect a subversive spirit. Even when they do not try directly to represent sign, it can inflect the meaning of their written English, creating what Mikhail Bakhtin calls double-voiced words. To return to Clerc's 1818 address: when he used "deaf" in an affirmative manner, he gave the word a meaning that more closely resembles the sign DEAF than traditional English. In modern ASL, a signer produces DEAF by first touching a raised index finger on the cheek near the ear, then again on the same cheek near the mouth (or vice versa); in the early nineteenth century, instead of near the mouth, the index finger might actually have been placed on the lips in a "sssh" gesture. DEAF not only means "does not hear," but also can connote "us," "uses sign language," "behaves in expected ways," and "shares deaf values."[32] DEAF has more positive colorings than the traditional English "deaf." In her study of late-twentieth-century ASL poetry and storytelling, Cynthia Peters argues that ASL functions as a carnivalesque discourse, frequently inverting and upending established meanings. In this respect, ASL parallels black English vernacular, which, as

Gates has shown, often signifies on, or repeats with a difference, Standard English. It seems likely that this carnivalesque element was present to some degree in nineteenth-century sign language as well. While sign cannot be directly written, it still can shape some of the meanings and messages that deaf authors produce in their writing. We occasionally can perceive Bakhtinian double-voiced words, that is, English words that are appropriated for deaf purposes, "by inserting a new semantic orientation into a word which already has—and retains—its own orientation" (qtd. in Gates, *Signifying* 50). "Double-voiced" is not the best term for the dynamic here, since of course ASL is not voiced at all; but nonetheless double-voiced helps to elucidate how deaf writing in English can be influenced by sign language. The challenge facing deaf authors is to master, as Jacques Derrida puts it, "the other's language without renouncing their own" ("Racism's" 333).

Burnet moves closer to this goal than previous deaf writers. In his creative pieces, he seeks to bring sign language and the deaf communal consciousness as close to the surface of his English text as he can, offering a sense of the exciting linguistic community he discovered at the New York Institution in 1830. His story "The Orphan Mute" is in many ways a conventional Victorian narrative, with a wealthy, corrupt uncle trying to keep two lovers apart. The sensibility of the story seems primarily hearing: we begin with hearing children finding Mary, a beautiful deaf girl who has been abandoned; we learn about Mary's progress at school mainly through a hearing principal; and at the end we share the thoughts of the hearing character, George, as he decides to propose. Yet Burnet bends these conventions at times to offer a deaf perspective centered on linguistic difference. For example, when the children find the orphan, they interpret her incoherent attempts at speech to mean she is French. Burnet casts deaf people as foreign rather than defective, humanizing them in the process. After she is adopted by the Wilson family, she and the son, George, develop a home sign that allows them to converse in a limited manner and for her to learn to write some English words. However, she does not fully blossom until she arrives at a school for deaf students, where the visual language of signs has a transformative effect. Presenting Mary as someone who has been living among "people of an unknown language," Burnet describes how at the school she finds "a community whose language [she] understands" (162), evoking the liberating linguistic richness of the environment:

> Those hidden thoughts which had been wont to pass from mind to mind, in such an invisible manner as to elude all the vigilance of her sense, seemed now to have become visible and palpable. The air was literally swarming with the creations of the mind; events past and future, thoughts, feelings and wishes, seemed floating around her, and that knowledge which she had hitherto sought so eagerly, and often so vainly, now knocked continually for admittance. (162)

The perspective has shifted; sign here appears normal, a welcome relief, even though Burnet laments that he "should vainly attempt to transfer [sign language] to paper" (167). From being on the outskirts of social interactions, Mary moves to the center of attention, part of a larger group of others like herself. The students cluster curiously around her, asking questions and making her feel welcome, leaving her "interested, pleased, tranquil, delighted" (162). These glimpses of deaf people interacting are almost entirely absent from previous written depictions. Later we learn that Mary has received a name sign, the signifier of her identity at the school: a finger placed behind the ear, where she has a scar. Burnet might subtly be paying tribute to Clerc, whose name sign—a brushing of the two forefinger tips on the right hand down the right cheek, near the mouth—also came from a scar, which he had received from a fall into a fireplace as an infant. In these ways, Burnet dramatizes the effects of deaf education that Clerc had upheld. Through English, he conveys Mary's movement from having little language to a rich visual one, from relative ignorance to knowledge, and from being an isolated deaf person to being a member of a community of peers.

In addition to showing Mary's acculturation into the signing deaf community, Burnet depicts her gradual learning of English, another aspect of nineteenth-century deaf Americans' identities that had not been represented much before in print. After learning to write her name and some individual words at home, Mary goes on to master the rudiments of English at school. She produces a short autobiographical sketch, which Burnet includes, allowing us as readers to experience her written voice directly. Recalling her childhood, Mary writes, "One day I was playing in the road, and a man drove his wagon, that ran over me, and crushed my head, and I was near dying; yet I got well, but I was deaf and dumb" (164). Mary's account resembles many student essays from the period that were published in the schools' annual reports. It is typical in its heartfelt, simple English. Burnet connects his representation to the actual deaf students he met at the New York Institution. Instead of just reading about a deaf character, we are suddenly reading words *by* a deaf character; Burnet manages to allow Mary to have a voice, a deaf "I." Shortly before Mary's graduation, George (with whom she grew up) reappears. Having forgotten their home sign, George for a moment cannot think how to communicate with her, but remembering that Mary is now literate, he takes out his pencil and they begin a long written conversation. Burnet shows not only how the school has enabled Mary to become an independent, capable adult, but also how writing, again, can act as a bridge between educated deaf and hearing people.

Finally, with its sympathetic and bigoted characters, "The Orphan Mute" implicitly critiques hearing attitudes toward deaf people. George emerges as a model of positive hearing behavior. He treats Mary respectfully and attentively, developing a home sign with her when they are young and, after she returns from school, learning "the eloquent and poetic language of gestures" so he can readily communicate with her (168). Ironically, George finds that he can express his feelings in this language "much more forcibly and clearly than words could do," indicating that sign is a valuable form of communication in its own right (168). In contrast, his uncle epitomizes the most derogatory hearing attitudes. He calls Mary "no better than a well-taught parrot, a beautiful automaton," and refuses George's request for permission to marry her (176). The uncle does not believe that Mary is fully human. Coming from a deaf author, and especially in conjunction with his earlier essay on prejudice, it seems likely that Burnet must have had personal experience with such bigotry. The uncle's disapproval of a deaf-hearing union has parallels to the taboo on mixed marriages; they are proscribed because they are perceived as the mixing of superior with inferior people, of blending species that should be segregated. In the conclusion of the sentimental plot, George happily weds Mary and gains his inheritance, representing the triumph of progressive hearing attitudes toward deaf people.

Not content to depict the value of sign, education, and community only through prose, Burnet also includes a poem, "Emma," that further drives home these themes. Unlike in "The Orphan Mute," here Burnet extends Clerc's early missionary rhetoric, describing Emma, a girl who becomes deaf due to illness, in inflated imagery of gloom and entombment before she goes to school. Going against his own words elsewhere against "highly colored" depictions of uneducated deaf people (47), Burnet reveals the pervasive influence of such imagery. After these bleak images of isolation, he shows the emancipating effects of school, presenting a jubilant account of community and connection:

> I see an hundred of the deaf and dumb,—
> Collected from full many a distant home,—
> Within this noble pile,—whose walls—to them
> Open'd another world,—a fairy realm;
> A realm of a new language,—all their own,
> Where mind was visible,—and knowledge shone. . . .
> *Here*, from the speaking limbs, and face divine,
> At nature's bidding, thoughts and feelings shine,
> That in thin air no more her sense elude,—
> Each understands,—by each is understood.
> Here can each feeling gush forth, unrepressed,
> To mix with feelings of a kindred breast. (196)

Skillfully evoking the headiness of sign language and deaf culture, Burnet gives a sense of the liberation and self-discovery that many deaf students experienced at residential schools. With "I see," he again calls attention to vision, emphasizing visual language rather than the lack of hearing.[33] While the dashes give a broken movement to the lines, the occasional off-rhymes add to the energy and excitement; we are in iambic pentameter, but it is not quite predictable. He goes on to describe the deaf students in chapel watching prayers and lessons "from the hand with graceful gesture flung" (197), showing how sign helps to bring Emma and deaf students like her into the Christian faith. With his poem and story, Burnet takes Clerc's advocacy of sign and deaf education, and Nack's efforts to create a deaf self in verse, and revises and expands these precedents to offer a new vision of deaf experience in print, one that illustrates why most educated deaf Americans cared deeply about their language, community, and schools.

Together, Clerc, Nack, and Burnet achieved a voice through their writing that expressed not just themselves individually, but also, by extension, all deaf Americans. As white males, they enjoyed privileges not available to many deaf people, but through their pioneering works they began to open the way for more deaf Americans to succeed in antebellum society. From being mute and powerless on the social margins, they sought to write deaf people into national understanding by sharing their point of view and contesting some of the ways that hearing people imagined them. In the process, they used many of the same subaltern strategies as other minority authors to express themselves to the public. In their written works they oscillate between two different social constructions of identity, an "ethnic" one based on sign language and a deaf communal consciousness, and a "colonial" one based on the views of the dominant culture that saw them as inferior.[34] This self-division sometimes causes them to offer seemingly contradictory statements of pity and pride as they express the ambiguities of their conflicted state. However, it also leads them to imbue their writing with a double vision that both uses hearing values and threatens them by arguing against the existing hegemony.

For all the differences in their writing style and form, Clerc, Nack, and Burnet all explicitly or implicitly argue for social change. They attack the notions that deaf people are subhuman, ineducable, and dense, that they are beings without language or feeling, are incapable of literary expression, and have nothing to contribute to American society. Emphasizing their commonality with hearing people, they nevertheless assert one basic difference. While sometimes they present this difference in auditory terms, at others they frame it as a matter of vision. Clerc and Burnet both present themselves as using a visual language and sharing a visual community; "*their eyes supply the place of ears*," Burnet repeatedly reminds hearing readers (*Tales* 15). Even Nack, who does not mention sign in his poetry, positions himself as more visually perceptive than his hearing counterparts, as if deafness has sharpened his acuity with this sense and afforded him special insight. If deaf Americans were given respect, access to visual language, and education, these writers argue, they would thrive and society would be more just. "Let the deaf and dumb, then, be regarded as your own brethren," Burnet concludes (50). Through writing, these deaf authors, none of whom spoke much vocally in person, were able to find a distinct voice. It remains to be seen just how well they were heeded.

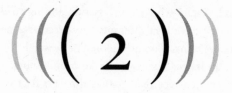

Essaying the Unsayable

THE DEAF PRESENCE IN ANTEBELLUM AMERICAN LITERATURE

*"Just and venerable Delaware. . . . Be deaf to yonder
artful and remorseless monster, who poisons thy ears with
falsehoods, to feed his thirst for blood."*
James Fenimore Cooper, *The Last of the Mohicans* (1826)

*The re-examination of founding literature of the
United States for the unspeakable unspoken may reveal those
texts to have deeper and other meanings, deeper and other
power, deeper and other significances.*
Toni Morrison (1989)

In 1835, John Burnet contended that hearing novelists had never depicted a deaf person. "We have often been surprised that among the host of novel writers who are incessantly aiming to delineate new characters, none have ever attempted to describe a deaf mute," he wrote. "Here, we think, is an unexplored field, worthy of the genius of a Cooper, or an Irving" (229). While we could quibble with Burnet's claim,[1] he seems correct that at that time no deaf characters had appeared in American literature. As we will see, later hearing authors like Herman Melville, Walt Whitman, Ambrose Bierce, and Mark Twain did portray deaf characters in their work. Yet even in early canonical literature that ostensibly has nothing to do with deafness, we can detect an engagement with the hearing line through authors' depiction of silence and gesture and use of deaf-related images and metaphors. Taken together, these elements contribute to what I, following Toni Morrison's concept of an Africanist presence, call a "deaf presence" in early American writing, an abiding discourse that, while subtle, rarely seems distant from these works. To me this deaf presence adds to the power of such literature, making it even more intriguing, complex, and rich. Yet scholars seem to have either overlooked this presence or taken the assumptions behind it for granted, an omission that resembles earlier critical lacunas about such topics as gender and race. In recent decades scholars working in these areas have broadened our understanding of American writing by pointing out the complex ways in which it addresses women, African Americans, and other groups. Building upon these insights, I call attention to the hearing parts of the equation and inspect the ways that canonical authors wrote deafness. By exploring how the deaf presence appears within these works, we can see how writers consciously or unconsciously use it to define not just deaf individuals, but also themselves as hearing people. In other words, they effectively construct and probe the hearing line.

In making this argument, I am drawing especially from Morrison, who in her book *Playing in the Dark* (1992) calls for a reinterpretation of our national literature to take into account the ways that it negotiates racial identity. Morrison identifies an "Africanist presence" in our literary canon, which she defines as "the denotative and connotative blackness that African peoples have come to signify, as well as the entire range of views, assumptions, readings, and misreadings that accompany Eurocentric learning about these people" (6–7). She contends that this presence gives force to classics by Edgar Allan Poe, Nathaniel Hawthorne, Melville, Twain, and others. "The contemplation of this black presence is central to any understanding of our national literature and should not be permitted to hover at the margins of the literary imagination," she maintains (5). In insisting that we need to be conscious of how race informs the work of white males, Morrison extends the arguments of earlier critics like Du Bois, who, in *The Souls of Black Folk* (1903), argued that white American culture is bound up with black American culture, and Ralph Ellison, who found it difficult to believe that white people "can be so absurdly self-deluded over the true interrelatedness of blackness and whiteness" (*Shadow* 55). Such insights have helped us to appreciate how our national literature relates to all Americans, navigating and producing identities in the process.

Morrison's theory can be extended quite effectively to deaf Americans and the canon. Even though the literary works are written by, "about," and for hearing people, we can often detect an implicit meditation on what it means to hear and speak or not to do so. It is as if, in creating their written speech acts, authors felt compelled to contemplate the absence of speech and hearing, concerns that they could readily express through tropes of deafness. Often this deaf presence shows up indirectly, in portrayals of silence and nonverbal communication or use of deaf-related imagery. As we will see in the next chapter, it appears more overtly in the representation of physically deaf people starting around 1840. Our founding literature does seem to convey the dominant mindset of the young republic, expressing popular attitudes and occasionally questioning or exorcizing them.

Hearing authors address a wide variety of topics with the deaf presence, frequently in language of both attraction and dread. Deafness offers a convenient way to explore and police such issues as language, hearing, speech, and nonvocal communication; civilization, difference, compassion, and religion; the unknown, danger, disorder, limitation, fear, and power.[2] Their imaginative renderings of deafness reveal a jumble of terror and fascination that also characterizes European portrayals of the Orient, white apprehensions of blackness, and male fantasies about women. I explore this mix of longing and dread in more depth in the next chapter. For now, we can note that the deaf presence offers writers a way to suggest the ineffable, to approach the unknowable, and to grapple with human difference as they treat deafness with a paradoxical mixture of anxiety and yearning.

Through tropes of deafness, antebellum hearing authors contribute to what we might call the national auditory consciousness, the way that the hearing majority conceptualized and thought about individuals who were deaf as well as about their own identities as hearing, speaking people. Just as Morrison put literary whiteness on the table for critical investigation, prompting an outpouring of scholarship,[3] so I suggest that literary "hearingness" is equally ripe for critical inquiry. The fact that hearingness is not even a word underscores how formulations of auditory identity have rarely been probed. We have blackness, whiteness, maleness, femaleness, deafness, blindness, Americanness, a myriad of nesses that serve to demarcate, identify, and label, but no equivalent term to describe the state of having auditory ability. While deafness has been discussed since ancient times, hearingness has been left largely unremarked, for hearing people deem it unremarkable, a state of predictable normalcy that does not deserve inspection. George Lipsitz's observation about whiteness holds equally true for hearingness: it "never has to speak its name, never has to acknowledge its role as an organizing principle in social or cultural relations" (369). Whereas Richard Dyer asserts that "white power secures its dominance by seeming not to be anything in particular," we could say the same thing about hearing hegemony in our society (qtd. in Lipsitz 369). We are so unaccustomed to thinking about hearingness that we routinely accept and replicate hidden signs of aural superiority. By examining the deaf presence, we begin to see that hearingness is not an absolute or a given, but something subjectively imagined and formed. Canonical authors use the unknown, imagined expanse of deafness reflexively to negotiate their own identities as hearing people.

In the remainder of this chapter and in chapters 3 and 5 I examine specific instances of the deaf presence in nineteenth-century American literature by hearing authors, moving from figurative representations of deafness to depictions of physically deaf characters and of hearing characters acting deaf. Through my discussion, I hope to enrich our understanding of the complexity, power, and scope of these texts. My goal is not to enforce a strict allegorical schema upon them or to reduce their many meanings through one critical approach. Nor do I wish to pass judgment on the merits of these works for the ways in which they do or do not contain prejudice, ignorance, or progressivism. Along with Morrison, I want "to enhance canon readings without enshrining them" ("Unspeakable" 19). What intrigues me is how early American writers imaginatively address matters of hearing, speech, and related topics, the very concerns that deaf and hearing citizens had to negotiate as they began increasingly to come into contact with one another in nineteenth-century society. The deaf presence illustrates the universality of the canon in a specific new way. Three writers who are particularly rewarding to consider in this light are Washington Irving, James Fenimore Cooper, and Herman Melville, whose best-known work revolves around a fabricated deafness.

SILENCE AS DEAFNESS

The most frequent and elusive way that the deaf presence appears in antebellum canonical literature is through depictions of silence. Hearing Americans routinely imagined deaf people as silent, even if early deaf writers like Clerc, Nack, and Burnet seldom described themselves with this term. While deaf authors often emphasized the visual, hearing people tended to stress the auditory. Because silence conveys both the absence of sound (deafness) and the absence of speech (muteness), hearing writers found it an apt descriptor of deaf people. For example, in an 1819 poem to celebrate the opening of the New York Institution, Moses Scott said deaf people are individuals "in whom eternal silence reigns profound!" (6). They are "Silent on Earth" (9), "the *silent* throng" (12, emphasis in original), walking manifestations of soundlessness. In 1845 the poet Lydia Huntley Sigourney referred to deaf students as "silent beings" (242), while in 1852 Henry Barnard, the head of the Connecticut school system, pronounced them "the sons and daughters of silence" (9). Such tropes became par for the course, a convenient shorthand for evoking and denoting deafness. A cursory glance at American poetry about deaf people from the period turns up countless titles with silence, including "The Silent Path," "Silent

Voices," "Our Silent Ones," "A Silent Life," "The Silent Children," and "Sacred Silence."[4] The expression "children of silence" emerged as an especially popular catchphrase. In chapter 3 I explore how, when hearing authors began to depict deaf people, they almost always made them soundless. As we will see, silence is a problematic metaphor for deaf experience, and one that later deaf writers sometimes contested; deafness is not silence, but many hearing people in the nineteenth century, like today, routinely conflated the two. By considering hearing authors' representations of silence, we can therefore perhaps begin to discern some of their unconscious attitudes toward deafness and toward themselves as hearing people. However, the meanings that silence assumes in these texts are not straightforward.

Silence and deafness do resemble one another in that both seem to lie beyond language and rational understanding. As Henry David Thoreau lamented in 1849, "It were vain for me to endeavor to interpret the Silence. She cannot be done into English" (*A Week* 420). To Thoreau, silence remains a "sealed book" despite six thousand years of human commentary upon it. Critical exegesis will always fail because ultimately silence lies beyond language; to grasp any one aspect of silence risks missing a great deal more. Any effort to try to define silence (or deafness) ultimately must appear incomplete, for they are always larger, always beyond the scope of human comprehension.

Moreover, just as silence takes on significance based on sound and vice versa, so the meaning of deafness is dependent on hearingness. George Steiner and Adam Jaworski have shown that Western culture is organized frequently to discourage silence. Words, logos, discourses of history, and other verbal strategies try to minimize stillness. Yet while silence appears the opposite of speech and literary acts, it is also entwined with them. Lennard J. Davis has pointed out that silence not only precedes and supersedes a text, but also occurs within a literary work, in space between words, breaks, ellipses, and even, to an extent, in authors' paradoxical efforts to represent silence through language (*Enforcing* 116–17). Silence functions as a complex element in dialogue. "'Silence' never ceases to imply its opposite and to depend on its presence," Susan Sontag writes. "One must acknowledge a surrounding environment of sound or language in order to recognize silence" (187). Sound and silence are connected and depend on one another. We could say the same thing about deafness: without hearingness, deafness would have no meaning. There would be no hearing line.

Finally, silence and deafness resemble each other in that their significance is not universal or inherent, but rather culturally specific. Antebellum texts illustrate how the meanings of silence, which may appear absolute, are actually shifting and subjective, revealing more about the characters, authors, cultural moment, and reader than about the negative states of silence and deafness themselves. In their works hearing authors reveal a fundamental ambivalence where the appealing connotations of silence never seem too distant from the disturbing ones. These contradictory treatments of silence provide a useful template for understanding how hearing Americans may have imagined deafness in the first half of the nineteenth century. Although they ostensibly have nothing to do with deafness, two of Washington Irving's classic stories, "Rip Van Winkle" and "The Legend of Sleepy Hollow" (1819–20), serve as representative examples. Interestingly, they appeared just a few years after Irving was the shipmate of Thomas Hopkins Gallaudet in 1815 during the latter's voyage to Europe to learn how to teach deaf students.[5]

Irving begins both tales by presenting a pastoral vision of silence as offering a welcome refuge from the clamor of life. In "The Legend of Sleepy Hollow," the narrator nostalgically describes the valley as "one of the quietest places in the whole world," with almost "uniform tranquility" that allows one to escape "the world and its distractions" (291–92). Irving establishes a sharp contrast between the noisy pace of rapidly modernizing society, which is "restless" and "making such incessant changes," and the charming, peaceful stillness of Sleepy Hollow (293). In "Rip Van Winkle" such quiet is precisely what the title character seeks. At the opening of the story Rip is assailed by his nagging wife, who "kept continually dinning his ears about his idleness. . . . Morning, noon, and night, her tongue was incessantly going" (36). Dame Van Winkle's ceaseless noise drives Rip out of the house, first to a tavern, and then, when she follows him there, into the Catskill Mountains, where the "still solitudes" of the woods, along with the sight of the Hudson River moving in its "silent but majestic course," give him a feeling of utter tranquility (38). The mountain's stillness serves as a haven, for it is the complete antithesis of his cacophonous home. Such depictions play off the romantic conception of nature as place of rebirth and regeneration. Silence takes on positive meaning in these cases because of its juxtaposition to the unsettling clamor of Dame Van Winkle and society; the disruption of human sound makes silence appear soothing. Given the linkage between silence and deafness in hearing minds, we can imagine how nineteenth-century hearing Americans might sometimes construe deafness as a peaceful state, an escape from the busy tumult of the modern world.

If silence appears natural and comforting in the first part of these tales, it quickly becomes unnatural and ominous when strangers do not speak to each other. When a short man in old-fashioned Dutch clothes appears to Rip carrying a keg, he does not say anything, although he presumably had called Rip's name a moment before. He merely gestures for Rip to help him. The silence soon becomes uncomfortable: "During the whole time Rip and his companion . . . labored on in silence; for though the former marveled greatly what could be the object of carrying a keg of liquor up this wild mountain, yet there was something strange and incomprehensible about the unknown, that inspired awe and checked familiarity" (39). Far from calming, this silence is eerie. By not speaking, the man violates the rules of European American culture, which call for strangers meeting for the first time to greet each other or introduce themselves. In this silence, Rip is disempowered, participating in something outlandish he does not understand. The sense of something amiss grows when Rip meets the band of cheerless men playing ninepins. They maintain "the most mysterious silence," so that "nothing interrupted the stillness of the scene but the noise of the balls, which . . . echoed . . . like rumbling peals of thunder" (40). Once again Irving draws out a meaning of silence by juxtaposing it with sound; the thunderous crashes underscore the threatening nature of the company's speechlessness, a threat made more apparent by the players' menacing expressions. Unlike the serene silence in the first half of the story, this silence causes "fear and trembling" in Rip (40).

A similar movement occurs in "Sleepy Hollow," where the initial consoling stillness of the valley soon gives way to the intimidating soundlessness of the Headless Horseman. Although Ichabod Crane is an expert purveyor of sound, he cannot elude the visceral terrors of silence. A master singer in the area, he teaches psalmody; people admire him for his "superior address," "great erudition," and tales of witches, and he has an "authoritative voice" as teacher in the school-room (296, 294). Yet just as Rip encounters the silent figures in the mountains, so Ichabod confronts the imposingly speechless Horse-man. He rides home through a "dead hush of midnight" that is only interrupted by the far-off sounds of a dog barking and of other ani-mals (312). Except for the darkness, this silence does not significantly differ from the restful quiet at the opening of the story, but to Ichabod, with his head full of ghost stories, the midnight stillness is distressing. He tries to calm himself first by whistling, then by singing to himself; again we have a contrast of sound and silence. However, his voice fails once he meets the Headless Horseman, who frightens him by not responding to his queries: "There was something in the moody and dogged silence of this pertinacious companion, that was mysterious and appalling" (314). Once again, a figure who fails to speak is omi-nous, and such silence is associated with the supernatural and un-known. When the horseman hurls something that appears to be his head at Ichabod, the latter flees Sleepy Hollow forever in terror.

These episodes with silent, spectral figures who may or may not be alive display elements of Freudian uncanniness, even if Irving under-cuts much of the anxiety with his folksy humor. In his account of the uncanny, Freud implies that positive and negative meanings of silence may actually not be an opposition at all. Calling the *unheimlich* ("un-canny") a subcategory of the *heimlich* ("homelike"), he argues that "this uncanny is in reality nothing new or foreign, but something familiar and old-established in the mind that has been estranged only by the process of repression" (241). When a person recalls these re-pressed desires and ways of thinking, anxiety can result. Among other things, Freud contends that silence (like darkness and solitude) may arouse feelings of danger by reviving repressed fears that begin in infancy when a child dreads the loss of love. In this view, silence can seem threatening because it can make people feel vulnerable and at risk of losing connection with others. Freud's suggestive analysis also implies that silence can represent the chilling proximity of death, which is why it so often appears in Gothic tales. Again, such depictions perhaps offer insight into how early-nineteenth-century hearing Americans sometimes imagined deafness. Just as Rip and Ichabod feel

Ichabod flees the Headless Horseman. (Engraving by Richardson.)
From The Legend of Sleepy Hollow, and the Spectre Bridegroom
(Philadelphia: J. B. Lippincott Company, 1886).

frightened and mystified by the speechless figures they encounter, so early-nineteenth-century hearing people may have sometimes felt afraid of deaf individuals who did not speak, seeing them as both familiar and foreign, as otherworldly reminders of the danger of isolation or even as a kind of living death. Yet Irving's literary silences do not quite create uncanny moments for us as readers. The narrator's comical tone reduces the tension; while Rip and Ichabod tremble, we may be more inclined to smile. Readers usually suspect that the roguish Brom Bones is the Horseman, and that the dreamlike figures are all part of Rip's imagination. After all, when Rip returns to town he varies on the details of his story before settling on a single version. While Irving thus provides a useful glimpse of the uncanniness of silence (and deafness) in hearing minds, he distances us from it through the reassuring buffer of humor.

Even as he moves from one construction of silence to another, Irving mixes positive and negative aspects, pointing to how the significance of silence is finally unstable and ambiguous. At the end of "Sleepy Hollow" we may ask: Is the valley's stillness comforting or eerie, especially given the local superstition that Ichabod's ghostly voice remains, "chanting a melancholy psalm tune among tranquil solitudes of Sleepy Hollow" (318)? The silence seems both reassuring and spooky, and neither, vague, indefinite, always containing new possibility and beyond any one assigned meaning. A similar ambivalence toward silence appears at the end of "Rip Van Winkle." Rip's twenty-year descent into the quiet, unconscious world of sleep culminates his progression from noise toward silence, but the meaning of his silent slumber at the heart of the story seems contradictory. On the one hand, his lengthy nap serves as the ultimate sanctuary, enabling him to escape not only his "terrible virago" of a wife once and for all, but also the strife and commotion of the Revolutionary War (38). However, his slumber is also profoundly disorienting. It takes just a fraction of a second in the reading of the narrative, yet by the end it looms as an enormous blank silence, a moment of amnesia or aphasia, a disconnection from all around him, even a sort of death. When Rip returns to town, his descent into silence has made him into a figure of isolation. His friends and family are gone, and when he calls for his wife and daughters at his desolate house, "the lonely chambers rang for a moment with his voice, and then all again was silence," a moment of Freudian *unheimlich* (which connotes both familiar and unhomelike) if there ever was one (42–43). Although Rip gradually manages to rejoin the world of sound and the human community, finding his son and daughter and regaling citizens with his wild tale, the meaning of his adventure remains unclear. The story concludes with other henpecked husbands yearning for a "quieting draught of Rip Van Winkle's flagon" (48). They, too, desire silence, but as Rip's story shows, silence is not uniformly attractive: it can just as easily be dangerous, disorienting, and isolating as it can be a refuge. In both stories, the meaning of silence ultimately is indefinite, shot through with ambivalence. I do not wish completely to collapse silence into deafness or argue that they are always equal in hearing imaginations, but nonetheless Irving's tales provide an early indication that hearing Americans felt similarly conflicted about those whom they often conceived as beings of silence, deaf people.

Irving's example provides a fitting introduction to the intricate ways that silence functions in the founding literature of the United States, for a quick survey reveals that subsequent hearing authors represent it in a similarly equivocal manner. In *The Last of the Mohicans* (1826), Cooper presents an archetypical wilderness whose persistent stillness is at once majestic, part of the serene wonder of nature, and threatening, since lurking out of sight in that silence are hostile Huron Indians. With murderers potentially hidden behind every tree, Hawk-eye's party must whisper and can rarely relax; silence here is again uncanny, a produced stillness rather than simply an absence of sound. Adding to positive depictions of quietude, in *A Week on the Concord and Merrimack Rivers* (1849) Thoreau praises silence as "the universal refuge, the sequel to all dull discourses and all foolish acts, a balm to every chagrin, as welcome after satiety as after disappointment" (418). He wrote the book largely while living at Walden Pond, finding that the stillness enhanced his reflectiveness and literary output, an interpretation that hearkens back to the Zen view of silence as promoting meditation and wisdom.[6] In *Walden* (1854) Thoreau also presents silence as part of his communion with nature, but even he sought to break the stillness by hosting frequent visitors at his hut and walking into town to learn the latest news, suggesting that while temporary silence may be appealing, permanent silence is less desirable. In Melville's *Moby-Dick* (1851), we again encounter slippage between positive and threatening depictions of silence when Ishmael describes standing on the masthead of the whaling ship. Initially he finds it an "exceedingly pleasant . . . delight" to stand in the calm silence where "you hear no news" (169), away from verbal excess of society. Yet just as we accept this peaceful vision, Ishmael abruptly warns how silence can be treacherous: "Lulled into such an opium-like listlessness of vacant, unconscious reverie is this absentminded youth by the blending cadence of waves with thoughts, that at last he loses his identity" (172). The stillness, broken only by the sound of the ocean's waves, can become so mesmerizing that it destroys one's self and casts one into oblivion. The uncanniness here stems not from the presence of another speechless person, but from the vast emptiness of silence itself. Under the guise of serene escape, silence endangers: it can trap you, like a soundless Siren, and lure you into the abyss. Later, when a sailor falls from the masthead to his death in the sea, this danger seems to be realized.

Inevitably the clash between logos and silence comes back to the impossibility of ever defining, describing, or fully grasping the absence of sound.[7] We may well assert about silence, as Ishmael does of whiteness, that "to analyze it, would seem impossible" (209). Nonetheless, we can detect how antebellum hearing authors tend to oscillate between positive and negative interpretations of silence, presenting it as serene at one moment, frightening the next, sliding from the *heimlich* into the *unheimlich* and back again. These shifting interpretations point to how silence itself has no essential meaning. Silence may be physically present, but it is opaque, its significance socially and culturally produced and dependent on sound. The various meanings that people project onto silence spring from their own minds, their own fears and wishes, which arguably include the meanings I identify in my exegesis above.

Because hearing Americans commonly associated deafness with silence (as the next chapter demonstrates more clearly), these literary encounters with silence offer insight into how hearing people may have imagined lack of speech or hearing in the early nineteenth century. From Rip's descent into silence to Cooper's ominous forests to Thoreau's paean to quietude, these works all implicitly confront deafness.

Furthermore, they produce hearingness: against the vast emptiness of imagined silences, the meaning of speaking vocally with others and responding to sound comes into sharper focus. Again, we see the deafness and hearingness are interrelated and dependent on each other.

Yet how accurate is silence as a metaphor for deaf experience? Silence does appear to resemble deafness in the way that it cannot be captured in words, and in the way that its significance depends on its opposite and its meanings are culturally produced. Nevertheless, silence is not quite an accurate representation of deaf people. Despite the ubiquity of the trope in nineteenth-century hearing accounts of deaf people, metaphors of silence mistakenly make it appear that deaf people live in an utterly soundless world and are soundless themselves, as we will see in chapter 4. Furthermore, as Douglas Baynton argues, while hearing people tend to imagine silence as an absence, deaf people typically do not experience deafness that way, unless they have recently lost their hearing. This argument helps to explain why Clerc, Nack, and Burnet tend to portray themselves in visual rather than auditory terms. Metaphors of silence also fail to represent deaf experience because they focus only on the inability to hear or speak, leaving out deaf people's community, language, and manner of being. In writing about silence, antebellum hearing authors point to the way that hearing people can, in a sense, temporarily experience deafness. I have been arguing that Rip's immersion in silence metaphorically serves as an immersion in deafness, since hearing people in the nineteenth century equated the two. Yet it is crucial to note that experiencing the diminishment of sound is not the same as becoming a deaf person, any more than donning blackface makes a white person African American. Deaf people's community, values, and language are formed by being deaf over a period of time and are socially produced. Deafness, as an identity, extends far beyond audiograms and eardrums. As Baynton puts it: "When hearing people think of the world of the deaf as silent, they are comparing and reducing an identity, a way of life, an infinitely complex set of social and cultural relationships to a simple and concrete phenomenon: a temporary absence of sound" (24). Despite these shortcomings, hearing Americans continued to employ imagery of silence to describe deaf people, and, as we will see in chapter 4, some subsequent deaf authors responded by using tropes of silence themselves, creating a gap between written representations and actual deaf experience similar to what we observed with hyperbolic rhetoric of brutishness in the previous chapter.

Some early works hint at other, non-audiological aspects of deaf people's identity through their depiction of gesture, which forms another component of the deaf presence in literature. The manner in which early canonical authors envisioned visual-gestural communication in general suggests how hearing Americans may have conceived the sign language of deaf people. As we will see, in these works body language and gestures can play an important role, sometimes augmenting spoken discourse and sometimes undermining or replacing it. Let us return briefly to "Rip Van Winkle," which in many ways serves as a prototype of attitudes toward silence and gesture in early-nineteenth-century America. In it, Irving comically presents the power of body language. We have already seen how the strange man commands Rip with a motion to help him, while the silent ninepin players intimidate him with their threatening looks. Silent expressiveness also gives Nicholas Vedder, the proprietor of the local tavern, a certain authority. Although he is "rarely heard to speak," Vedder "completely controlled" the languid discussions among the regulars, for the others understand his opinions from the way he smokes his pipe: vehemently when displeased, peacefully when contented, and nodding when approving (37). In contrast to the idle talk, which appears rather inconsequential, Vedder's silent body language is full of meaning and gives him clout. Similarly, Rip appears to obtain strength from nonvocal communication. When facing his wife's shrill condemnations, "he shrugged his shoulders, shook his head, cast up his eyes, but said nothing" (36). The meaning of Rip's reaction is not immediately clear; his gesture could just as easily be a mark of passive resistance as of agreement and submission. After he returns at the end of the story, whenever he hears the name of his deceased wife, he repeats his habitual silent shrug and head shake, which "might pass either for an expression of resignation to his fate, or joy at his deliverance" (47). Despite such seeming ambiguity, we can scarcely doubt that Rip feels relief to be free of his wife's harangues, especially given the gender stereotype at work here. In the end, his silent body language prevails over Dame Van Winkle's strident voice.

The characters' visual cues relate to deaf people's sign language by showing that effective communication is possible without vocal speech. Whether menacing, approving, or ambiguous, the characters' body language often carries more weight than the speech of others, which frequently resembles so much blather. In this way, the tale occasionally questions the conception of hearingness as a consistent mark of superiority. However, the situation is complicated by the fact that Rip is a tale-teller who entrances, entertains, and finds connection with others through his spoken words. Just as we see Janus-faced, ambivalent portrayals of silence, so Irving seems to have it both ways here, displaying the pleasures of vocal discourse while simultaneously pointing to the potentially advantageous aspects of nonvocal ways of communicating and being. As we will see, he is not the only canonical author to approach the deaf presence in such a two-sided fashion.

COOPER AND THE FRONTIERS OF DEAFNESS

James Fenimore Cooper makes sound, silence, speech, and gesture even more prominent in his work than Irving, but he treats them in a similarly equivocal manner. Pointing to Cooper's role as an important cartographer of early American consciousness, critics have discussed how, in *The Last of the Mohicans*, he takes on central issues that were confronting the young republic, including the relationship between civilization and wilderness, between whites and Native Americans, and between licit and elicit desires, but his elaborate exploration of hearingness and deafness has received scant attention.[8] The first words of the novel are "Mine ear is open," taken from Shakespeare's *Richard II* as the beginning of an epigraph to chapter 1 (11). The auditory emphasis is appropriate, for aural imagery dominates the novel. Earlier I mentioned how Cooper depicts a silent, sublime wilderness that is alternatively peaceful and frightening, where the smallest sound can indicate imminent death. In this landscape the Indians and whites have profoundly different attitudes toward speech, sound, and gesture, pointing again to how the significance of these things is not universal but culturally dependent. While Cooper's Native Americans dwell comfortably within silence, often using hand signals to communicate, especially in the first part of the novel, his white characters struggle to come to terms with a place where speech is not always valued or effective. Through the resulting disjunction, Cooper inter-rogates the hearing line. Although he sometimes treats deaf attributes respectfully and hearing characteristics more skeptically, in the end he seems to affirm the ability to hear (along with whiteness and male-ness) as marks of superiority.

The discrepancy between the two groups with regard to sound becomes apparent in the opening pages of the novel, when Alice meets the treacherous Huron Magua (who poses as a guide) for the first time. She asks Heyward to get Magua to speak so she can tell what kind of character he has. "Foolish though it may be, you have often heard me avow my faith in the tones of the human voice!" she says (21). From the outset, Cooper associates reliance on speech and hear-ingness with whites, especially white women. In contrast, silence and deafness is the province of Native Americans and masculinity: Magua is quiet, willful (he would refuse to speak, Heyward tells Alice), and, as we later learn, a fierce warrior. Already a dichotomy has been estab-lished, and already we can discern a certain ambivalence on Cooper's part. That Magua does not speak and turns out to be an enemy seems to vindicate Alice's logocentric instincts; yet in imbuing Magua with dignity and wordless power, Cooper previews his concomitant admi-ration for Native American—and perhaps deaf—ways of being.[9]

Throughout the novel, Cooper draws out this connection between Native Americans and stillness; like deaf people, the Indians are fre-quently imagined as beings of silence, quite different from the highly verbal world of white, hearing society. When we first encounter Chin-gachgook with Hawk-eye, the chief allows a "silence of a minute" to pass before he answers a question (31). After Chingachgook's son Uncas appears, they both say nothing for several minutes, "each ap-pearing to await the moment, when he might speak, without betray-ing womanish curiosity or childish impatience" (33). Such behavior is at odds with white social mores, where a question or the appearance of a family member would normally require verbal acknowledgment, but because the participants share the same cultural understanding of silence these moments are comfortable rather than uncanny. Gener-ally, the more important the occasion, the longer the Native American characters are silent. Before Chingachgook, Uncas, and Hawk-eye have a terse debate, they sit passing a pipe "amid the most profound silence" (198). When Heyward goes in disguise to a Huron meeting, he must adapt to different codes of conduct. "A long and grave pause succeeded," the narrator says. "Duncan, who knew that silence was a virtue amongst his hosts, gladly had recourse to the custom, in order to arrange his ideas" (234). We also observe this appreciation for silence after Magua returns from battle; the chief sits quietly with his fellow Hurons for "ten minutes, which appeared so many ages to Duncan" (246). The silence, which seems appropriate to the Native Americans, discomfits Heyward because it is alien to his experience.[10] The Indians' silences add to their charisma, mystery, and allure. They become a regular feature in the narrative, mirroring the narrator's repeated comments on the silence of the wilderness and aligning the Native Americans with nature.

The Native Americans also resemble deaf people somewhat in their use of nonvocal communication, for Cooper's Indians are probably the most eloquent signers in antebellum literature by hearing authors. For instance, when giving an address to his fellow Hurons, Magua employs "those significant gestures with which an Indian always illustrates his eloquence" (106). He not only tells the others about a warrior's tragic death, but also reenacts it in graphic pantomime. These gestures add to Magua's persuasiveness and help to solidify his position as leader of the tribe. We encounter similar silent communication throughout the novel. We are told that Chingachgook's "gestures were impressive, and at times, energetic" (226). Magua sometimes orders others with signals, as when he "made a sign" for Cora to mount a horse (178). After Magua professes peace to the Delaware chief, the latter "acknowledged the pacific compliment by a gesture of the hand, and remained silent" (288). Gestures serve as a quick and effective way to communicate in the narrative; Cooper presents such movements as unmediated expressions of truth. Uncas and Chingachgook's gesticulations are "direct and natural," easy for an outsider like Duncan Heyward to understand (198). Unlike spoken languages, which typically separate the white characters and the various Indian tribes from each other, gestures are simple, natural, and universally comprehensible.[11] In this way, the Native Americans form a deaf presence at times, and the novel appears to valorize their commanding discourse of signs over speech.

In contrast to the Indians, the white outsiders' reliance on speech and discomfort with silence establishes them as figures of hearingness. Heyward's uneasiness among the quiet Hurons, as well as Alice's opening remark about Magua, point to how they put a premium on speech and sound. Native Americans like Magua think that the whites talk too much. "[T]he pale faces are prattling women!" he says at one point, connecting loquaciousness with both race (whites) and gender (females) once more (91).[12] While the Indians prove highly skilled at blending in with the quiet forest around them, the European Americans do not know how to navigate the quietude of the wilderness. "[S]peak not a syllable; it is rare for a white voice to pitch itself properly in the woods," Hawk-eye cautions Heyward, Gamut, Alice, and Cora (201). Moreover, the white characters prove less adept with nonverbal communication. For example, as Heyward watches Uncas, Chingachgook, and Hawk-eye debate in the Native Americans' language, he understands the Indians because of their gestures, but Hawk-eye's comments are unclear because he "affected the cold and inartificial manner, which characterizes all classes of Anglo-Americans, when unexcited" (199). Only when it appears that he will lose the argument does Hawk-eye, a liminal figure who has lived among Native Americans for many years, begin expressively to gesticulate. European Americans, for all their supposed civilization and racial superiority, lack the Indian's powerful skill of communicating visually. We might even suggest that the novel presents gestures as the remedy to what Ralph Waldo Emerson would later lament in *Nature* as the tiredness and the corruption of language.[13] At any rate, the Native American's comfort with silence and sign throws the white characters' hearingness into high relief, in effect allowing hearingness to exist, and it initially does not seem of much value. In Cooper's natural world, expertise with nonaural modes of living at first seems more beneficial.

Yet as David Gamut, the character who most epitomizes the primacy of aural-oral forms in European American culture, reveals, Cooper's take on speech and hearing is far from straightforward. From the moment he joins the party so he can "partake of social communion" and talk with others, Gamut is linked with speech and sound (24). Like Ichabod Crane, Gamut is at once clownish and an expert singer, a psalmist who is the antithesis of deaf: his ears are called "exquisite organs," and at one point he jokes, "[I]f dumb, there would be an end to my calling" (324, 24). Through his character, we see both the weakness and strength of white society's privileging of the voice. On one hand, the awkward and effeminate Gamut is completely out of place in the forest, unable to assist with physical labor or fighting enemies. "The Lord never intended that the man should place all his endeavours in his throat, to the neglect of other and better gifts!" Hawk-eye exclaims to him in exasperation (224). For all his verbal skills, Gamut often seems quite helpless; in this respect, Cooper again makes the logocentric European Americans appear behind the game, less vigorous and farther from nature than their deaf-like Indian counterparts, who resemble versions of Rousseau's conception of natural man. However, as the novel unfolds, Gamut's vocal talents give him special potency. Like the biblical David, whom he consciously emulates, Gamut affects others through his music. This power becomes most evident during the massacre at Fort William Henry, when Gamut improbably begins to sing and the astonished attackers do not harm him, Alice, or Cora. By late in the novel Gamut's voice has helped him to rise above the violent circumstances; he lives unmolested in a Huron camp, where the Native Americans view him as deranged but benign. Taking Thomas Philbrick's observation that Gamut serves as a figure of an artist (36), we could recall that Cooper, as an author, accords similar high value to verbal forms. Cooper seems to oscillate between admiration for Gamut's verbal attainments on the one hand and esteem for those who thrive without emphasizing the voice on the other. Even as he implicitly constructs hearingness and deafness in the narrative, he appears to vacillate on the value of both.

Thus far, I have argued that Cooper's Native Americans parallel deaf people in some telling ways, while his white characters frequently exemplify the hearingness of European American society. When the two groups come into contact, Cooper often interrogates assumptions about hearing and speech. For example, we could read Heyward's discomfort among the silent Hurons as similar to a hearing person's unease among deaf individuals, while Gamut's effort to teach Native American children Christian songs has tinges of an oral educator coaching deaf children on how to speak vocally. (Gamut gives up in frustration when the children merely whoop and howl.) Along the same lines, the narrator's description of Uncas endeavoring to speak English to Alice and Cora contains echos of accounts of a deaf person essaying to speak: "He made use of English broken and imperfect, but sufficiently intelligible . . . that it never failed to cause both ladies to look up in admiration and astonishment" (56). The sisters' amazement resembles the wonder we find in hearing people's reports in the nineteenth century of a congenitally deaf person speaking vocally. A Native American speaking English, like a deaf person learning to articulate, suggests that the color or hearing line has been temporarily transcended; for a moment, the other becomes closer to "normal," to the white, hearing, civilized *we* that occupies the center of American literature. In this way, just as Cooper's Native American characters help to define and demarcate whiteness, so their deaf attributes allow hearingness to exist. We become more conscious of European American hearingness because Cooper contrasts it, along with race, gender, and culture, with Native American ways of being.

The character who seems most successfully to bridge the two worlds is Hawk-eye, who resembles Thomas Hopkins Gallaudet, Lewis Weld, and other hearing people in the early 1800s who learned American Sign Language and interacted effectively with deaf individuals. Having lived in the forest among Indians for years, the scout appears relatively comfortable with silence (he laughs noiselessly to avoid detection) and knows how to track, speak the language of the Mohicans, and use Indian gestures, although not nearly as well as the Native Americans. Hawk-eye often advocates Native American ways to the white outsiders, much as Gallaudet and others explained and defended deaf people to the hearing majority. Yet for all his understanding, Hawk-eye's white identity never recedes. He continually reminds us that he is "a man without a cross," that is, has pure white blood, and he communicates most readily in spoken English. Moreover, just as Gallaudet saw deaf people with both admiration and paternalism,[14] so Hawk-eye alternatively displays fascination and condescension to Native Americans, calling them "savage" one moment, "deliberate and wise" the next (119, 189).

This ambivalence indicates a final salient way that Cooper's Native Americans resemble deaf Americans: influenced by evangelical epistemology and the romanticization of natural man, the white hearing

Hawk-eye gestures to Chingachgook. (Painting ca. 1840; artist unknown.)
Courtesy of the American Antiquarian Society.

majority perceives both groups with a contradictory mixture of desire ✓ and dread. In the previous chapter, we saw how Gallaudet referred to uneducated deaf people as "ignorant heathen" who lacked enlightenment and knowledge of the gospel ("Duty" 217). Gamut frequently expresses a similar missionary spirit in *Mohicans*, calling the Native Americans "heathen" and "among the profanest of the idolatrous" (226). He is not the only one. During one battle Hawk-eye calls the enemy Indians "the children of the devil," and the narrator (who is presumably white and hearing) sometimes refers to the Hurons as "demons" and "savages" (76, 107). Such language plays off of what John Cawelti calls the original American myth of the frontier, which "originated with the Puritan 'errand into the wilderness' to bring light and Calvinist Christianity into the heathen darkness" (157). In representing this view, Cooper successfully encrypts a dominant mode of consciousness of the period. This idea upheld European American civilization, religion, and culture as superior, and served as the justification for what, two decades after *Mohicans*, would be called the Manifest Destiny. Yet at the same time, Cooper consistently undercuts such views. Just as Gallaudet praised deaf people's intelligence and sign language, so the narrator writes admiring descriptions of Native Americans' silence, visual communication, and connection with the natural world. Uncas, in particular, emerges as larger than life, almost an ideal. Next to such a courageous and heroic figure, Gamut's ungainly foolishness makes it difficult for us to take him too seriously. Furthermore, Hawk-eye argues against assertions of the Native Americans' supposed heathenism and inferiority. "'Tis a wicked fabrication of the whites" that Indians do not worship the true God, he asserts (226). After Chingachgook identifies a scalp, he declaims, "What right have christian whites to boast of their learning, when a savage can read a language that would prove too much for the wisest of them all!" (196). In this way, the novel creates a tension between positive and negative interpretations of otherness. Just as Cooper presents "the uncorrupted natives" with a mixture of longing and horror (53), so many hearing people at the time were becoming fascinated with uneducated deaf Americans while thinking them uncivilized or unredeemed. In these respects, Cooper's Indians could be said to serve as stand-in "deaf" characters in early American fiction.

However, the equation is more intricate than I have acknowledged thus far, for while Cooper's Native Americans do have striking similarities with deaf people, they are of course *hearing*, and can hear astoundingly well, as Hawk-eye points out on several occasions. "[Uncas] has Indian senses, and may hear what is hid from us," he observes (192). This dynamic turns the tables somewhat and paradoxically makes the whites, who elsewhere display qualities of hearingness, seem more deaf-like. Here Cooper uses deafness to convey white failings, just as their un-deaf quality of depending on speech hinders them at other times. The correlation between whiteness and deafness is therefore complex. While in many ways whiteness aligns with hearingness in the narrative, when it comes to actual aural skill, whites appear more deaf-like than their Native American counterparts. Cooper uses the deaf presence to question not just white hearing people's reliance on speech, but also their artificial separation from the natural world and concomitant loss of skills such as aural acuity. Through their excessive volubility and diminished hearing, Cooper represents the primitive potency that over-civilized whites have lost. For all its sympathy for nonvocal communication, the novel winds up unequivocally championing the ability to hear.

Because hearing is necessary to survive in this world, the ability figuratively to deafen others becomes a mark of power. Since the party often finds itself surrounded by darkness, woods, or other visual barriers, hearing serves as a precious sense, the main way to detect the approach of a threat. Cooper's representation of Native American figures of speech sometimes buttresses this view. We are told that the skilled Chingachgook would never be detected by "the ears of one he wished to be deaf" (96); after Heyward tries to trick a Delaware chief, the latter asks, "Why did you wish to stop my ears?" (300); and Uncas scornfully asks his captors, "Has a Huron no ears?" (241). In these cases deafness signifies weakness, unawareness, and being duped, and the Indians, especially, have the metaphoric ability to "deafen" others. Those who hear well, in addition to being able to move silently, have control and prevail. The only times such deaf rhetoric has positive colorings is when it is voluntary. When Cora pleads for Tamenund to "be deaf to yonder artful and remorseless monster," Magua, she is complimenting Tamenund's authority, his power to decide what he wants to approve (303). However, even in this case, Tamenund can hear. On the surface, then, the novel consistently promotes aural skill as an esteemed attribute, a mark of potency and perception, even as it celebrates the ability to live in silence and communicate nonverbally at the same time.

Cooper seems most ambivalent when it comes to speech, calling its value into question even as he points to its power. Another way that the Native Americans do not correspond to deaf people is that they do of course routinely speak and use their voices. As we learn through the brief story of Reeds-that-bends, who is executed because his "tongue is loud in the village, but in battle it is still," the Indians have specific rules about when and where to use one's voice (242). The Indians give unnerving war whoops and death halloos; Uncas and Chingachgook converse in low, musical tones; and Magua emerges as a persuasive orator who ironically "in a more advanced state of society, would have . . . the reputation of a skillful diplomatist" (290). By making the narrative's villain the most eloquent speaker in the novel, Cooper calls into question the value of speech. If the most impressive singer is the clownish Gamut, and the most accomplished speaker the wily Magua, how can the narrative uphold verbal achievement as a mark of superiority? As a Delaware chief puts it, often "the mouth has spoken, while the heart has said nothing" (296). Significantly, the novel only questions the truthfulness of speech, never of gestures, which are invariably "direct . . . and natural" when made by an Indian (198). Just as Cooper seems to respect Native American silence over the whites' logorrhea, so he appears to maintain special admiration for nonverbal forms of communication.

In the final scene, Cooper seems to offer a vision of harmony through the voice; the characters mourn Uncas and Cora, and the Native American women, Gamut, and Chingachgook alternatively sing. We learn that the Native Americans pass on the story of Uncas and Cora orally, through storytelling, again aligning Cooper's writing with verbal art. However, it seems clear that the Native American and white views on speech and gesture will never come together; rather, the European American privileging of the voice will reign supreme. "The pale-faces are masters of the earth," Tamenund says at the end, acknowledging the rise not just of the European American race, religion, and civilization, but also of white logocentrism (350). The deaf presence helps us to see how, even as Cooper writes in English, he feels conflicted over its dominance. His whole treatment of the hearing line is shot through with ambivalence, and while the novel ultimately seems to value hearingness, its nostalgic portrayals of the Native Americans' skill with nonverbal forms show that Cooper, like Irving and many hearing Americans in the 1820s, had reservations about a hearing society that seemed more cut off from silence, gesture, and nature, and that increasingly experienced reality through seemingly arbitrary words. In this way, the novel appears to set the stage for the emergence of deaf Americans, who could offer a means, like Cooper's Indians, for white hearing peoples to escape their seemingly artificial logocentric culture and reconnect with nature and their past.

MELVILLE'S QUEST FOR THE INEFFABLE

Herman Melville shares some common themes with Cooper, whom he called "a great, robust-souled man" (*Letters* 145). Like his predecessor, Melville sometimes writes critically of white society and missionary forays into other cultures. In early works like *Typee* (1846) and *Omoo* (1847), and also with Queequeg and the multicultural crew in *Moby-Dick*, he interrogates concepts such as "civilized" and "heathen," often portraying non-European-American ways of life with admiration. While Cooper situates the Leatherstocking novels in the western frontier, Melville explores the frontier of the sea. Expanding on Cooper's silent, sublime wilderness, he presents vast oceans that beckon and intimidate. Moreover, just as Cooper frequently confronts the role of hearing, speech, sound, silence, and gesture, so Melville creates a hidden but pervasive deaf presence in his works. Yet he takes things further; especially in *Moby-Dick*, he uses tropes of deafness to convey the tantalizing, terrifying nature of what lies beyond human comprehension.

Perhaps the best way to introduce Melville's use of deafness is to examine how, in three of his novels—*Redburn* (1849), *Moby-Dick*, and *The Confidence-Man* (1857)—he has mysterious individuals come on board ship who explicitly or implicitly resemble deaf people. In each case, the deaf presence both intrigues and discomfits the others on board, and they try to understand it through speech and conjecture, sometimes penetrating the enigma, sometimes not. In *Redburn*, the early novel he wrote for a mass audience so as to earn money, Melville makes the connection to deafness overt. When a man comes on the ship who does not speak to anyone and keeps studiously to himself, the narrator immediately speculates: "Perhaps he was a deputy from the Deaf and Dumb Institution in New York, going over to London to address the public in pantomime at Exeter Hall concerning the signs of the times" (106). Because of the passenger's silence and isolation, the narrator associates him with deafness. The comment demonstrates that Melville knew about the New York Institution, which opened in 1818, a year before his birth. One wonders if he saw a public exhibition at the school (they were quite popular at midcentury), or what kind of contact he might have had with deaf people in New York City. Perhaps he knew of Laurent Clerc's mission to America in 1816, for he imagines a similar role for the mysterious passenger (although in this case the deaf emissary goes from the New World to the Old). With his punning reference to "the signs of the times," he reveals an awareness of sign language while slyly mocking deaf people's knowledge of the world: here, a deaf person addressing the public appears slightly absurd. At any rate, the unaccountable stranger fascinates the sailors, who speculate exhaustively about the man's identity. Among other suppositions, they hypothesize that he is a secret messenger, a bigamist, bank-robber, burglar, or a murderer overwhelmed with speechless remorse. All of the interpretations are negative; the passenger's deaf characteristics not only intrigue the crew, but also cause them with some relish to imagine him as lawless. Only when the sailors tie him to the rigging do we learn that he is not deaf, but merely has a bad stutter. "Wha-wha-what i-i-is this f-f-for?" he cries (108). The deaf presence recedes, the mystery and danger dissolve into harmless farce, and the passenger emerges as another humorous, curious character that Redburn encounters on his voyage. The brief episode not only reveals cultural attitudes toward the deaf other, but also, through the interrogation of a silent passenger, serves to test and affirm the identity of everyone on board as hearing.

Melville repeats the pattern more prominently in the last novel he published in his lifetime, *The Confidence-Man*, which opens with an apparently deaf beggar coming on board a Mississippi steamboat. Like the mysterious passenger in *Redburn*, this man appears profoundly different from the other people: he is "in the extremest sense of the word, a stranger" (7). He silently writes on a slate quotations from I Corinthians about charity, but the passengers push him aside, jeer, and finally punch him. When he is hit by a heavy trunk, he reveals his deafness through "a peculiar inarticulate moan, and a pathetic tele-graphing of his fingers" (10). Again, the appearance of a deaf other intrigues the people on board, who speculate while he sleeps who he might be. Some call him an innocent, a "poor fellow" and "Moon-calf," while others view him as an "Odd fish," "Green prophet," a manipulator, escaped convict, and one to beware (12). Into the void of his deafness, they project their own imaginings, coming up with any number of possible explanations, none of which is definitely valid.

Unlike in *Redburn*, here the deaf mystery is never dispelled. The strange outsider slips away unnoticed, leaving us to wonder who he is and whether he is really deaf. None of the passengers seems to suspect he might be an impostor, although, as I discuss in chapter 5, hearing people sometimes acted deaf for fun and profit in nineteenth-century America. In this novel about confidence men and charades, we must wonder if he is genuine. The stranger comes on board just as the passengers are reading a placard warning of a skillful impostor who has recently arrived from the East. Later, the narrator remarks that the deaf man's cream-colored suit looks "almost linty, as if, travelling night and day from some far country beyond the prairies, he had long been without the solace of a bed," implicitly linking him with the recently arrived confidence man (11). Stephen Matterson notes that the deaf man's writings about charity soften up the passengers and set the stage for subsequent appeals to altruism; later a lady is seen read-ing the same passage of Corinthians that the stranger cited, and she contributes twenty dollars to the man in gray (xxx). Furthermore, the stranger introduces a thematic deafness that appears later; Melville titles chapter 6 "At the Outset of Which Certain Passengers Prove Deaf to the Call of Charity." More than just recycling an idiom, Melville seems to be playing off the identity of the deaf character. The irony, of course, is that the hearing passengers ignore the stranger's pleas for contributions; in other words, they are unheeding, or figuratively deaf, to the man who appears physically deaf. Melville sets up a rhetorical hall of mirrors where the true significance of deafness seems impossible to ascertain. The deaf stranger could be an early avatar of the confidence man; significantly, he departs before Black Guinea, a confidence man disguised as an African American disabled person, comes on board. Yet he could just as easily be an innocent foil for the confidence man's (or men's, since it is also not clear if there is more than one confidence man here) subsequent guises. While all the other masquerades in the novel are apparent, Melville employs a figure of deafness to convey an unknown, an enigma that resists explanation. In both *Redburn* and *The Confidence-Man* Melville thus uses deafness overtly to suggest the unfathomable, to hint at what lies beyond words and understanding.

In between these two novels, he wrote his grand, chaotic master-piece, *Moby-Dick*, which employs a similar strategy, although in a more subtle and profound way. Just as he explicitly associates the unknown strangers in *Redburn* and *The Confidence-Man* with deaf-ness, so Melville imbues Ahab with deaf-related qualities. When he appears, Ahab is characterized by mysterious stillness: "Not a word he spoke; nor did his officers say aught to him" (135). Meals with the ship's officers take place in "awful silence," although Ahab does not forbid conversation: "only he himself was dumb" (163). Like the "deaf" outsiders in *Redburn* and *The Confidence-Man*, the silent Ahab inspires uneasiness, curiosity, and fascination; Ishmael feels awe and an impatience at "the mystery in him" (89). Again, people try to penetrate the deaf vacuum through rumor and supposition; Captain Peleg and Elijah tell Ishmael about Ahab's legendary past, and the crew speculates about the origin of his ghastly scar. In the pivotal scene on the quarterdeck, Ahab breaks out of the deaf aura. His hortatory address to the crew, with its impassioned call for pursuit of the white whale, unites him and the other people on board as speaking, hearing individuals. Interestingly, though, the deaf presence does not quite disappear. Ahab himself returns to moody silence throughout the book; Ishmael refers to him as "inscrutable Ahab," "wordless Ahab," and so forth (243, 256). More significantly, the deaf presence around Ahab proves a microcosm for the larger ways in which it envelops whales, God, fate, and the entire universe.

Throughout the novel, Melville describes whales, particularly the

white whale, as essentially unknowable and beyond language, characteristics that he subtly equates with deafness. At the outset, Ishmael
calls Moby Dick a "portentous and mysterious monster" (8). This
baffling creature becomes linked to speechlessness in the great chapter
"The Quarter-Deck," when Starbuck refers to the whale as "a dumb
thing": Moby Dick, like Melville's other deaf figures, is silent and mute
(178). Ishmael refers to "the white, silent stillness of death" in the
Great White Shark (206), a phrase we could equally apply to Moby
Dick himself, who after all remains silent beneath the surface of the
ocean for most of the novel and destroys the *Pequod* and its crew at the
end. By later saying that "blind and deaf, the whale plunged forward,"
Ishmael makes the deaf presence slightly more explicit (421). Through
the trope of deafness (and also blindness), he evokes not just the
whale's obduracy, but also its strangeness, its vast inscrutability. As in
the case of the "deaf" strangers in *Redburn* and *The Confidence-Man*,
so here people try to fill in the deaf void with speculations. Ishmael
reports "wild rumors" whose "wonderfulness and fearfulness" add to
the Moby Dick's terror (195–96), as sailors conjecture that the white
whale has supernatural powers, is intelligent, malicious, ubiquitous,
or even immortal. Once again, people project their own desires and
fears onto a silent, speechless, deaf other.

To Ishmael and Ahab, the white whale seems to embody the secrets
of the universe. In the opening chapter, Ishmael calls Moby Dick a
"grand hooded phantom," linking him to the "ungraspable phantom
of life" that he had mentioned just before (8, 5). For his part, Ahab
cannot tolerate the ambiguity of the whale. "The inscrutable thing is
chiefly what I hate, and be the white whale agent, or be the white whale
principal, I will wreak that hate upon him," he declares (178). His
monomaniacal quest appears to be not so much about revenge for his
missing limb as about apprehending the incomprehensible nature of
the world; he fears that there is "naught beyond," that aimless inscrutability is all he will ever discover. Yet, as Raney Stanford points
out, Ahab paradoxically does gain a certain self-affirmation from his
quest: "In a very real sense, Ahab does worship the power beyond
man's ken and control, for it is through assaulting it in rebellion that
he achieves significance, even identity," Stanford contends (36). How-

ever foolish his mission, by insistently taking on the deaf presence, Ahab defines himself as a vital hearing person.

Both Ahab and Ishmael come up empty in their endeavor to penetrate this deaf mystery. Ahab's obsessive desire to grasp the enigma of the whale becomes particularly evident during his address to the sperm whale head:

> Speak, mighty head, and tell us the secret thing that is in thee. Of all divers, thou hast dived the deepest. That head upon which the upper sun now gleams, has moved amid this world's foundations. . . . Thou hast been where bell or diver never went; hast slept by many a sailor's side, where the sleepless mothers would give their lives to lay them down. . . . O head! thou hast seen enough to split the planets and make an infidel of Abraham, and not one syllable is thine! (339–40)

Ahab believes the whale knows "the secret thing," the answers to the questions he so ardently seeks. By imploring the head to speak, he asks it to enter the logocentric world of speech, hearing, and rationality, to explain the unexplainable. Through sheer force of will, he wants to determine one clear meaning in a disorderly world. Yet of course the head remains silent, impervious to speech. Ishmael appears more comfortable with the whale's deaf-like nature, but he, too, tries to decipher it. Throughout the novel, he brings all his encyclopedic knowledge to bear on whales, categorizing them and dissecting their various body parts and functions. In "Cetology," he even groups whales into books and chapters, making obvious how he is trying to write the whale, to cast the unknowable into known systems. Yet he repeatedly admits the impossibility of this quest to discover the mystery of whales. "This whole book is but a draught, nay, but the draught of a draught," he says (157). He tells us we cannot find out precisely what a whale looks like. He describes how the whale has no true face and dares us to "read it if you can" (380). He decries his "inability to express" the whale's tail; "dissect him how I may, I know him not, and never will," he concludes (414). The act of trying to write the whale wearies him, for no matter how much knowledge, how many words, he brings to the task, the whale's "incommunicable contemplations" lie beyond human understanding (409). In this way, the deaf presence in the novel lurks in the background and continually threatens to overwhelm the poised logocentrism of Ishmael's opening invitation to speech, "Call me. . . ."

Strikingly, Melville's whales are perceived, with mixed comedy and wonder, to have their own gestural system that lies beyond human comprehension. As Ishmael speculates on how whales may use their tails to signal each other, we sense his frustration at the limits of English, speech, and hearingness:

> The more I consider this mighty tail, the more do I deplore my ability to express it. At times there are gestures in it, which, though they would well grace the hand of man, remain wholly inexplicable. In an extensive herd, so remarkable, occasionally, are these mystic gestures, that I have heard hunters who have declared them akin to Free-Mason signs and symbols; that the whale, indeed, by these methods intelligently conversed with the world. . . . Dissect him how I may, then, I but go skin deep; I know him not, and never will. (414)

Ishmael sees the whales' gestures as a cryptic code that leaves him feeling once again vulnerable and in the dark. Confronted by the whales' community and indecipherable language, Ishmael's knowledge and language come up short. He is left wanting, just as some hearing observers, encountering a group of deaf people energetically signing to each other, may have felt left out, constricted by their hearingness. For example, after watching a deaf minister preach in sign language in 1869, a hearing correspondent wrote: "He is so expert, so facile, so swift, so fleet, he fills us with ever increasing wonder; and forces us to think it is we who are imperfect, and not he, who leaves us so deeply impressed" ("Sign" 199). In this way, the whales' perceived signals correlate with sign language, subverting the hegemony of logocentrism and disrupting the usual reign of hearingness over deafness. Like Irving and Cooper, Melville points to the potency of nonverbal cues, but unlike his literary predecessors he does not seem to subvert that authority somewhat with a confident narrative voice. Perhaps we could interpret Ishmael's increased vulnerability and dissatisfaction with hearingness as a mark of how the national consciousness had evolved between 1820 and 1850, a period during which deaf Americans went from seeing their first schools opened to gathering together in public by the hundreds to celebrate their shared communal identity.

Implicit in Ahab's quest for meaning and order is a search for some higher being, and the underlying fear seems to be that God is deaf, shut off from human prayers and suffering. The trope was not uncommon in the nineteenth century. Emerson wrote in 1856 of "Jove . . . deaf to prayers" (*Conduct* 157), while the poet Emma Lazarus asked, "Why offer prayers unanswered and unheard / To blank, deaf heavens that will not heed her pain?" (146). Meanwhile, in *Uncle Tom's Cabin* (1852) Stowe assures readers that "the ear of One . . . is not deaf, though he be long silent" (202). Ahab longs for a world in which God is ever-present and loving, but instead Melville presents us with an indifferent divinity toward the end of *Moby-Dick*, when Ishmael describes a mute, deaf "weaver-god": "The weaver-god, he weaves; and by that weaving is he deafened, that he hears no mortal voice," he says (490). Deafness becomes a shorthand for humanity's existential condition, for its estrangement from a god who knows or cares. Ishmael goes on to suggest that the deafness is contagious: "by that humming we, too, who look on the loom are deafened." We could make a connection to how Ahab, in his rage against a deaf universe, becomes effectively "deaf" to the crew. He has seen the loom and been deafened by it. This impervious, unreasoning meaning of deafness reappears in the person of the carpenter, an automaton-like man who "did not seem to work so much by reason or instinct" as by "a kind of deaf and dumb, spontaneous literal process" (510). The carpenter, like the weaver-god, is "deaf" in that he does not think or feel: he is cut off from humanity. It is a condition that Ahab paradoxically both decries and replicates in his own relations with the crew.

As we can see, Melville structures his novel around an elusive deaf presence that allures, horrifies, and almost invariably remains ungraspable and unknown. To try to write this deaf phenomenon, to say the unsayable, is of course a paradoxical undertaking. "To grope down into the bottom of the sea . . . among the *unspeakable* foundations . . . of the world: this is a fearful thing," Ishmael remarks (147, my emphasis). Yet through his reams of verbal discourse, Melville effectively sets himself up as opposite to the silent deaf other. He defines himself as a hearing, speaking, logocentric individual, albeit one preoccupied with the limits of human understanding. Friends who knew him around midcentury commented on his interest in the unknowable. On October 1, 1856, the editor and literary critic Evert Duyckinck recorded in a diary that "Herman Melville passed the evening with me—fresh from his mountain charged to the muzzle with his sailor metaphysics and jargon of things unknowable" (qtd. in Parker 291). A month later Nathaniel Hawthorne commented in his notebook that "Melville, as he always does, began to reason of Providence and futurity, and of everything that lies beyond human ken" (163). Other moments in *Moby-Dick* further reveal a similar concern with knowledge and interpretation: the doubloon and Queequeg's tattoos, for example, are signs whose definite meaning no one can decipher. With the deaf presence, Melville neatly conveys this ineffable inscrutability, this sense of something at once quite close and quite far from rational comprehension. We might even suggest that this "deaf" incomprehensibility of life defines life itself. That is, just as deafness helps to produce hearingness, so rationality in a way owes its existence to the presence of an unknowable "deaf" other.

Since scholars rediscovered *Moby-Dick* in the 1920s, they have interpreted it in myriad ways. It has been viewed as a political allegory of impending sectional conflict, with Ahab as John C. Calhoun (or Daniel Webster, or William Lloyd Garrison), Starbuck as New England caution, and Stubb as the zealous westerner. It has been scoured for its commentary on democracy, on capitalism and corruption, on God and humanity, and (most often) on the individual versus a brutal, impassive Nature. Michael Rogin and Toni Morrison, among others, have identified its powerful connections with race and slavery. I do not wish to suggest that any of these readings are invalid. Surely, much of the greatness of *Moby-Dick* lies in its profound relevance to so many aspects of its historical and cultural moment and the general human condition. Yet in pursuing any one line of explication, we run the risk of reducing Melville's boisterous epic to a medieval morality play. Ishmael himself somewhat ingeniously warns of this danger: "So ignorant are most landsmen of some of the plainest and most palpable wonders of the world," he says, "they might scout at Moby Dick as a monstrous fable, or still worse and more detestable, a hideous and intolerable allegory" (223). The deaf paradigm I have been tracing may allow us to avoid this potential hermeneutical dilemma. It helps us to see how various critical interpretations finally resemble the passengers' endless speculating about the identities of "deaf" passengers in *Redburn* and *The Confidence-Man*: all potentially valid, and some quite persuasive, but none definitely true, for Melville organizes *Moby-Dick* around a beguiling, horrifying deaf presence that is never quite explained.

My goal in this chapter has been to recover some of how hearing Americans imagined deafness during the first part of the nineteenth century and how they used the deaf presence to define their own identities as hearing people. I have sought to show how, even when they did not write directly about deaf people, they approached aspects of deafness with oscillating admiration and horror, and how they tended to associate deafness with unfathomable silence, powerful nonvocal communication, and the vast natural world. While they clearly value the ability to speak vocally and to hear, they regularly evince anxiety about the ability of reason, speech, hearing, and words, and of civilization more generally, to apprehend fundamental truths of existence. The deaf presence reveals their persistently shifting feelings of superiority and inferiority, condescension and vulnerability, and shows how the meanings of deafness and hearingness are invariably dependent on each other. With these insights, we can now turn to hearing authors' more direct representations of deaf people in nineteenth-century literature.

Powers of Deafness

DEAF CHARACTERS BY HEARING AUTHORS

I flung her from me, even though she clung to my vesture,
and with a wild cry of agony I burst from the apartment!—
She was dumb! Great God, she was dumb! DUMB AND DEAF!
Herman Melville, "Fragments from a Writing Desk, No. 2" (1839)

For, being an Angel, thou dost use an Angel's tongue,
Silence, God's holy language, sweeter far than Song.
T. H. Chivers, "The Beautiful Silence: Composed on
Seeing a Beautiful Deaf Mute Lady" (1851)

[There] is a mobile, conflictual fusion of power, fear and
desire in the construction of subjectivity.
Peter Stallybrass and Allon White (1986)

As the nineteenth century progressed, hearing authors began including deaf characters in their work more often (albeit in mostly minor roles), which I take as a sign of deaf Americans' increasing prominence in society and in the popular consciousness. While the Africanist presence in literature is connected to the presence of African peoples in the United States, the deaf presence is tied to the growing visibility of deaf people in public. For all their differences, African Americans and deaf people both raised perplexing questions for the majority, and in the literature of the period we can observe white, hearing authors addressing or evading these concerns. By writing about deaf people, along with African Americans, Native Americans, working-class citizens, disabled people, and immigrants, authors like Melville, Walt Whitman, and Mark Twain created more realistic and democratic portraits of the United States. Their representations of deaf people embody and extend many of the features of the deaf presence that I identified in the last chapter. They almost always imagine deaf people as incorporations of silence who rarely speak or make noise. Their deaf characters sometimes appear as peaceful, innocent beings and at other times as threatening figures of horror. This commingled fascination and repulsion frequently amounts to abjection, as Julia Kristeva describes it, connecting deaf characters to other marginalized people in literature. It also reflects the influence of the Bible and religious thought, which tended to position deafness as a mark of either evil or innocence. Through deaf characters, hearing authors often reveal what Rosemarie Garland-Thomson calls the "uneasy human impulse to textualize, to explain, to contain our most unexpected corporeal manifestations" (*Freakery* 3). With writing, they seek to name and domesticate deafness, which resists easy classification, lurking like silence as an enigmatic void forever beyond the reach of logocentric comprehension. Deaf characters stand at the limits of knowing, serving as mediative figures on the threshold of difference. Hearing authors regularly give them metaphorical significance but seldom illuminate much about the actual lived nature of deaf experience or about deaf people as a cultural group. More than any other aspect of the deaf presence, deaf characters allow hearing authors to express their own anxieties and desires and to attempt to demarcate their identities as hearing people.

These textual renderings of deaf people tend to contain competing views of deafness, creating a shifting, unstable portrait that confirms and elaborates ambivalent attitudes toward the deaf presence that we have seen so far. For example, as hearing authors created deaf characters, they were influenced by conflicting notions about speechlessness. As mentioned in chapter 1, since ancient times many people subscribed to the belief that the ability to speak is what makes one human, so not surprisingly, sometimes silent deaf characters appear almost beyond the human pale. On the other hand, as we began to see in the last chapter, influential thinkers in the eighteenth and nineteenth centuries began to question the superiority of speech and indeed all civilization. Rousseau famously argued that the uncivilized state was in some ways preferable to the refined language and culture of civilization, which could corrupt the morals of humankind. Poets such as Friedrich Hölderlin and John Keats helped to shape an appreciation for quietude, where silence stood in opposition to the verbal excess of society. Along the same lines, people began to privilege actions increasingly over words. "Speech that leads not to action," wrote Thomas Carlyle, "still more that hinders it, is a nuisance on the Earth" (qtd. in Steiner, *Language* 48). Given such views, we can see why some authors might romanticize deaf people, just as Cooper occasionally romanticized his Indians, celebrating their silence as something noble and pure. During the nineteenth century, at least two rival interpretations of human silence prevailed: one that saw it as a mark of inferiority and another that revered it as closer than words to truth and goodness. Given such manners of thinking, we can better grasp why hearing authors read so much into those "children of silence," deaf people, creating portrayals that often border on the sensational. It was not a tremendous leap for them to interpret the supposed silence of deaf people as idiocy, bestiality, imprisonment, innocence, virtue, or the supernatural.

Overlapping with these two divergent takes on speechlessness are several influential religious interpretations of deaf people, complicating hearing authors' depictions of deaf characters still more. As I have suggested, the Bible sometimes depicts deafness in a negative light, presenting it (along with all disability and disease) as a sign of evil. In Isaiah we learn that when the Messiah comes, "The eyes of the blind shall be opened, and the ears of the deaf unstopped" (35:5). In the New

Testament Jesus begins to fulfill this prophecy by curing a deaf man with the cry of "Ephphatha," or "Be opened" (Mark 7:33–35). These passages make deafness into a sign of humanity's fallen condition, evidence that humans are not godly and pure. Elsewhere Zechariah is struck mute when he doubts the words of the angel Gabriel, which equates speechlessness with divine punishment (Luke 1:20–22). Literal-minded believers could take these biblical accounts as evidence from God that deafness and muteness represent sin or a curse. Furthermore, many hearing Christians interpreted Paul's assertion that "Faith comes by hearing" (Romans 10:17) to mean that their deaf counterparts were unredeemable because they purportedly could not understand the Gospel and be saved. In the fourth century, St. Augustine stated that "those born deaf are incapable of ever exercising the Christian faith, for they cannot hear the Word, and they cannot read the Word."[1] Augustine's proclamation effectively shut deaf people out of the church, barring them from communion and even marriage. In medieval times, some people saw deafness as evidence of possession by the devil, a view that was still common in the eighteenth century. The Abbé de l'Epée reported that when he founded the first school for deaf students in France in the 1760s, some respected priests publicly condemned his undertaking on theological grounds (Barnard, *Observations* 5). According to Epée, many parents thought themselves disgraced if they had a deaf child and would conceal it from outsiders. The deaf person was a mark of shame to be repressed or expelled. If the Bible has historically contributed to the oppression of homosexuals and women, it thus has also done so with deaf people. Religion led many people, including nineteenth-century authors, to interpret deafness as sinful, malevolent, even as the sign of Satan. Such views may help to explain F. A. P. Barnard's observation in 1834 that hearing Americans often displayed "a species of contempt . . . or an absolute aversion" toward deaf people, attitudes that he no doubt experienced himself after he lost his hearing as a young adult (6).

Yet again these negative perspectives of deaf people were counterbalanced by more positive ones, which also shaped hearing writers' depictions. With the Old Testament injunction that "you shall not revile the deaf" (Leviticus 19:14), the Bible explicitly forbids hateful attitudes toward deaf people. In the New Testament, Christ advocates an empathetic attitude toward people who are sick, lame, or spurned by society. As we saw in chapter 1, deaf education arose largely because of an evangelical impulse to bring the gospel to deaf people and save them from their pagan ignorance. Once hearing Americans accepted that deaf individuals could be educated, they began to see them not as visible marks of evil but merely as unenlightened humans in need of assistance. In an 1819 poem, the hearing poet Moses Scott described uneducated deaf people as beings "Whose struggling Genius still is doom'd to dwell, / An angel hermit, in a doorless cell" (6). Their intelligence and benevolent "angel" are dormant inside, only needing to be freed through education and literacy. Along the same lines, in 1824 Thomas Hopkins Gallaudet called uneducated deaf people "long-neglected heathen" while praising their potential fully to learn spiritual and intellectual truths ("Duty" 217). In the same sermon, Gallaudet points to still another religious interpretation of deafness that cast it in a more positive light: he describes deaf people as exempt from "the scandal, the abuse, the falsehood, the profanity, and the blasphemy which their ears cannot hear nor their tongues utter" (219). Instead of serving as a harbinger of evil, here deafness makes deaf people purer than their hearing counterparts, above the corrupt fallen world of various iniquities that spoken language enables. Together with the increasing appreciation for the ennobling aspects of silence, this view of deafness as a sign of innocence gained credence during the nineteenth century. It added yet another theoretical model with which Americans could try to fathom the enigmatic, recalcitrant disruption of deafness. Such opposing views often coexist in hearing authors' portrayals of deaf people, forming a dialectic of danger and attraction, a blending of the perilous with the wondrous that they seek to negotiate and work out.

Deaf characters in canonical literature represent a certain threatening epistemological disorder. They typically lurk on the edges of narratives or appear indistinctly in poems even seemingly about them, not quite clearly defined, transgressing conventional boundaries and ways of thinking. In her seminal work *Purity and Danger* (1966), Mary Douglas argues that those in a marginal state have an indefinable status that symbolizes both danger and power. We see this potency in the ineffable silence of deaf characters, which violates the speech-based system of rationality. As René Girard puts it: "Difference that exists outside the system is terrifying because it reveals the truth of the system, its relativity, its fragility, and its mortality" (33). Deaf characters not only help to prop up hearing identities, but also endanger them by revealing their flimsy, unresolved nature. Just as whiteness depends on blackness for its authority, so hearingness paradoxically relies on deafness for its systemic power. Lurking on the margins, silent deaf characters frequently become figures of uncanniness. Unlike ethnic minorities or blind or one-legged people, deaf people appear "normal," like one of "us" (assuming the "us" is hearing, as nineteenth-century hearing authors invariably did). Because deafness is invisible, it only emerges through behavior, when a person does not respond to sound, uses sign language, or perhaps speaks in an unusual manner. In this respect, deafness resembles Foucault's description of madness: "[It] is always absent, in a perpetual retreat where it is inaccessible, without phenomenal or positive character; and yet it is present and perfectly visible in the singular evidence of the madman."[2] Deafness is a gap, an absence at borders of spoken language, and its elusiveness and impenetrability seem part of its power. As we will see, much of the shock of deaf characters comes when their deafness is exposed, when they are revealed not to be an "us" but a "them." Because deaf people typically are born into hearing families, deafness is always potentially close to hearing people; when we recall that any hearing person can become deaf and that many people have partial hearing loss, we are back in the realm of *unheimlich*, that unsettling combination of the familiar and the unknown. The hearing line emerges as somewhat less fixed than the color or gender lines, more permeable and at least equally problematic. The distinction between deaf and nondeaf, between them and us, perhaps is not so stark as it may first appear.

This sense of deaf characters defying boundaries and upsetting order takes us close to what Kristeva calls abjection. In *Powers of Horror* (1982), she describes abjection as "what disturbs identity, system, order"—a descriptor we could equally apply to deafness in literature by hearing authors (4). Like deafness, the abject threatens to break down meaning and both attracts and repels. We simultaneously want to confront the abject and rid ourselves of it. In Kristeva's lyrical description, the abject "beseeches, worries, fascinates desire, which, nonetheless, does not let itself be seduced. Apprehensive, desire turns aside; sickened, it rejects" (1). By psychologically trying to exclude the abjectness that endangers one's sense of identity, people seek to escape it. However, because the abject can never be completely expelled, it always returns. The cycle is invariably repeated and the abject seems at once "unapproachable and intimate" (6). It is related to Freud's familiar yet foreign uncanniness but even more horrifying because it disrupts the tidy division of self and other. We might make a similar statement about deafness, which can never quite be controlled or purged from hearing people's lives.

Perhaps the strongest link between hearing authors' treatment of deafness and Kristeva's concept of the abject comes through their relation to language. Kristeva argues that people who suffer from abjection are either cut off from language or live on its margins, much like the bafflingly silent deaf characters in literature by hearing authors. In Kristeva's view, the adult is defined by speaking, much as earlier philosophers believed that humans were defined by speech. Yet all people once lived in a condition of abjection, since before infants learn to speak, they inhabit an abject borderline state (the Latin word *infans* means "incapable of speech"). In this infant state, identity is undefined, without boundary. According to Kristeva, abjection is in everyone's past and something of the unnameable condition of infancy remains forever in all people. If we insert the speechless deaf characters into this paradigm, we see that they can appear as if infants, never growing to adulthood through speech, remaining permanently infantilized in silence. Strikingly, most deaf characters in nineteenth-century American canonical literature are children or women; in writing deaf people, hearing authors seemed to need to infantilize or feminize them, perhaps to minimize the danger of their silent transgression. We do not encounter strong deaf males in these pages.

Finally, in these texts we can detect an effort to define and control the abjection of deafness through the written word. Kristeva maintains that "purification is something that only the Logos is capable of" (*Power* 27). She upholds the literary act, the verbal reason of logos, as a means of surviving and transcending abjection. Literature, Kristeva avers, is "the ultimate coding of our crises, of our most intimate and most serious apocalypses" (208). Writing offers a way to try to name the unnameable silence of deafness. According to Jeffrey Jerome Cohen, the fascination with different bodies such as deaf people springs from "the twin desire to name that which is difficult to apprehend and to domesticate (and therefore disempower) that which threatens" (viii). Through writing, one can attempt to identify, understand, and subdue, to bring order to the disorder in existence. However, as we have seen, silence and deafness always exist beyond the reach of logocentric comprehension. Confronted by the vast vacuum of silence and deafness, hearing authors paradoxically (and sometimes heroically) attempted, with words, to define and come to terms with something that could not quite be written.

Despite her celebration of the literary act, Kristeva, like Freud before her, occasionally expresses a wish for the abject, prelinguistic form of being. Freud sometimes intimates that humans have a backward longing, a "covert wish for re-immersion in an earlier, inarticulate state of organic existence" (Steiner, *Language* 36). Similarly, in *Powers of Horror* Kristeva occasionally betrays a yearning for a form of being outside of language, outside of religious, moral, and ideological codes, without boundary or rule.[3] Shaped by these competing interpretations of silence and deafness, deaf characters serve as the means through which hearing authors could investigate their own fears, questions, and desires. By attempting to write deafness, they wrote themselves.

SENTIMENTALIZING THE HEARING LINE

Sometimes deaf characters are easy to miss. Hearing authors occasionally mention deaf people in passing, making them hover indistinctly in the background in a manner that brings hearingness into sharper focus. For example, in the midst of one of his typically expansive catalogs of people and places, Whitman mentions "the blind, the deaf and dumb, idiots, hunchbacks, lunatics" (109) in "Salut Au Monde!" (1856). Similarly, he places deaf people between the blind and prisoners in "The Sleepers" (1855). Such lists are joyously inclusive, running the gamut of the American population and often, as in "The Sleepers," gently emphasizing the shared humanity of all people—rich and poor, black and white, hearing and deaf. However, by placing deaf people under "the defective," Whitman reinforces negative perceptions of them even as he calls attention to their commonality with others (105). Twain mentions deaf people in a somewhat similar fashion in his novel *Roughing It* (1871). Describing a sensational trial, he remarks that "of course all men not deaf and dumb and idiotic, talked about it" (341). Twain acknowledges deaf people's place in society but makes them seem dense and oblivious; they serve as a not-quite-real backdrop to help define the behavior of "normal" hearing individuals. Although such categorical depictions do reflect inclusive sensibilities, they are hardly egalitarian, reifying impressions of deaf people as ignorant and broken. Even in such brief evocations, the hearing line is constructed and affirmed.

We can see more clearly how hearing identity depends on the deafness it abjects when we turn to some of the popular verse of the period. Almost always sentimental in the favored style of the day, these poems were usually composed by hearing poets after they had personal contact with deaf people, offering a window into how they interpreted such encounters. In an early example, Moses Scott wrote "The Deaf and Dumb" (1819) shortly after visiting the newly opened New York Institution and its students (including, presumably, the ten-year-old James Nack).[4] It presents deaf people in piteous terms that throw the pleasures of hearingness into high relief:

To him, in vain, is pour'd the melting song,
Vain falls the streamlet, murmuring along. . . .
While strains of harmony *our* spirits buoy,
He may but see, and wonder at our joy. . . .
Then let us *hear*, rememb'ring *those* around
In whom eternal silence reigns profound! (6)

The unabashed joy and gratitude for hearing relies on the silent deaf "they" to exist, as the final couplet makes clear. The "us" here refers to adult hearing readers and the poet, while Scott positions deaf people as "*Affliction's children*," silent figures of *infans* in need of hearing care (5). In some ways this adult-child dynamic makes sense, since Scott had the children at the New York Institution in mind and was writing to elicit financial support from hearing readers. Yet however well intentioned, the adult-child rhetoric fosters what Baynton calls "the trap of paternalism," producing an impression of deaf people as weak, incomplete, and dependent, and hearing people as strong, self-reliant, and happy (150). Although he acknowledges deaf potential, Scott neglects to mention sign language and only seems to have a dim idea of how such potential might be realized. In his portrayal deaf people are defined by what they cannot do, which not only begins to demarcate and tame deafness, but also allows hearingness to be formed.

If Scott imagines a dichotomy with piteous deaf children on one side and grateful hearing adults on the other, subsequent hearing poets reinforce and complicate this dynamic. They frequently depict deaf people in religious terms, creating a recognizable genre of emotive, pious work that tends to pity or idealize deaf people, inevitably setting them apart from the hearing norm. Their poems are part of a larger trend that David Reynolds has called "the new religious style" in antebellum American culture, where religious discourse was no longer merely in doctrinal tracts but permeated much imaginative literature (15). Written in polite, conventional rhythms, such verses appealed to nineteenth-century Americans for the same reasons that they have since fallen out of favor. Among the many minor poets who wrote about deaf people, the most prominent was Lydia Huntley Sigourney, who by midcentury had probably become America's most famous female poet. Known at the height of her popularity as "the Sweet Singer of Hartford," she was a dedicated supporter of the American Asylum from its founding in 1817 and had a remarkable amount of contact with deaf people.[5] Along with ardent verse on other subjects, Sigourney produced poems about a bright deaf girl, Alice Cogswell, whom she taught for a while in 1814 (and who played a pivotal role in American deaf history by inspiring Thomas Hopkins Gallaudet to found a school for deaf students);[6] about Julia Brace, whom she referred to as "the deaf, dumb, and blind girl";[7] and about deaf students in chapel. The poems of Sigourney and her peers introduced many hearing Americans to deaf people. In one example of these poets' influence, their verses about Laura Bridgman, a deaf-blind student at the Perkins Institution for the Blind in Boston, helped to draw a record crowd of more than eleven hundred visitors to view the child on July 6, 1844 (Gitter 106). However affected such verse may seem to us today, it deserves our attention because it resonated with nineteenth-century

Lydia Huntley Sigourney. From James Herring, ed.,
The National Portrait Gallery of Distinguished Americans: with
Biographical Sketches, *vol. 4 (1858). Courtesy of Special Collections,*
University of Virginia Library.

readers, offering another glimpse into the national mindset about deafness.

One common way that such poets depicted deaf people was by dramatizing Isaiah's prophecy of them becoming hearing in heaven. Often designed to console, these verses present deaf people as both suffering and pure—and by implication their hearing counterparts as happier and perhaps more liable to sin. Consider "Alice" (1838), in which Sigourney imagines her former pupil, Alice Cogswell (who had died a few years before), speaking from above:

> The seal is melted from my ear
>   By love divine,
> And what through life I pined to hear
>   Is mine! Is mine! (274)

Intended to comfort members of Alice's hearing family, the poem expresses values that Sigourney and they hold dear. By showing a formerly deaf person in heaven, she implicitly asserts Alice's goodness, contesting the centuries-old view of deafness as a curse or mark of evil. Moreover, Alice is now one of the privileged, hearing "we," a spokesperson for hearing claims of greater happiness and superiority. Through her, Sigourney ventriloquizes the hearing belief that deaf people constantly "pined to hear," whereas, as we saw in chapter 1, early deaf Americans typically did not think that way.[8] In this manner, the poem implies that the actual deaf Alice on Earth was both benevolent and pitiable. We encounter a similar paradigm in Francis Scott Key's "Lines Given to William Darlington, A Deaf and Dumb Boy" (1857):

> The dumb shall speak, and the deaf shall hear,
>   In the brighter days to come,
> When they've passed through the troubled scenes of life
>   To a higher and happier home.
>
> They shall hear the trumpet's fearful blast,
>   And the crash of the rending tomb,
> And the sinner's cry of agony,
>   As he wakes to his dreaded doom.

And the conqueror's shout, and the ransomed's song,
   On their opened ears shall fall;
And the tongue of the dumb, in the chorus of praise
   Shall be louder and higher than all. (134)

The formerly deaf people escape the "troubled scenes" and sorrow of their deafness and, like Sigourney's Alice, find happiness in hearing, which Key underscores by having them joyously sing above all the others, as if making up for lost time. Once again we see a clear power dynamic at work where hearingness appears celestial and felicitous in contrast to the degradation of deafness. Yet Key also hints at a possible blessing in deafness: the formerly deaf people in heaven are separate from the sinner, whose cry they hear, suggesting that they have not sinned or are forgiven. By portraying deaf people on Earth as both inferior and virtuous, Key and Sigourney affirm the value of hearing, even if hearing may offer greater opportunity for corruption in this life.

With their simultaneous pity and idealization of deaf people, these heartfelt verses marshal mixed dread and longing for the deaf other, returning us again to Kristevan abjection. In presenting deaf people on Earth as piteous beings, Sigourney, Key, and their peers write from the Christian view that pity is a good quality that motivates charitable acts. Yet as many philosophers have pointed out, pity is often problematic because it relies on feelings of superiority and frequently contains disgust. In the words of Aaron Ben-Ze'ev, pity is "sympathetic sorrow" for someone "who is considered inferior in some aspect" and includes "contempt of the object" (3, 4). We certainly discern antipathy and condescension toward earthly deaf people in the treatments above, but the emotions seem more complex than that. In *Time and Free Will* (1910), Henri Bergson offers a more nuanced view that is perhaps applicable here. Conceding that pity probably has horror at its base, Bergson goes on to contend that pity is actually a process, a "transition from repugnance to fear, from fear to sympathy, and from sympathy itself to humility" (19). If we accept this model, we could say that Sigourney and Key are working out their initial revulsion at deafness, intrepidly trying to transform it into more uplifting thoughts and feelings for themselves and their readers. The humility at the end of this process may be their suggestion that deaf people are purer than they are. Such romanticization converts deafness into something appealing and manageable, but, Kristeva would argue, the allure is entangled with the horror, and abjection always returns. Mark Edmundson makes the same point in a different context, observing that "images of easy transcendence often act as antidotes, usually only partially successful, to pressing Gothic fears" (77). The aversion inherent in such piteous depictions is never quite suppressed, and deaf abjection remains, bringing hearing identity into clearer light.

This phenomenon is especially apparent in Sigourney's "Marriage of the Deaf and Dumb" (1848), where she moves from repulsion toward humility in an effort to discipline deafness. With palpable wonder and uneasiness, she begins by describing the wedding of a deaf couple:

> No word! No sound! But still yon holy man
> With strong and graceful gesture doth impose
> The irrevocable vow, and with meek prayer
> Present it to be registered in Heaven.
>   Methinks this silence heavily doth brood
> Upon the spirit. . . .
>   Mute! mute! 'Tis passing strange!
>   Like necromancy all. (241)

Once again we are in the realm of the uncanny. The familiar scene of a wedding is rendered "passing strange" by the silence of the participants and the minister's compelling but indecipherable gestures. Like Rip before the speechless ninepin players, like Ichabod before the headless horseman, Sigourney finds the soundless ceremony weird and unsettling, even, with "necromancy," likening the bridal couple to spirits of the dead. Her exclamations emphasize her hearingness, positioning her as a reassuring intermediary to the event for hearing readers. However, she soon strives to contain the latent fear; "yet, 'tis well," she says, and goes on to assert that love does not require speech. As she tells the couple:

> ye may build as firm
> Your silent altar in each other's hearts
> And catch the sunshine through the clouds of time
> As cheerily, as though the pomp of speech
> Did herald forth the deed. (242)

Enacting Bergson's notion of pity as a progression, Sigourney endeavors to transform her repugnance into respect by stating that deaf people can love as well and happily as hearing people. Yet beneath that affirmative claim of equality, conflicting emotions remain. She imagines the couple mourning their lack of speech and hearing, revealing persistent condescension and disgust. These feelings overlap with a subtle romanticization of deaf people when she uses their silence to identify a grandiloquent "pomp" in hearing people's speech. Never quite disciplined, the revulsion, fear, sympathy, and admiration overlap with and inflect each other; the poem mostly valorizes hearingness, but presents all people as somehow flawed. Sigourney's final strategy for taming such disorder is again to invoke heaven, where she imagines hearing and deaf alike basking in "the eternal dialect of love," allowing sorrowful deaf people to escape their silence and hearing people the arrogant artificiality of their speech.[9]

Taking her idealization of deaf people further, in other poems Sigourney uses them to indicate more explicitly the drawbacks and value of hearingness. Strikingly, although she had exposure to sign language and occasionally refers to it in her verse, in these poems Sigourney consistently defines deaf people not as a linguistic group but in terms of silence, the better to illuminate speech and hearing. She did appreciate sign, as she acknowledges in a reminiscence of her deaf student Alice Cogswell: "I was indebted to her for a new idea, that the hand and eye possessed an eloquence which had been heretofore claimed as the exclusive privilege of the tongue; that the language of the speechless might find an avenue to the soul" (*Letters* 253). Yet when she portrays Alice in verse, this enabling sign language is nowhere to be seen. Take "Answer to a Question" (1845), which Sigourney addresses to Alice in response to a query a hearing spectator posed at one of Sicard's exhibitions in Paris: Are deaf people unhappy?

> Oh! could the kind inquirer gaze
>   Upon thy brow, with gladness fraught,
> Its smile, like inspiration's rays,
>   Would give the answer to his thought. . . .
>
> Thy active life, thy look of bliss
>   The sparkling of thy magic eye,

Would all his skeptic doubts dismiss,
    And bid him lay his pity by,—

To bless the ear that ne'er has known
    The voice of censure, pride, or art,
Nor trembled at that sterner tone,
    Which, while it tortures, chills the heart.

To bless the lip that ne'er could tell
    Of human woes the vast amount
Nor pour those idle words that swell
    The terror of our last account.

For sure the stream of *silent* course
    May flow as deep, as pure, as blest,
As that which rolls in torrents hoarse,
    Or whitens o'er the mountain's breast. (*Scenes* 244–45)

Contradicting her own depictions elsewhere, Sigourney argues for Alice's (and deaf people's) happiness on Earth. While deaf authors such as Clerc (whom she knew) and Burnet celebrate sign language as part of deaf people's felicity, Sigourney romantically locates their happiness in their supposed ignorance of sadness and evil. She conveniently elides the fact that one can learn "censure, pride, or art" as readily through sign as through speech, just as one can tell of human tragedy. Despite the assertion of deaf-hearing equality at the end, we again discern both idealization (deaf people are pure) and condescension (they are ignorant) that serve to define hearing people as both more aware and more susceptible to sin and sorrow.

Sigourney's "Prayers of the Deaf and Dumb" (1845) extends this pattern. Describing deaf students in chapel at the American Asylum, she initially laments their inability to voice prayers as hearing people do. Yet, alluding to Paul's assertion that the "Spirit intercedes with sighs too deep for words" (Romans 8:26), she contends that connection with God does not require speech, which actually may impede it. The poem concludes:

The pomp of words may sometimes clog
    The ethereal spirit's flight,

But in the silence of their souls
  Burns one long Sabbath light,—

If God doth in that temple dwell,
  Their fancied loss is gain;
Ye perfect listeners to His voice!
  Say, is our pity vain? (*Scenes* 240)

Drawing on the religious tradition of silent meditation,[10] as well as views of silence as closer than speech to the ideal, Sigourney moves to contain fear and notions of deafness as a piteous mark of the Fall. Paradoxically, she suggests that the deaf worshipers are "perfect listeners," better hearers than hearing people distracted by portentous speech. Adding to the irony is that Sigourney, a poet, questions the effectiveness of words even as her meter and rhyme schemes chug along. We do not get any of Emily Dickinson's dashes and gaps here, so as readers we are not forced to experience silence. Sigourney's final, tentative query suggests that perhaps it is hearing people who are inferior, for deaf people may have closer connection with God. Language of condescension gives way to language of esteem, but of course neither quite disappears, and either way, Sigourney romanticizes deaf people, using their perceived difference to define the hearing "we."

In these verses Sigourney and her peers use the spirit of their times to interpret deafness. Harlan Lane has criticized Sigourney for ennobling deaf people as a result of disappointments in her own life, including an unhappy marriage. In Alice and other deaf people, Lane asserts, Sigourney found symbols of her own isolation. "Turned in on herself, forswearing men and the world, feasting on her own sensibility, the poetess tried desperately to represent that isolation yielded richness of inner experience for Alice and for herself," he says (*When* 181). Lane concludes that Sigourney's idealization of deaf people is a result of egoistic self-love. He has a point, for Sigourney, like all hearing authors who attempted to portray deaf people, inevitably projected her own insecurities, fears, and desires onto those characters. Yet Lane largely bypasses the context in which Sigourney wrote. Both women and deaf people endured oppression, so it seems unsurprising that Sigourney identified with her deaf subjects in terms of an emotional piety that the culture valued. Furthermore, quite a few other nineteenth-century poets, especially women, produced religious, sentimental poems about abnegation. Dickinson, the greatest female poet of the century, celebrates isolation and meditative silence even more than Sigourney. Sigourney's distinction lies in the way that she imagined these values, saw them embodied and expressed, in the deaf children she met at the American Asylum in Hartford. Furthermore, if female poets produced a lot of this verse, men did too, as Key reminds us. One of the more idealistic portrayals of the period was produced by a Barton Hill, who, after seeing a young deaf girl perform the Lord's Prayer in sign language, wrote a poem extolling her purity. Calling the girl a "sweet lamb of innocence," Hill asserts that God "blessed thee with a soul / Only to angels given" (Hodgson 194). Such emotional portrayals became the rule rather than the exception in nineteenth-century American verse. As Elisabeth Gitter points out, while Nathaniel Hawthorne and Melville struggled for readers, Sigourney and her peers found an appreciative audience by writing to the "general public's appetite for angelic heroines and uplifting pathos" (107). Sigourney emerges as an able recorder of both her own and her nation's evolving, ambivalent attitudes toward the mysterious, elusive deaf "they."

What seems constant in all these religiously informed poems of deafness is that deaf people are seldom just people. In using a religious framework to apprehend deaf Americans, hearing poets inevitably exaggerate their condition, expressing overlapping sensations of condescension, disgust, and reverence that further form and buttress the hearing line. Seeking to name and order the unruliness of deafness, they produce poems where the adult hearing voice is always calmly in control, which is to say, it depends on deafness for its control. For their part, the deaf characters appear virtually indistinguishable from each other. They are almost always children and almost always silent, a dynamic that further infantilizes those figures of *infans*, the deaf. No one wrote a poem about Laurent Clerc, as Charles Willson Peale painted him, or about deaf people signing with each other. At a time when educated deaf adults were gaining prominence in society, it seems telling that deaf children dominate verse. Such characters seem to function more as symbols and metaphors than living human beings, which aligns them with many disabled characters in literature. As David Mitchell puts it, "While disability as an experience is rarely narrated in terms of its own significance, disability as a metaphor allows writers to access concerns on a metaphysical scale" ("Narrative" 25). These poems use deaf figures to grapple with such larger topics as God, faith, and the utility of hearing and speech, serving to bring hearing identity into focus.

My overview of sentimental portrayals of deaf children may help to illuminate a more prominent deaf character in American literature, Jim's daughter 'Lizabeth in *Adventures of Huckleberry Finn* (1885). Just as Sigourney, Scott, and Key wrote about deaf characters after meeting deaf people, so Twain may have been inspired by his personal experience with deafness. As I discuss in chapter 5, Twain's boyhood friend Tom Nash caught scarlet fever and became deaf at age fifteen; similarly, 'Lizabeth gets scarlet fever and becomes deaf in *Huck Finn*. We learn about 'Lizabeth through a brief exchange between Huck and Jim as they float down the Mississippi on their raft. Jim tells Huck that soon after 'Lizabeth recovered from her illness, at about age four, he asked her to shut the door. In his narrative, she does not respond and "jis' stood dah, kiner' smilin' up at me" (156). Jim yells and, when 'Lizabeth still does not obey, strikes her. Moments later, the wind bangs the door shut and Jim notices that his daughter does not react to the noise. He says:

> De chile never move'! My breff mos' hop outer me; en I feel so— so—I doan' know *how* I feel. I crope out, all a-tremblin', en crope aroun' en open de do' easy en slow, en poke my head in behine de child, sof' en still, en all uv a sudden, I says *pow!* jus' as loud as I could yell. *She never budge!* Oh, Huck, I bust out a-cryin' en grab her up in my arms, en say, 'Oh, de po' little thing!' . . . Oh, she was plumb deaf en dumb, Huck, plum deaf en dumb—en I'd ben a-treat'n her so! (156)

Twain seems to trade a bit upon the growing literary tradition of using deaf children for sentimental purposes. "Po' little 'Lizabeth" has more in common with Sigourney's Alice than with Twain's other deaf characters (perhaps because she is Twain's only female deaf character) (155). She is a helpless, angelic victim; like all deaf characters in this sentimental vein, she appears completely passive. 'Lizabeth's muteness and obliviousness add to her vulnerability; they underscore the helpless deaf girl's dependence on her hearing father. Some aspects of the account seem a bit far-fetched. She probably would not have lost her ability to speak so soon after losing her hearing, and it is somewhat difficult to believe that she could not feel the vibrations of the door slamming shut just a few feet away from her. Such elements may reveal the limits of Twain's knowledge and show how he presents a somewhat narrow account of the deaf experience. At any rate, the scene sets up the duke comically acting deaf soon thereafter, as I discuss in chapter 5. Moreover, Twain skillfully uses the episode further to humanize Jim, both for Huck (who earlier is surprised to learn that a "nigger" like Jim even cares about his family) and for us as readers. But most important, the incident makes Huck and Jim's racial difference recede more. Against the startling void of 'Lizabeth's deafness, they are united as hearing people.

ATTRACTION AND HORROR

Thus far I have considered literary treatments of deaf children or of a generalized deaf "they" where deafness is rarely overtly threatening; it seems safely infantilized, kept apart from the adult hearing speaker who controls the narrative. While individual deaf men seldom show up in these poems and stories, adult deaf women do appear, and they frequently endanger the orderly balance. If Twain's 'Lizabeth points to how the hearing line can complicate and sometimes trump the color line, these women characters illustrate more clearly how the hearing line is also invariably gendered, reflecting pervasive assumptions about the meanings of femininity and masculinity in American society. Such deaf female figures (usually written by hearing men) often embody both exceptional purity and menacing sexuality, exhibiting another side of hearing authors' conflicting reactions to the deafness they abject. Moreover, these destabilizing deaf characters almost always have metaphorical significance, allowing authors to address larger themes even as they use them further to define and police the boundaries of hearingness.

Several works separate deaf women from hearing people by idealizing them to the point of adoration. Beneath such veneration we can sometimes again discern a certain revulsion, as male hearing narrators seem unwilling to contemplate a romantic deaf-hearing relationship.

In "The Deaf Girl" (1836), a melodramatic story by an anonymous hearing author, the threat to the social order is the strikingly beautiful, "*angelic*," and vivacious title character (278). Although eighteen, Marianne has not been allowed to grow up; she has never been out of sight of her family's house and remains "as free from guile as an infant" (281). Kept in this state of *infans* by her overprotective parents, she apparently has not received an education, met another deaf person, or learned sign language. When an aunt takes her to Albany, she is courted by a hearing officer who has no intention of marrying her. "Could she but speak," he says, "I should prefer her to any woman on earth" (281). We learn that the father would never have consented to such a deaf-hearing pairing, and even the narrator seems to agree that Marianne's speechlessness is an insurmountable barrier: "a beauty who cannot speak," he says, "is no more to our intellectual beaux than a statue" (276). For all her virtues, Marianne's muteness and deafness causes the hearing narrator and characters to view her as incapable of living an adult life, consigning her to a permanent, suffocating childhood. Devastated by her suitor's dishonesty, unaware of "the promises of Christianity" that the narrator says would have consoled her, Marianne soon perishes. "She had worshiped truth—she found the world false," and "her spirit was not formed to endure it," the narrator concludes (283). In this way, the author uses deafness to enhance feminine purity to the point where life is no longer possible. Through Marianne, he reveals not only the treachery of hearing society, but also hearing people's position as adult, in control, sexual, and marriageable. In contrast to deaf author John Burnet's portrayal of a joyful deaf-hearing marriage in "The Orphan Mute," this story works against deaf-hearing unions, perhaps out of fear that such a pairing would diminish the integrity of hearingness. (Notably, white segregationists commonly accused abolitionists and, later, supporters of equal rights for African Americans of plotting the destruction of the white race through miscegenation.) In the interests of preserving the dominant order, Marianne's social, romantic, and sexual needs as an adult woman are squelched, and at the end her disruptive presence is effaced.

Just as author of "The Deaf Girl" esteems Marianne while denying her full humanity, so in "The Beautiful Silence: Composed on Seeing a

Beautiful Deaf Mute Lady" (1853) Thomas Holley Chivers rhapsodizes over a deaf woman he chanced to observe without any apparent interest in her as a real person. Going beyond any idealization we have seen thus far, Chivers glorifies the woman as a celestial being, using her to reveal hearing people as both more alive and more corrupt than their deaf counterparts. He begins with an ecstatic religious interpretation of her beauty and silence:

> Thou art the Angel of the voiceful silence
>   Christ left behind him when he went to God. . . .
>
> Thy knowledge comes to thee down-flowing,
>   As does an Angel's, free from earthly sin,
> Out of the life divine of God all-knowing—
>   Ours from without—thine to thy soul within—
> And, Angel-like, although thy lips are mute,
> Like Israfel in Heaven, thy heartstrings are a lute.
>
> All those discordant, ever-jarring noises,
>   Which grate upon our souls, thou hast not heard;
> But thou doest hear, unheard to us, the heavenly Voices
>   Made audible to thee through God's most holy Word;
> For, being an Angel, thou dost use an Angel's tongue,
> Silence, God's holy language, sweeter far than Song.

Seeing the woman's ineffable silence in positive terms, Chivers, like Sigourney and Hill, presents deaf people as having special communion with God, but he goes further still, revering the woman as an angel. Turning Sigourney's conjecture at the end of "Prayers of the Deaf and Dumb" into a firm assertion, Chivers depicts the deaf woman as a better hearer of "heavenly Voices" than hearing people, who are ironically made deaf to God by the clamor of their daily lives. In this way, he extols her as someone sinless who represents celestial harmony, exposing the "discordant," fallen, hearing world.

Making the woman into an emblem of everything missing in his life, Chivers goes on to express his ardent desire to unite with her, a wish that seems more romantic than realistic. In the midst of his paean to her pure, angelic character, he expresses palpable physical attraction:

So, thy dear soul sits here in peace secure,
Shrined in the milk-white Temple of thy body pure.

Chivers's earnest language, which may invite ridicule today, reveals how his interpretation of the deaf woman is inflected by his yearning for her race ("milk-white"), sexuality ("Temple of thy body"), and, if we include the title, beauty and class ("lady"). In other words, she conforms to the hegemonic ideals of the time, except for her deafness, which in Chivers's eyes adds to her feminine innocence and pushes her into the realm of the divine. Seeing her as an opportunity for physical and spiritual release, he concludes:

God could bestow on me no heavenlier Vision
    Than gazing on thy form, dear heavenly One!
Thinking of thee, I rove through Fields Elysian,
    In mental walks, with His dear blessed Son!
For, where thou art, there Christ must ever be;
And there, or not, thy presence makes him there to me.

Thou art more beautiful than milk-white Una—
    Meeker than Mercy, gentler than sweet Sleep—
Fairer to me than to Endymion Luna—
    Coming from Heaven to teach me how to weep,
With piteous love, for thy dear, blessed sake—
Whose lamb-like innocence should make the World's heart
    break. . . .

Oh! God! if this dear, heavenly creature
    Were only mine, what would I do for thee?
Seeing her wearing here each God-like feature
    Of Christ, while Incarnating Heaven for me;
And living here on earth the life divine,
And, Star-like, singing, shining while she makes me shine.

For Chivers, the beautiful deaf woman offers salvation of every kind; if she unites with him, all the pain and loss of the fallen hearing world will be relieved. Through their union, he seems to believe he would have the bliss of overcoming many barriers: the boundaries between male and female, hearing and deaf, sound and silence, sin and redemption, the fallen and the divine. His poem marks the most extreme glorification of a deaf person in the literature of the period, an example that makes Sigourney's excesses seem conservative by comparison. Such romanticization tells us almost nothing about the actual deaf woman that Chivers saw, and with whom, as far as we can tell, he did not communicate. If we remember "Rip Van Winkle," another part of the allure probably lies in the idea of a woman who does not speak.[11] As the reference to "Una" suggests, both thematically and prosodically Spenser seems to be the model here, for Chivers makes the woman into an allegorical emblem with no more humanity than, say, Dante's Beatrice. Once again, the deaf character is passive, with her own personality, desires, and fears absent from the picture. We cannot know if this woman could sign, if she was educated, or whether she could read this poem that Chivers wrote. For all his soulful yearning, we get no evidence he believes he can win this woman or even that he will see her again. Part of his pleasure seems to lie in her very distance, in the impossibility of boundaries being transgressed, of him ever having his wishes granted—or his romantic illusions destroyed. Against her ethereal presence, Chivers and all hearing people emerge as more distant from God but also more human.

In the literary depictions of deaf people we have examined so far, the revulsion at deafness has been largely hidden from view. While discomfort and paternalism often turn up, such as in the portrayal of deaf people as inferior and shut out from the joyful sounds of life, or in the treatment of Marianne's inability to speak, for the most part hearing authors succeed in naming and corralling deafness, placing it into reassuring categories that minimize its disruption and shore up their own identities as hearing people. Elsewhere, however, the horror of deafness spills out, shocking hearing characters and readers alike at the end of works with its unexpected appearance.

Perhaps an early story by Melville best exemplifies this mode. In "Fragments from a Writing Desk, No. 2" (1839), which he published when he was just nineteen, Melville presents a collision between hearingness and deafness. The narrator, a young hearing man, is a figure of Logos who not only addresses readers with his words, but also is steeped in books of romance and adventure. At the beginning he casts aside an ancient Greek lexicon, and he frequently uses literary allusions, quoting from *The Rivals* and *Romeo and Juliet* and comparing an arbor to something out of Atlantis and an elegant chamber to one from *Arabian Nights*. Affected by such readings, he longs for the "days of romance," despite Burke's claim that "the days of chivalry are over!" (197). When he goes outside in the evening to clear his head, a mysterious woman wearing a cloak gives him his chance: she drops a romantic note at his feet that asks him to follow the bearer. His curiosity and ardor aroused, the narrator pursues this "tantalizing stranger," who beckons and gestures to him but laughingly stays ahead, out of the range of speech (198). Is the messenger deaf? We never find out, although the narrator's reactions to "a being so perfectly inexplicable" fluctuate between fascination and distress, paralleling many hearing people's response to deafness (201). Unable to fathom the enigma of her silence, he follows her out of the town, into a forest, and eventually to a mansion in a "harsh, gloomy, and forbidding" place, where the "profound stillness [and] solitude . . . were enough of themselves to strike panic into the stoutest heart" (201). Disturbed by this silent Gothic environment, the narrator, who puts so much value in speech and words, increasingly wishes he had never come.

When he enters the mansion, the latent attraction and horror of deafness burst forth. He comes into an elaborate chamber, complete with draperies, perfumes, carpet, chandeliers, and mirrors, and espies a beautiful woman reclining on an ottoman. Wearing a white robe, with roses in her hair and a bracelet of heart-shaped rubies, this "glorious being" (203) has "loveliness . . . which as no obscurity could diminish, so, no art could heighten" (202). Before she notices the narrator, the woman has a mournful, melancholy air, which suggests the isolation and unhappiness that hearing people tended to imagine deaf individuals enduring. Upon seeing him, she brightens, and he immediately falls upon his knees and declares his love. Calling her "thou sweet Divinity," he gives in to the same kind of ecstatic rapture that Chivers displays in his poem. Like Chivers, the narrator takes the woman's silence and beauty as signs of the celestial, but when he kisses her hand and asks her to speak to seal their love, the woman does not respond. The story rushes to its conclusion:

She was silent; gracious God! what horrible apprehension crossed my soul?—Frantic with the thought, I held her from me, looking in her face, I met the same impassioned gaze; her lips moved—my senses ached with the intensity with which I listened,—all was still,—and they uttered no sound; I flung her from me, even though she clung to my vesture, and with a wild cry of agony I burst from the apartment! —She was dumb! Great God, she was dumb! DUMB AND DEAF! (204)

The narrator's powerful attraction quickly turns to equally potent terror. He flees, presumably back to his world of speech, sound, and language, although the story ends with his cry and fittingly descends into wordless silence itself.

Why does the narrator react so adversely? His fervent nature doubtless has something to do with it, as does the disorder of deafness threatening conventional boundaries. Even before he meets the deaf woman, the narrator reveals his tendency toward emotional histrionics. When he cannot catch the messenger, he expresses his anger in a way that "savored . . . of the jolly cavaliers" and even considers committing suicide to put a "romantic end" to his existence (198, 199). Given such self-dramatization, his panicked departure at the end hardly surprises. Furthermore, to this young man deafness clearly does not betoken the divine. Its sudden appearance where it is not expected shocks, producing feelings of transgression, of being tricked and threatened with violation. Because she presumably sent the note inviting the narrator, the deaf woman is more active (and thus unfeminine) than other deaf characters we have seen, and hence more disruptive and in need of purging. Douglas's comment on human reactions to pollution may help here: "Our pollution behavior is the reaction which condemns any object or idea likely to confuse or contradict cherished classifications," she says (48). In Melville's tale, deafness seems a sort of pollution that threatens to sully the boundaries around identity. Kristeva's words neatly summarize the narrator's horrified reaction: "if these limits are not sufficiently stable . . . our reaction can be a violent one of disgust, rejection and hate" (qtd. in Nooy 162). Invisible deafness imperils the distinction between reason and unreason, self and other, and may be forcefully expelled. The narrator's loathing at his attraction to the deaf woman has parallels,

(((POWERS OF DEAFNESS)))

again, to repugnance at miscegenation, at the mixing and perceived diminishing of racial identity. The potential for sexual blending of hearingness and deafness seems to hold similar terror. Like racism, sexism, and homophobia, audism (a relatively new term for discrimination against individuals based on hearing ability) often betrays insecurity, a fear that the boundaries between self and other are too weak, too porous, and too flimsy to protect one's identity from threats to its meaning.[12] By naming the abjection of deafness at the end—"DUMB AND DEAF!"—the narrator seeks control over it, to reestablish his own difference as a hearing, speaking individual. "Deaf" emerges once again as an epistemological device, a category that helps form identity.

Rather than endeavoring to portray an actual deaf person, in his dreamlike tale Melville seems to use deafness more symbolically to comment on the loss of romance in the modern world, but still we can see the hearing line being tested and formed. With the failure of ardent speech in the face of deafness at the end, Burke's pronouncement, quoted at the start of the story, seems verified: "The days of chivalry are over!" (197). Only foolish young bachelors and melancholy deaf women seek romance. For their apparent differences, the two characters are alike in that they both desperately yearn to enact and experience romantic connection. But the hearing line, at least as it is understood by the narrator, prevents them from coming together. Or, more forcefully, the hearing line may exist, or be put there, precisely to block their similarity, to abject the deaf female body. Just as the young officer will not consider marrying Marianne, just as Chivers displays no intention of approaching his deaf beauty, so, again, the possibility of a deaf-hearing union is written out of the realm of possibility, a prospect too fantastic and frightening to consider. While Melville, through his foppish narrator, illustrates the folly of hearing people relying too much on words and speech, he also reinforces the apparent taboo against deaf-hearing relationships, segregating the deaf character from the hearing one to maintain the social structure.

The dormant terrors of deafness were driven home later in the century by Ambrose Bierce in one of his most memorable stories, "Chickamauga" (1889). The title alone would have reminded many nineteenth-century Americans of the disastrous Civil War battle in Chickamauga, Tennessee. Fought in a thick forest over several days in

September 1863, the conflict left over 37,000 soldiers dead, missing, or wounded. Bierce himself witnessed the carnage firsthand as a young officer in the Union army. For modern readers who may not be familiar with the battle, the story packs even more wallop (students respond to it strongly). Deafness plays an integral part in its effect.

Like Melville in "Fragments from a Writing Desk," Bierce shields deafness from view, bringing it out in the end as part of a tragic, gruesome surprise. The story begins innocently enough as a boy about six years old, the son of a southern farmer, ventures away from his home pretending to conquer imaginary foes with a wooden sword. However, we soon sense that something is amiss. Wandering into the forest, the boy is terrified by a harmless rabbit, which causes him to cry and run deeper into the undergrowth where, exhausted, he falls asleep. When he awakens, he sees a hideous sight: scores of wounded soldiers crawling painfully toward a creek. However, the boy does not quite comprehend what they are. "Something in this," the narrator says, "something too, perhaps, in their grotesque attitudes and movements—reminded him of the painted clown who he had seen last summer in the circus, and he laughed as he watched them" (51). Adding to the incongruity, the boy remembers how the slaves at home give him rides on their backs and so jumps onto the back of a jawless soldier crawling by. The garish contrast between the laughing boy and the dying men becomes even more apparent as the boy takes the head of the procession. Happily waving his sword, he leads the macabre crew toward the water and a bright light in the distance. As the soldiers collapse and die near the creek, the boy approaches the light and suddenly realizes it is his home on fire. He discovers the body of a woman, presumably his mother, lying in a field, her brains leaking out from her shattered skull. Adding shock upon shock, Bierce concludes:

> The child moved his little hands, making wild, uncertain gestures. He uttered a series of inarticulate and indescribable cries—something between the chattering of an ape and the gobbling of a turkey —a startling, soulless, unholy sound, the language of a devil. The child was a deaf mute.
>
> Then he stood motionless, with quivering lips, looking down upon the wreck. (57)

(((POWERS OF DEAFNESS)))

Once again, the unexpected appearance of deafness destabilizes and surprises. Just as the abjection of deafness shows up in a beautiful woman in Melville's tale, so here it appears in the person of an innocent boy, and its horror lies partially in its presence in what is familiar and attractive. Through deafness, the known becomes mixed with the unknown, producing again an uncanny, unsettling disturbance of expected boundaries. As in other episodes, the deaf character is a child, described to us by the adult, hearing narrator. The boy's "wild, uncertain gestures" (the sign language of a distraught deaf child?) and inarticulate cries contrast with the narrator's eloquent, assured voice. By comparing the boy's sounds to those of an ape or turkey, Bierce reifies the old interpretation of deaf people as animalistic, while his linkage of the boy's voice to a "soulless, unholy sound, the language of a devil" taps into the old interpretation of deafness as a mark of evil and sin. Finally, the boy's ignorance of the battle and obliviousness to the soldiers' pain reinforces stereotypes of deaf people being dense and lacking in compassion. In a few sentences, Bierce manages to evoke almost all the negative interpretations of deafness we have seen thus far and cast the whole story in new light.

In retrospect, we can discern Bierce planting subtle clues of the boy's deafness throughout the piece. The boy is a visual person; he fashions the wooden sword because of engravings he has seen in his father's military books. After seeing the rabbit, he calls out for his mother with "inarticulate cries," suggesting his muteness (48). The rabbit itself turns out to be something of an inside joke, for the boy is scared of its "long, menacing ears" (50). The narrator does not talk much of sound except when the boy goes to sleep; then he describes the birds singing, the squirrels barking, and a "strange, muffled thunder" in the distance, which proves to be the noise of battle (48). Later in the story the narrator informs us that the soldiers had marched past the sleeping boy on every side. "Almost within a stone's throw of where he lay they had fought a battle; but all unheard by him were the roar of the musketry, the shock of the cannon" (54). Like Twain's depiction of 'Lizabeth not sensing the slamming door, this description seems a bit far-fetched, for surely the boy would at least have felt the vibrations of the cannon or of so many soldiers marching by. As the story progresses, we as readers have a sense of something awry, not just with this destructive world, but with the boy in particular. Our position somewhat resembles that of a hearing parent of a deaf child. We watch his actions, notice some unusual behavior, but it takes time for the clues to add up and for us to deduce his status. In this way, our shock at the end distantly resembles the trauma hearing parents often experience when discovering their child is deaf.

Bierce uses deafness not just to offer a fresh and vivid take on the horrors of the Civil War, but also, on a more symbolic level, to satirize the behavior of misguided generals during the conflict. Throughout the story, the child inhabits the role of commanding officer. The narrator describes his wandering into the forest in terms of military maneuver, saying he "committed the common enough military error of pushing the pursuit to a dangerous extreme" (47). The child's general-like status becomes especially evident at the end, when he triumphantly leads the wounded soldiers. Commanders in the Civil War, Bierce implies, were often, like the deaf boy, arrogant, insensitive to their soldiers' suffering, and "deaf" to the reality of the situation. The boy finding his home burning may be a metaphor for how the foolhardy Civil War leaders in effect burned Americans' home, turning some cities and sections of the country into desolated wasteland. Just as Melville uses deafness to comment on the loss of the age of romance, so Bierce employs it to convey the incompetence of Civil War leadership.

If these portrayals of the terror of deafness seem more vivid and stimulating than the rather pious takes on deaf people I examined earlier, we might remember Frederic Jameson's comment that "the enjoyment of the shock and commotion fear brings to the human organism" is a fundamental part of pleasure (72).[13] Kristeva reiterates the complicity of abjection and the experience of astonishing beauty throughout *Powers of Horror*. The pleasure and fear are interconnected; as Peter Stallybrass and Allon White put it, "disgust bears the impress of desire" (77). Hearing authors' attraction and revulsion at the prospect of deafness are never far from one another as these writers display the operative ambivalence that characterizes so much writing about difference.

To sum up, deaf characters in this literature do a great deal of cultural work. Through them, hearing authors not only acknowledge and seek to come to terms with the growing presence of deaf Americans in society, but also think about and define themselves as hearing people. From Sigourney's sentimental poems to Bierce's horrific tale, we can see how hearing identity relies on the deafness it abjects. In *Orientalism*, Said argues that Europe came up with the myth of the Middle East and Asia to legitimate its own authority, and we can make a similar connection here. With their deaf characters, hearing authors legitimate themselves as adult, rational, human, alive, and often happy, grateful, in control, and sympathetic.[14] At the same time, deaf figures allow hearing authors to express anxieties about the effectiveness of speech and hearing, fears that they are arrogant, prone to corruption, and have lost connection with God, as well as views on larger cultural topics like romance and war. By almost always portraying deaf people as passive children and women, hearing authors work to tame latent disgust and condescension and discover humility toward them. However, when deaf characters become active, like Melville's woman or Bierce's boy, they become frightening agents who threaten the established order, a danger that authors usually deal with by firmly excluding deaf figures who imperil the boundaries of hearing identity (notably, deafness is not expelled in Bierce's "Chickamauga," which seems part of its intended horror). Such moments remind us how linked their attraction and fear are, and illustrate how difficult it would be to achieve meaningful deaf-hearing equality. Since these depictions rarely give us insight into actual deaf experience, we could easily dismiss them as inaccurate, biased, and therefore counterproductive. Yet if they do not quite humanize deaf people, these portrayals do regularly attack the old notion that deafness is a mark of evil. In addition, just by including deaf characters, however flat, in their visions, these writers raised consciousness of deaf people in mainstream society. By contributing to the discourse over the hearing line, Sigourney, Melville, Twain, and their peers further opened the way for deaf people to counter with their own literary points of view. In the next chapter we will see how deaf authors at midcentury grappled with these challenges and sought to find a welcoming place for themselves in America.

My favorite deaf character by a hearing author may not be deaf at all. Melville's "deaf and dumb stranger" in *The Confidence-Man*, as we have seen, could easily be a hearing impostor (12). Yet even if the man is a con artist, he enacts the kind of deaf American mostly absent from the literature: adult, educated, literate, familiar with the Bible, and able to sign. (He is also a grown man, another rarity in a deaf character by a hearing writer.) As such, he seems the most progressive representation of a deaf person by a hearing author during this time. This observation may appear odd, given the corrosive nature of the novel's satire, but nonetheless it seems true. Like Duncan Campbell in early-eighteenth-century literature, Melville's stranger, whether he is a fraud or not, reveals attitudes and thinking about deafness in his time. The man embodies many other features of deaf characters that we have seen: he is not only innocent, pious, and pitiable, but also potentially threatening and duplicitous, perhaps a mercenary out to take people's money. Finally, he is unknowable, beyond comprehension from our limited perspectives, a mysterious cipher that we can endlessly interpret without ever naming conclusively. In all these depictions by hearing authors, there always seems much that is left unsaid.

A Sense of Two-ness

DEAF DOUBLE CONSCIOUSNESS
AT MIDCENTURY

I move—a silent exile on this earth . . .
No gleam of hope this darken'd mind assures
That the blest power of speech shall e'er be known.
John Carlin, "The Mute's Lament" (1847)

We do attest that we are capable of many [things]
which the prejudice, and sometimes even malignance of our
hearing brethren, deprive us!
John Jacobus Flournoy (1856)

Every colonized people . . . finds itself face
to face with the language of the civilizing nation.
Frantz Fanon (1952)

In this literary environment, with its welter of images of deafness, deaf Americans continued to strive to assert their own identities through writing. While hearing authors typically imagined deaf people as a homogeneous "they," deaf writers distinguished themselves both as individuals and as members of a heterogeneous deaf "we." In their work the deaf community emerges as a dialogic place not just with a strong shared sense of identity but with disagreement and prejudices of its own. While hearing authors created phantasmic depictions that abjected figures of deafness and buttressed hearing identity, deaf authors at midcentury contended with contradictory notions of self. Building on the early work of Clerc, Nack, and Burnet, they sought to write themselves out of the subordinate space that hearing people assigned to them by demonstrating their equal intellect and richness of feeling. Yet like these predecessors, they sometimes replicated dominant imagery that positioned them as inferior, revealing once again an abiding double consciousness where they saw themselves both from within and through the eyes of hearing people. While this doubly inscribed mentality aligns them with minority and colonized groups, deaf Americans were unique in that they associated their collective identity with the majority, with hearing educators and philanthropists who helped to establish and run the schools that brought them together. As a result, deaf authors reveal an ever-shifting mix of gratitude, pride, self-deprecation, and occasionally resentment as they struggle to escape their sense of division and, in Du Bois's words, "merge [the] double self into a better and truer self" (11). If hearing authors frequently seek to establish boundaries and delimit deafness and hearingness, even as they explore ways that deaf and hearing people are alike, deaf authors do too. They investigate both their similarities to hearing people and their differences, further showing how the hearing line serves as a double-boundary, continually imagined, interrogated, and formed from both sides.

As the American deaf community coalesced, its oral (perhaps "manual" is a better term, since of course sign is not vocal) culture centered on sign language flourished, while its literacy in English grew, too, with the manual and literate discourses existing side by side in distinct but mutually interactive ways. Because nineteenth-century American Sign Language is mostly lost to us today,[1] it is easy to underestimate its importance. But in the classroom and the dormitory, at chapel services and deaf association meetings, in deaf-deaf marriages and in virtually all of deaf people's face-to-face contact with each other, sign was the preferred and most comfortable means of communication, a principal bond that held deaf people together. As a deaf student at the Missouri school named Laura Redden (later Searing) observed in 1858:

> Signs are the natural language of the mute. Writing may be used in his intercourse with others, but when conversing with those who are, like himself, deprived of hearing and speech, you will always find that he prefers signs to every other mode of intercourse; and every other established means of communicating his thoughts, no matter what facility he may have acquired in it, is no more nor less than what a foreign language is to those who hear and speak. ("A Few" 178)

While sign remained deaf people's language of choice, written English continued to play a role in the formation of their collective identity. As more deaf people became literate, they used writing to communicate not just with hearing nonsigners, but also with each other when they were separated by space or time. Near midcentury deaf-related periodicals began to be founded, giving them more opportunities to publish their work; in 1847 the American Asylum began producing the *American Annals of the Deaf and Dumb*, in 1849 the North Carolina Institution for the Deaf and Dumb and the Blind started *Deaf Mute*, and others followed. Such periodicals contained essays, poetry, and news of deaf people, giving further evidence of the emergence of a strong deaf "we," a "we" that does not appear in hearing authors' poetry or fiction. In this way, deaf writers continued occasionally to decolonize the English language and the whole structure of hearing assumptions, even if at other times they replicated and reified them.

Yet if writing appears a democratic form open to all deaf Americans, we should note that only a small portion of deaf people actually wrote for publication. Many signers continued to feel uncomfortable expressing themselves to the public through written English, as Searing noted in her 1858 essay. "A mute may be never so eloquent when expressing his thoughts in pantomime, but be utterly powerless to reproduce the same on paper," she wrote (179).[2] Some of the most compelling signers were never recorded, reminding us again of how the deaf community was a manual culture, where news, stories, and folklore were passed down through live face-to-face contact without the intercession of writing. To overcome deaf people's reluctance to publish, the editor of *The Deaf-Mutes' Friend*, William Chamberlain, pleaded in 1869 for readers to submit their work. "There are many among our class whose ideas, if written, would be of much interest, but who are afraid to write lest they should not be understood by those not accustomed to the peculiar expressions often used by mutes," he wrote ("Salutatory" 18). By "peculiar expressions," Chamberlain probably means deaf people writing English words in the order of American Sign Language, or ASL, idioms.[3] He partially circumvented this problem by having William Swett, a well-known sign language performer who mesmerized deaf audiences with his tales, sign autobiographical narratives to him, which he then translated and published in English. Swett was one of the few nineteenth-century deaf Americans to make it into print without having to contend with a pen, although one suspects that something was lost in the transfer to the printed page. Through print, the content of Swett's tales became available to readers who had never met him, just as, after major deaf meetings, the periodicals often carried English translations of the signed addresses for readers who could not attend. Deaf people's manual and literate forms thus had a complex relationship and sometimes reinforced each other. As Ruth Finnegan points out, such forms exist on a continuum: "Orality and literacy are not two separate and independent things; nor (to put it more concretely) are oral and written modes two mutually exclusive and opposed processes for representing and communicating information" (175). Paradoxically, deaf Americans used the written form of the majority's language, a language foreign to many of them, further to unify themselves on a national level, revealing both how distinct their communal identity was and how it intertwined with the larger hearing society in which they lived.

While discomfort with English deterred many deaf people from seeking to express themselves in print, so too did the nation's racial and gender prejudices, which infused the community. The deaf authors who published were uniformly white and mostly male. As previously noted, deaf people of color seldom received an education and, as far as I can determine, did not participate in deaf community events at midcentury or publish, adding another shameful facet to the oppressive racism of the period.[4] White deaf women often were educated and literate, but they were taught at the schools and elsewhere to adopt a domestic role and remain out of the public eye, indicating again the significant effect gender had in the construction of the hearing line. Margaret Fuller lamented in 1844 that all women had long been discouraged from "the use of the pen . . . that help to free-agency" (1628). Notably, the few deaf women who did publish at midcentury tended to be unmarried, which apparently gave them the freedom or the monetary need to thwart cultural expectations and write for publication.[5] Adele Jewel, an impoverished deaf woman in Michigan, only composed her brief life story so she could earn money selling it to passersby on the streets. "I shrunk from [writing] it, and could never have done so, had it not been really necessary for me to do something for my own maintenance," she explains (17). Laura Redden Searing embarked on a successful career as a journalist and poet, but did so by publishing under the name of Howard Glyndon; some of her readers thought she was a hearing man ("Poetry" 592).[6] Even as deaf people struggled to find autonomous voices in print, then, hegemonic forces helped to determine who would write and the hierarchical structure of their community.

Not surprisingly, the leaders of the deaf community tended to be the white deaf men who were more skilled in written English than other educated deaf people, who relied more on sign language. While sign bonded deaf Americans together and fascinated hearing people who observed them, and while skilled signers like Swett had special cachet in the community, English remained the language of power. As we saw in chapter 1, in the nineteenth century African Americans, Native Americans, deaf people, and others turned to written English to gain a voice in public discourse, demonstrate their reason to the public, and strive for equal rights; writing was seen as evidence of their humanity. This state of affairs parallels that sometimes found in colonial situations. For example, Frantz Fanon describes a similar dynamic among black Algerians under French colonial rule. Early in *Black Skin, White Masks* (1952), he asserts that an Algerian becomes "proportionately whiter—that is, he will come closer to being a real human being—in direct ratio to his mastery of the French language," the language of the colonizers (18). Skill in the dominant group's language gives oppressed people certain potency, which underscores again not just the importance of deaf authors' endeavors to convey themselves in print, but also the inherent contradictions of their seeking to do so in a language typically used to justify hearing normalcy and privilege.

Fanon illuminates these contradictions in his discerning analysis of the psychology of colonized Algerians, offering insights that apply to the mentality of many oppressed groups, including nineteenth-century deaf people, in telling ways. First, he maintains that black natives have been utterly objectified by the racial gaze of white colonizers. As Homi Bhabha summarizes Fanon's argument, such objectification makes the natives' "very presence . . . both 'overlooked'—in the double sense of social surveillance and psychic disavowal—and, at the same time, over-determined—psychically projected, made stereotypical and symptomatic" (236). Based on the evidence in the last chapter, we can assert that many hearing Americans similarly objectified deaf people: they attributed any number of stereotypical, metaphorical meanings to deaf figures—determining them to be angelic, pure, pitiable, or demonic—but rarely *saw* them as individual human beings. Fanon contends that this objectifying gaze is internalized by black Algerians, leading to a split consciousness. Building on Du Bois's ideas, he writes, "Overnight, the Negro has been given two frames of reference within which he has to place himself. . . . For not only must the black man be black; he must be black in relation to the white man" (110). In the same way, deaf Americans had to form their individual and collective notions of self through two distinct frames: their association with each other, through fluent sign language and shared experiences, and their interaction with hearing people, who rarely knew sign, spoke English, and, as we will see, sometimes responded to them with contempt or neglect. As a result of this dislocated subjective complexity, Fanon says that many black Algerians desire to become white, whether by seeking to lighten their skin color, sleep with white people, or imitate white ways. Again we can discern a similar mentality in deaf writing, as deaf people, surrounded by an environment that continually linked hearingness with power, control, and happiness, sometimes express a wish to be hearing. Such valorization of the majority culture also plays out linguistically, as some blacks and deaf people grow to value the dominant languages of French or English over their own. Yet no matter how much colonized natives or deaf people internalize white, hearing values, complete assimilation is impossible, for they will never be socially accepted as equals, leaving them feeling inferior and dependent. The tragedy is magnified because colonized blacks (like deaf Americans) likely will not realize that their degraded position is a result of social forces, and will fall into uncertainty or self-loathing, living, in the words of René Ménil, "in an unreal world determined by the ideals and *abstract ideas of another people*" (qtd. in Gibson 61).

Although Fanon provides a valuable schema for understanding the seeming contradictions in deaf writing, it is not completely applicable, for deaf Americans differed from colonized people and other minorities in crucial ways that made their identity unique and even more intertwined with the dominant group's. Most significantly, they usually did not pass on their language and culture through family. For his part, Fanon connects the psychological sickness ailing Algerians to contact with white people outside of the home, asserting that "a normal Negro child, having grown up within a normal family, will become abnormal on the slightest contact with the white world" (143). In contrast, because the majority of deaf children are born to hearing parents—over 95 percent, according to the most recent calculation—in Fanon's terms they become "abnormal" at birth, through contact with hearing family members who do not sign and who move their lips in indecipherable ways. For this reason Burnet strives in *Tales of the Deaf and Dumb* to persuade hearing parents to communicate with their deaf child visually, and deaf people often used metaphors of family to describe their arrival at deaf schools. For example, Edmund Booth, recalling how it felt to enter the American Asylum at Hartford, wrote: "It was all new to me . . . the innumerable motions of arms and hands. I was among strangers but knew I was at home" (qtd. in Lane, *When* 233). Except for deaf children of deaf parents, deaf people usually found a sense of normality outside of the biological family, at the schools that, somewhat paradoxically, were managed by hearing people, putting a new twist on a familiar colonial dynamic.

As a result, deaf Americans saw their group identity and past not as separate from their hearing counterparts, but bound up with them. While Fanon traces Algerians' sense of inferiority to the loss of their "long historical past" and "local cultural originality" under colonial rule (34, 16), as we saw in chapter 1 deaf Americans did not really have a collective identity or cultural institutions that preceded hearing people. Their most notable community in the eighteenth century, on Martha's Vineyard, where "everyone . . . spoke sign language" (Groce 2), included both deaf and hearing people, and deaf education was founded through the unique deaf-hearing partnership between Laurent Clerc and Thomas Hopkins Gallaudet.[7] Rather than as an occupied people, deaf Americans at midcentury understood themselves as a recently formed group that would not have come together without the efforts of hearing people like Sicard and Gallaudet. Even if they had a growing sense of the singularity of their language and collective self apart from hearing people, educated deaf people thus connected their very identity to the civilizing institutions that Fanon elsewhere finds so destructive.

These dynamics complicate not only deaf people's relationship to the hearing majority, but also notions of filiation and affiliation in the formation of their identities. In *The World, the Text, and the Critic* (1983), Edward Said uses the term filiation to refer to lines of heritage or descent "to be found in nature" and affiliation to denote the process of identification through culture (23). In colonized societies, indigenous filiative forms are distorted and replaced by affiliation as colonizers impose their own cultural and political institutions on natives. Ironically, this substitution often results in a new pattern of filiation where the colonizing nation is positioned as the parent ("mother England") and the colonized subjects as children. So where does the expanding network of residential schools for deaf students at midcentury fit in? At first they may seem clearly affiliative, as they are cultural institutions that took deaf children away from their families and placed them among people to whom they were unrelated by birth. As we will see, the schools promoted new filiative forms as deaf students were taught to think of hearing teachers and school directors as their parents, conforming to the theory of how affiliation, in Said's words, "surreptitiously duplicates the closed and tightly knit family structure that secures generational hierarchical relationships to one another" (*World* 21). On the other hand, the schools brought together people who shared a *biological* trait and an in-born proclivity for visual communication, which are features found in nature, of filiation. Deaf students discovered deep connection amounting to kinship with other deaf people; as adults, they frequently took deaf spouses.[8] When we recall that many deaf people also retained close ties to their hearing family members, we see the contradictory ways that the schools blurred the distinction between filiation and affiliation, how such institutions both empowered and patronized deaf people, all of which fed into deaf Americans' conflicted sense of self.

Through writing, deaf authors at midcentury sought to work out these complexities and assert their identities not just as deaf people, but as deaf people in relation to the hearing majority. While they conveyed pride in their flourishing communal identity and at deaf progress in society, they also bore poignant witness to the personal struggles they experienced among hearing people and to feelings of marginalization and inferiority. In the process, deaf authors endeavored to resolve their persistent sense of two-ness in midcentury America.

THE OTHER SIDE OF SILENCE

Perhaps the author who most epitomizes the contradictory manner in which deaf people saw themselves is John Carlin. Born deaf in 1813 and educated at the Pennsylvania Institution, he went on to become one of the most accomplished deaf Americans of the period as a painter, writer, sculptor, acquaintance of hearing leaders like Horace Greeley and William Seward, and an orator whose sign language presentations were in demand at deaf events. In his written works Carlin displays deep ambivalence toward his deaf identity, oscillating between viewing deaf people as inferior and asserting their equal intelligence and capability. Consider his poem "The Mute's Lament," which prominently appeared in the first issue of the *American Annals of the Deaf and Dumb* in 1847. From the opening line, when Carlin describes himself in terms of silence (a metaphor that previous deaf authors seldom employed), we are on notice that he is seeing himself through the majority's eyes, even as he implicitly questions this view. The poem begins:

John Carlin. Self-portrait, ca. 1850. Courtesy of Patricia Carlin Friese.

I move—a silent exile on this earth;
As in his dreary cell one doomed for life,
My tongue is mute, and closed ear heedeth not;
No gleam of hope this darken'd mind assures
That the blest power of speech shall e'er be known.
Murmuring gaily o'er their pebbly beds
The limpid streamlets as they onward flow
Through verdant meadows and responding woodlands,
Vocal with merry tones—*I hear them not*. . . . (15)

Like James Nack in "The Minstrel Boy," a precursor with which he was doubtless familiar, Carlin depicts himself as a miserable outcast, reflecting not just the disconnection he felt from the hearing people around him, but also a certain fashionable Byronic alienation. Also like Nack, Carlin omits sign language and any hint of the deaf community, presenting himself as a lonely deaf "I." Yet if Nack was affected by hearing models, Carlin was even more so, replicating the dominant ideology that abjects his identity so thoroughly that, according to the poem, little happiness is possible for him on Earth.

In this respect, "The Mute's Lament" is a classic expression of the inferiority complex as Fanon describes it, for Carlin appears to have internalized the majority's attitude that casts him as a subordinate other. Clearly influenced by hearing poets like Moses Scott, he applies Scott's images of deaf people being imprisoned in a cell, living in darkness and silence, to himself; while Scott joyfully enumerates all the sounds deaf people cannot perceive, Carlin laments not hearing birds, music, and eloquent orators. What is a bit odd is that Carlin, who was congenitally deaf, never directly experienced the "lyric of the lute divine" and "the cadence soft" of which he writes (15). These conventional depictions presumably came to him filtered through hearing writers, including one of his favorites, Milton, and their delight in such sounds probably made him feel deficient. The entire poem seems based on hearing epistemology, as the concluding lines, duplicating so many hearing authors' renderings of deaf people becoming hearing in heaven, suggest:

O, Hope! How sweetly smileth Heavenly Hope
On the sad, drooping soul and trembling heart. . . .

My ears shall be unsealed, and I shall hear;
My tongue shall be unbound, and I shall speak,
And happy with the angels sing forever! (16)

In some ways Carlin's attitude makes sense: he undoubtedly had a harder life because he was deaf, and it is customary to anticipate all worldly woes being removed in heaven. In the process, he affirms his commonality with hearing readers who are believers, showing that he is a Christian, too. Yet on closer inspection, his outlook is not unlike Fanon's natives who dream of "magically turning white" due to the privileged position whites have in society (44); in both cases, blackness and deafness are positioned as intrinsically inferior. Although earlier deaf authors like Clerc and Burnet typically emphasized how deaf marginalization was culturally fabricated, how society could be changed to make deaf Americans happy and productive, here Carlin, influenced by Isaiah and popular poetry like Sigourney's, adopts an essentialist position, firmly locating the problem in the body: because deaf people are deaf, they are inferior and unhappy. As a young man he yearned to become a "correct writer of verses," studying rhyming and pronunciation dictionaries and asking hearing poets for advice, but Carlin may have emulated hearing models too successfully ("Poetry" 589). As Nigel Gibson glosses Fanon's argument, "The slave who embraces the logos of the master can at best hope for only a pseudo-recognition" (30). In other words, no matter how well deaf people like Carlin accepted the majority's values and how much approbation they received, they could never achieve full recognition as equals since those very values held that deafness is a mark of lower status.

Yet even as he replicates prevailing stereotypes, Carlin manages implicitly to critique them through the poem's central paradox: the so-called mute who does not speak is nonetheless expressing himself directly to readers, finding a voice with a pen. If the work on a literal level confirms notions of deaf people's inferiority, just the fact that a deaf poet is writing contradicts some of its mournful images and moves us a step toward ironical satire. For example, while Carlin claims he has a "darken'd mind," he reveals that he is actually perceptive and intelligent, able to produce verse that, in the words of the hearing editor of the *Annals*, "would scarcely do discredit to many a writer of established reputation among us" (14).[9] Like Clerc applying Sicard's dramatic rhetoric to himself, Carlin's mimicry thus subtly exposes holes in dominant thinking even as it seems to subscribe to it. Through such subversive strategies, Carlin begins to write himself out of abjection and demonstrate that he is a capable deaf adult (even if one who feels inferior), a kind of representation decidedly absent from hearing authors' portrayals. The success of "The Mute's Lament" —it was prominently reprinted in *Harper's* for a national readership in 1884—may well have been due to the tension between the way it reifies hearing assumptions about deaf people and simultaneously undercuts some of them.

By appropriating hearing authors' use of silence to describe deaf people, Carlin contributed to a trend among subsequent nineteenth-century deaf Americans where they increasingly claimed the dominant label of silence even as they pointed to its inaccuracy. In the poem he refers to himself as a "silent exile" and says that to him "Deep silence reigned over all, and all seems lifeless," but we might wonder what significance the concept silence has to him, a person born deaf (15).[10] In 1869 William Chamberlain, who became deaf at age five, clarified deaf people's perception of sound:

Deaf-mutes are often able to hear sounds, although not distinctly enough to distinguish between articulation and mere noise; and even when entirely deaf, they are sensible of the concussion of jarring produced by heavy thunder, the report of a cannon, the rumbling of heavy wagons over the street pavements, beating a drum, stamping on the floor, &c., although they cannot always tell what produces the sound, or from what direction it proceeds, without the aid of sight. ("On deaf")

Deaf people are sometimes aware of aural stimulation around them. Today we know that most "deaf" people have some residual hearing, which usually varies across frequency; only about 10 percent of deaf individuals hear nothing at all (Rundle 1). They also produce sounds just by being living, breathing humans: they cough and laugh, and many use their voices. Burnet notes that "it is natural . . . for a deaf child to utter cries" (*Tales* 62), while Jewel, who was born deaf, recounted how as a child she would have been killed by an angry pet bear "had not my shrieks brought me instant relief" (8). Other deaf people, especially those who became deaf after learning to talk, broke the silence by speaking, with varying degrees of success. As an adult Burnet (who became deaf at age eight) did not have much luck articulating, except with people he knew well, while Chamberlain spoke well enough to sometimes pass as hearing. Yet even though silence is an imperfect descriptor of deaf experience, deaf authors after Carlin still sometimes applied the majority's metaphor to themselves. Writing about deaf conventions, Chamberlain opined that "we are in favor of these annual gatherings of the 'children of silence'" ("On calls" 242). Perhaps his quotation marks around the phrase indicate that he is being slightly ironical, that he does not mean the words literally, or that the expression is others' but not his own. Searing, too, put "silent ones" in quotation marks when she used it in 1858 ("A Few" 179). If Chamberlain and Searing call more attention than Carlin to the artificiality of the metaphor, they still recycle it, and gradually more deaf Americans came to embrace the term. *The Silent Worker* was on its way to becoming the most popular magazine for deaf people by the end of the century, while the Goodyear Silents, a deaf football team, achieved notable success in Ohio in the early twentieth century. Carlin helped to inaugurate this change where deaf Americans slowly claimed hearing people's metaphor for them, coming to apply it to themselves as a group later in the century in a good-natured, ironical way that both acknowledged the dominant interpretation of deafness and mocked its portentousness.

If in "The Mute's Lament" Carlin expresses his belief in deaf people's abilities only indirectly, he does so more explicitly in an essay he published seven years later, in 1854, although again contradictory feelings about deaf identity appear. Writing in the *Annals*, he issued a call for a national college for deaf Americans, a bold idea at a time when deaf people were at most expected to become teachers of deaf students or manual laborers and no colleges for deaf students existed anywhere in the world. Citing the examples of Clerc, Nack, and Burnet as evidence "that mutes of decided talents can be rendered as good scholars," Carlin shows his awareness and reliance upon the deaf authors who have come before him ("National" 179). He argues against the very notion of deaf inferiority he had seemed to promulgate in "The Mute's Lament," asserting that "there can be found no difference between speaking persons or deaf mutes, of the higher class, in imagination, strength of mind, depth of thought and quickness of perception" (176). Carlin posits the equality of deaf and hearing intellects, even if "higher class" seems elitist, excluding the majority of deaf Americans. Foreshadowing Du Bois's argument for developing a small group of gifted black people he called "the Talented Tenth," Carlin contends that a college would enable the most promising deaf students, though "few in number," to become achievers as "civil engineers, physicians, surgeons, lawyers and statesmen" who would benefit not only the deaf community, but also the nation as a whole (177, 179). His appeal, along with the force of a congenitally deaf person producing a learned essay with references to a variety of hearing intellectuals, made a public impression, and his vision became reality only a decade later. Unlike in "The Mute's Lament," here Carlin clearly directs attention to social forces that shape deaf people's "well-being, intelligence, happiness . . . and prosperity," showing how much deaf identity depends on cultural conditions apart from the body (183). But here, too, he mentions deaf people's "misfortune" and lack of "the blessed auditory sense," biological definitions that take us back to the literal thrust of "The Mute's Lament" (180). Carlin's essay and poem move between constructivist and essentialist notions of identity, between assertions of capability—if deaf people only receive opportunities—and reproduction of hearing values that lead to a certain self-loathing. Taken together, they dramatically reveal deaf double consciousness at midcentury, suggesting how potent feelings of inferiority and repressed potential coexisted in deaf minds.

AN IMAGINED COMMUNITY

Carlin's proposal for a college was part of a broader trend during the 1850s where deaf authors increasingly thought of their collective identity on a national scale. As they expressed themselves as individuals through print, they also contributed to the growth of what Benedict Anderson calls an "imagined community"; even when they were not immediately present to each other, their writing revealed a strong sense of commonality, of boundaries separating them from hearing people, of empowerment, and of comradeship, despite disagreement and inequalities among them. In Anderson's words, "Communities are to be distinguished, not by their falsity/genuineness, but by the style in which they are imagined" (15). Educated deaf Americans conceived themselves as connected by their sign language, deafness, shared experiences, schools and associations, and cultural heroes like Gallaudet and Clerc, and they used the medium of print to reinforce and extend these bonds. However, as Adele Jewel's autobiographical account reminds us, this sense of community was not always easily gained; deaf people, except for the few with deaf relatives, had to find their way to each other. Those who did so were extremely grateful to the hearing people who helped to found and support the schools that were the wellsprings of their communal consciousness. In written speeches at the first large deaf gatherings in 1850 and 1854, they expressed their sense of indebtedness to Gallaudet and other hearing benefactors, whom they esteemed as contributors to their deaf identity and whom they addressed in filial terms of children honoring parents. Yet later in the decade a deaf Georgian named John Jacobus Flournoy countered such filial rhetoric by insisting that deaf Americans prove their status as competent adults to an oppressive hearing society. To achieve this goal, he advocated that they, like free blacks and other subjugated groups at various points in the century, emigrate to a place where they could escape prejudice and manage their own affairs. While the nation as a whole edged toward civil war, the deaf community dealt with its own questions of identity and possible fissure, illustrating again how deaf Americans were bound up with the larger hearing culture and yet also distinct from it.

In her pamphlet *A Brief Narrative of the Life of Mrs. Adele M. Jewel, (Being Deaf and Dumb)* (ca. 1860), Jewel provides a vivid glimpse into the process by which many deaf Americans went from having no notion of community to a sense of belonging to a larger group of peers. Born deaf to hearing parents in 1834, Jewel recounts how she grew up in Michigan "wild and wayward, with no definite understanding of my relation to the world" because of the communication gap between her and the hearing people around her (11). Her parents, while loving, could not explain religion to her or what was happening when her father fell mortally ill, just as she could not tell them what had occurred when she accidentally set fire to the family home, burning it to the ground. Jewel's feelings of peculiarity and incomprehension increased when she was enrolled at a school for hearing students around age twelve; though she tried hard, she could not understand and withdrew in "despair . . . feeling, oh how bitterly, that I was not like the rest" (11). If her grief testifies to the recalcitrant reality of the hearing line, it also points to the social fabrication of her identity: just as Fanon's black Algerians feel abnormal because of contact with whites, so Jewel's sense of inadequacy stems from being surrounded by hearing people. A fortunate turning point came when, as a young teen, she met an educated young deaf woman named Almena Knight and realized that there were others like her. "She was the first mute I ever saw," Jewel writes, "and the mysterious ties of sympathy immediately established a friendly feeling between us" (14). Her words suggest a powerful connection based on the shared biological characteristic of deafness, an affinity that could be called filial in a way her relationship with her hearing parents was not. In this positive version of Foucault's "recognition by mirror," Jewel discovered that she was not alone, and she was "surprised and delighted" (14) to observe her potential to communicate adeptly, like Almena, through sign and writing. The sense of jubilation and emotional relief in this passage, characteristic of deaf accounts of deaf people coming together, continues as Almena becomes one of Jewel's closest friends, teaches her to sign ("by which we conversed very easily together [over] many pleasant seasons"), and inspires her eventually to enroll in the state's newly opened school for deaf students, where Jewel, "from being an entire stranger, soon became as a member of one large family" (14). Through the affiliative process of attending school, she finds an enabling new filial relationship with the "family" of the deaf community, a process repeated by thousands of other deaf Americans in the course of the century. Yet even as she thrived at the school, this new communal bond did not replace her filial connection with her mother; as we will see, like most deaf people, Jewel maintained the filial relationship with hearing family members.

In this way, Jewel's narrative shows how the filiative and affiliative factors that shaped deaf people's identities overlapped in convoluted fashion, as deaf and hearing people as well as biological and cultural forces played integral roles in the formation of their identities. Unlike most educated deaf people, Jewel did not go to school until the relatively late age of twenty.[11] If she had not met Almena, perhaps she never would have found sign, education, and community, reminding us of the untold numbers of deaf Americans, including deaf people of color, who did not manage to participate in the burgeoning community. For all the sense of deaf people empowering each other, hearing people beyond her parents played a crucial role, too: the Michigan state legislature, following the lead of other states, founded the school she attended, hearing teachers and administrators helped to run it, and hearing citizens of Jewel's hometown contributed the funds that enabled her to enroll. Later, when Jewel left school and could be seen, in the words of a hearing acquaintance, "conversing rapidly, in the sign language, to those who understood that method of speaking, or writing in a clear and graceful hand with a pencil, to others" (5), many people could take credit. Her entrance into the deaf community was inextricably intertwined with hearing involvement, a deaf-hearing collaboration that goes back to Gallaudet and Clerc's pioneering efforts to found the American Asylum in 1817. Although Jewel probably never met Gallaudet and Clerc, she surely knew about them, for they were cultural heroes to deaf Americans, who traced their education and community back to the two men even as they struggled to make their way in a society dominated by hearing people.

Nowhere is this genealogical view more evident than in the written addresses from the first formal gatherings of deaf Americans, where they honored Gallaudet and Clerc and used them to define and display their deaf communal identity to the public. In 1850, over four hundred deaf people assembled in Hartford to pay tribute to the two educators in what was believed to be the largest gathering of deaf people ever; four years later deaf people gathered again to dedicate a monument in memory of Gallaudet, who died in 1851. Although deaf Americans initiated both events, hearing people attended as well, including dignitaries like the American Asylum's board of directors, the mayor of Hartford, and the governor of Connecticut. While the deaf presenters delivered their addresses in sign language, most wrote their remarks in English beforehand so that hearing representatives could read them out loud for nonsigners and so their addresses could subsequently be published in the *Annals*. As speech acts, these presentations resembled Clerc's early addresses, except that they were written for audiences that included large numbers of deaf peers, which changed the dynamic. When, in 1850, on behalf of "the deaf mutes of New England," George Loring told Gallaudet, "We have long wished to make you some permanent testimonial of our gratitude," it was perhaps the most affirmative, assured deaf "we" to appear in American writing to that point (Rae, "Testimonial" 190, 195). As these presenters make clear, the deaf community had arrived and imagined itself in a distinct way.

Their rhetoric emphasized how they conceived themselves as rescued by Gallaudet and Clerc, whose efforts to bring deaf education to America they saw as making their communal identity possible. Employing dramatic language of conversion to express this effect, they followed and embellished the earlier example not just of Clerc, but also of influential hearing educators like Sicard and Gallaudet, who, as we saw in chapter 1, used imagery of nothingness and heathenism to describe uneducated deaf people. Thus in 1850 the deaf orator of the day, Fisher Ames Spofford, declared that, before the American Asylum opened, "the deaf mutes in this country were in the darkness of grossest ignorance. . . . Our ignorance was like chaos, without light or hope. But through the blessing of God, light has shone through the chaos and reduced it to order" (Rae, "Testimonial" 194).[12] Drawing on the cosmic imagery of Genesis, Spofford presents the advent of deaf education as nothing less than a creation story: prior to 1817, all was darkness and confusion for deaf Americans. In 1854 John Carlin used similarly heightened rhetoric, writing that before Gallaudet went to Europe, "all the deaf mutes of this country were ignorant heathen! Their minds were desolately blank!" (Rae, "Ceremonies" 33). Just as in 1816 Clerc used Sicard-inspired exaggerations to argue for deaf education, here Spofford and Carlin use such hyperbole to provide a stark contrast to the intelligent, respectable deaf people at the assemblies, underscoring their fortunate, empowered status and extreme debt to Gallaudet and Clerc. In Carlin's words, Gallaudet's work brought about "our deliverance from the degradation to which we were unavoidably consigned," hinting that deaf people felt literally and figuratively saved (34). Such depictions reveal that this mythos had become the conceptual paradigm by which educated deaf Americans at mid-century defined and thought of their community.

If strains of hearing educators' ideology inflect how deaf people imagined their communal beginnings, they also show up in the filial language deaf presenters used to describe their relationship to their hearing benefactors. In his 1850 acceptance speech, the sixty-two-year-old Gallaudet remarked that he thought of his former deaf students "with a father's love," and that every member of "your large deaf-mute family" should be grateful to the first hearing supporters of the school, who gave deaf students "a paternal and maternal care" (Rae, "Testimonial" 197). This filial rhetoric was repeated by deaf presenters, with Clerc admonishing deaf attendees to be thankful for "the directors in particular, who were like fathers of yours"; the organizer of the event, Thomas Brown, calling on deaf peers to cherish the American Asylum with "the sincere love of children"; and another graduate introducing a written resolution referring to Gallaudet as someone whom deaf people "revere . . . as a father" (199, 197, 201). Such a motif goes beyond conventional sentiment of alumni toward an alma mater, for deaf Americans viewed the schools and hearing people behind them, especially Gallaudet, as indispensable progenitors of their identity; they were keenly aware that without hearing involvement, they would have had a difficult time coming together. In his 1854 address, Carlin compared Gallaudet to George Washington, implicitly suggesting that as Washington was a founding father of the United States, Gallaudet was a founding father of the deaf American community. The filial rhetoric also reflects religious discourse, since the Bible not only refers favorably to the children of God and children of Israel, but also in the New Testament encourages believers to cultivate the trusting innocence of children.[13] At the same time, hearing educators' employment of parent-child language, however well-intentioned, contains vestiges of imperialist paternalism, not altogether unlike nineteenth-century government officials who, as Stan Steiner has argued, used the Great White Father myth to position themselves as superior, civilized guardians of Native American "children" (83). Deaf people's acceptance of such a model, in turn, suggests a Fanonesque internalization of dominant values that cast them as dependent and subordinate. Yet it is hard to isolate these elements, as the benevolence seems inextricably mixed with the paternalism, and the self-infantilization with the liberation. Strikingly, deaf authors never apply the trope of fatherhood to Clerc even as they esteem him, perhaps because Clerc was not among the original group of hearing residents of Hartford who in 1815 decided to establish the American Asylum, or, more likely, because they absorbed a system at the schools where deaf people had a largely horizontal filial bond with each other and a vertical one with hearing benefactors.[14]

In one sense the parent-child metaphor was fitting, for with hearing guidance, the deaf community gradually matured and became more autonomous. Deaf presenters celebrated this increasing capability and independence, which they saw as the product of Gallaudet's early efforts. At the dedication in 1854, Clerc noted with satisfaction that the $2,500 to construct the granite monument had been "wholly raised from the contributions of the deaf and dumb; for none who can hear and speak have been allowed to contribute one cent" (Rae, "Ceremonies" 24). Calling attention to how strong the deaf communal identity had become, Clerc reveals how deaf people formed the hearing line from their side, too, as they insisted on their own separate memorial for Gallaudet. That deaf people in many different states, few of whom were wealthy, could join to give such a sum was further evidence of their ability and shared commitment. Carlin, the orator of the day, took equal joy in the accomplishment. Demonstrating his pride not just as a deaf person, but as a deaf American whose national community was achieving what older deaf communities in Europe had not, he wrote: "As there is much reason to believe that this is the first monument in the world that has ever been erected by a community exclusively deaf and dumb, how exquisite is the satisfaction with which we look upon ourselves as its founders!" (31). Somewhat ironically, the memory of a hearing person became a force that united deaf Americans and helped further to coalesce the national community. The first association of deaf people, the New England Gallaudet Association of the Deaf, was given Gallaudet's name when it took shape in the 1850s, as was the first periodical expressly for deaf readers, *The Gallaudet Guide and Deaf-Mutes' Companion*, which began to appear in 1860. In deaf imaginations, to honor Gallaudet was also to celebrate their collective identity, for the two were intertwined.[15]

These perceptions fed into the contradictory ways that deaf authors thought about themselves at midcentury. On the one hand, writing from these events amply demonstrates their pleasure in their thriving community. In 1850 Thomas Brown referred to "our happy meeting," while Clerc wrote that "this is the most pleasant day we have ever had" (Rae, "Testimonial" 192, 198). Luzerne Rae, the hearing editor of the *Annals*, confirmed the delight among deaf attendees: "A more happy assemblage it was never our good fortune to behold. . . . It was most pleasant to see the joy that beamed from all their faces, and gave new vigor and animation to their expressive language of signs" ("Testimonial" 201). Challenging the assumption that deafness is a lamentable affliction, such words emphasize the joie de vivre and comfort deaf people found in each other's presence, where they were not abnormal and could easily understand and be understood. Yet while they relished this uplifting communal identity, deaf writers credited it to hearing benefactors who instilled in them a grateful language of benevolence that positioned them as children and hearing people as superior, so that notions of deaf capacity became entangled in notions of subordination. This double consciousness appears when Clerc, shortly after expressing his happiness at being with his deaf former students, referred to deaf children as divine "chastisements" and, in a surprising departure from his early addresses, concluded with the now-familiar vision of becoming hearing in heaven: "My prayer is that when we must leave this world, we may all be ushered into another where our ears shall be unstopped and our mouths opened—where our happiness shall have no alloy" (200, 201). Like Carlin in "The Mute's Lament," Clerc echos the prophecy in Isaiah and the example of hearing poets like Sigourney to espouse an essentialist vision of deaf people as biologically subordinate and unhappier than their hearing counterparts on Earth. It is difficult for modern ASL users to imagine Clerc talking in this manner when signing informally with deaf peers, but because Clerc's signs are lost to us, we have no sense of how stylized this rhetoric is, how much a product of English discourse and the formal occasion with influential hearing people in the audience, and how much a fully internalized worldview. (And how much a result of age: interestingly, when he was asked in London in 1815 if deaf people are unhappy, the twenty-nine-year-old Clerc said no.)[16] Such depictions may have pleased hearing readers and audience members by reassuring them of the correctness of their suppositions and of their superiority, and deaf readers and audience members by extending the logic of revered figures like Gallaudet and of the Bible that they had grown up with in the schools. As they imagined their community, then, deaf authors at midcentury simultaneously felt proud and inferior, socially ascendent and wanting. To revisit Fanon's formulation, if they were happy being deaf among themselves, they were often less so being deaf in relation to hearing people. For them to protest grateful language of subordination would be to go against the roots of the community and the very way it was imagined. Yet as the decade unfolded and deaf Americans, through associations and periodicals, participated more in their collective welfare, some writers began boldly to deliberate their place in society away from the schools among hearing citizens who did not sign, and to look for new ways to resolve their split sense of self.

DEBATE AND DISSENT

In 1855 a colorful and eccentric deaf Georgian named John Jacobus Flournoy issued a circular to deaf people in the United States and Europe proposing that deaf people so inclined should emigrate west and form a state of their own, away from "rejections and consignments to inferior places" by hearing people (83). Like Mormons and other subjugated groups, and true to Frederick Turner's frontier thesis, Flournoy turned to the western frontier as a place where individuals could escape restraints to free circumstances. His perception of prejudice may have stemmed from the fact that he grew up hearing; unlike other deaf writers we have considered, Flournoy became deaf as a young adult and so could easily compare his treatment before and after he crossed the hearing line. Yet his feelings of marginalization were also connected to his sometimes erratic behavior. The son of a wealthy slave owner (and, somewhat bizarrely for someone who railed against prejudice, the holder of some slaves himself as an adult), Flournoy struggled to deal not only with deafness and loss of his ability to speak comprehensibly, but also with seizures, and apparently acted in peculiar ways.[17] When he sought public office, hearing audiences laughed at his attempts to make speeches and he received few votes, leaving him with feelings of injustice and rage that resemble *ressentiment* as Nietzsche and Scheler account for it. Elaborating on his proposal in the 1856 *Annals*, Flournoy asserted that "in the South we are contemned, spurned, degraded and abhorred, and I see no redemption but in forming a powerful oligarchy of our own to control a State at the West,—a Deaf-mute Republic" (124). However radical, Flournoy's idea resonated with deaf readers enough for them to engage in a lively written debate over the next several years in the pages of *Annals* that led to some of the most spontaneous and illuminating deaf writing of the century. The contestatory, dialogic nature of the community, as well as their common values, came into sharper focus as they argued over the happiness of deaf Americans in hearing society, the merits of assimilation versus separation, and the feasibility of the commonwealth plan. In advocating a deaf state, Flournoy tried to enact not just a physical separation to a safer place for deaf people, but also an epistemological revolution in deaf thought, linking him to other early minority and colonized authors of resistance literature.

Condemning discrimination against deaf people much more forcefully than any of his predecessors, in his letters to the *Annals* Flournoy described widespread bias on both the personal and institutional levels that routinely denied deaf people dignity and opportunity. In his interactions with hearing people, he stated he was "treated with neglect" and faced numbing intellectual isolation: "There is not a hearing man, that, except for occasional novelty and to while away a *tedium*, would *like* to hold written converse with any of us," he wrote. "It is too irksome. . . . And such hearing people as know the sign language, or alphabet of our class, never make it a point to convey to us one ninety-ninth of the information they constantly impart to each other by oral converse" (146, 141). Flournoy testifies that written English and sign language, so celebrated by Clerc and Burnet as enablers for deaf people, were sometimes imperfect means of socialization in the broader hearing society, and that, in turn, led to disenfranchisement in the workplace and in government. "Especially in the Middle and Southern States, few deaf men have employment of respectability," he asserted, arguing that prevailing prejudices made it almost impossible for deaf people to accrue wealth and weakened the United States as a whole (45). Assailing the way he perceived hearing people to stereotype deaf people's ignorance (in a process of overdetermination that we, following Fanon, might call the fact of deafness), Flournoy expressed a strong sense of injustice. "We do attest that we are capable of many [things] which the prejudice, and sometimes even malignance of our hearing brethren, deprive us!" he wrote, angrily adding that he himself had "thousands of . . . hearing *inferiors*" (122, 123). Such declarations reveal *ressentiment* that, according to Nietzsche and Scheler, arises out of inequality in social conditions. Typically featuring feelings of anger, envy, and impotence in the face of dominant values, *ressentiment* begins and ends with a defiant conviction of self-worth, as Flournoy shows.

In making his case, Flournoy built on Clerc, Burnet, and Carlin's earlier assertions of deaf potential, but emphatically extended them to assert equality with hearing people. Responding to claims that deaf people were not oppressed but had natural limitations because they could not hear, he turned attention from essentialist notions of difference to the way society was constructed, pointing out that with suitable support he could accomplish a great deal. "Place *me* for an example in any Capitol with Legislative sanctity, and I will move for an *aid*, a hearer and an amanuensis, to reveal to me what is said, what to be done, what to do, and to read my speeches. And by this way I can get along supremely well, as Legislator" (123). With such language, Flournoy resists all insinuations of deaf people as subordinate and insists on his equal capability with appropriate accommodations. At other points, he expanded his argument to include not just deaf Americans, but all those stigmatized because of physical differences. Becoming one of the first published deaf American writers to use the word "disabilities" in conjunction with deaf people, he wrote, "The old cry about the incapacity of men's minds from physical disabilities, I think it were time, now in this intelligent age, to *explode*!" (121). Even as he focuses on deaf people, Flournoy calls attention to how all disabled people are stereotyped, illustrating again how nineteenth-century deaf authors implicitly and explicitly helped to pioneer arguments of the later disability rights movement. Although he acknowledged that some hearing individuals gave deaf people "respectful or affectionate consideration," he maintained that the mass of hearing Americans treated their deaf counterparts contemptuously or patronizingly: "When we would claim equality, it offends" (142, 146).

To Flournoy, the only way deaf people could escape such entrenched injustice would be to establish a state where they could manage their own affairs, demonstrate their competence, and interact apart from hearing people. In his view, this was the "measure by which alone our class of people can attain the dignity and honor of Human Nature" and realize their potential (122). As his detractors pointed out, in many respects Flournoy had not thought through the idea, including the location and constitution. Yet even as he revised himself on the size and structure of the state (or territory, as he also called it) in sequential letters, Flournoy held true to the main vision: "*this Government is to be sacred to the Deaf alone*" (123). Deaf people would hold all positions of power and, to demonstrate their independence, would not accept land as charity but would instead purchase it by the acre. In this way, Flournoy extended the proud self-sufficiency displayed by deaf people earlier in their tributes to Gallaudet and Clerc. "My plan is to make a HOME for the mutes, for mutual intercourse and improvement, and to show the world our abilities," he stated, implicitly pointing out that deaf Americans, unlike most other linguistic groups, had no geographical homeland other than the schools (143). In this state deaf people could freely communicate, attend church and lectures in sign language, and discover peace and happiness that was not "attainable in their scattered condition" (44). When critics argued that, since most deaf parents have hearing children, the state's population would dwindle in just one generation, Flournoy was unperturbed. New groups of deaf people might emigrate, he suggested, but even if the deaf population died out, the enterprise was worth undertaking, for "we shall have proved to the other nations and our own, that deaf and dumb people are capable of many things; and to our successors in misfortune, offices and employment may be opened. They may be treated as men and women of *some use* to society and to the country, and respected accordingly" (45). If Clerc, Burnet, and other writers advocated segregated schools for deaf students so they could become productive members of society, Flournoy took things further, arguing for complete segregation until society was more just and accessible. Yet even as he insisted on deaf equality and competence, Flournoy's use of "misfortune" suggests that he had a double conscious view of himself similar to that of Clerc and Carlin, where he saw himself not just as eminently capable, but also, in comparison with the hearing majority, as lacking, a familiar psychic split that shows up repeatedly in these texts.

In the process, Flournoy sought to recast notions of deaf people's filiation by situating them as adults rather than children and privileging their connection with other deaf people over biological family bonds. Countering the parent-child rhetoric of the 1850 and 1854 events, which he likely read in the *Annals*, he repeatedly positioned deaf people as grown-ups—usually male grown-ups, gendering this distinction as well—who were equal to their hearing counterparts. If deaf people remained in hearing society, he asserted, they would be "perpetual children" in subordinate spaces of dependency (124). "But we are men," he averred, "enterprising and resolute deaf men" who would move to the new state (44, 121). If Flournoy defiantly maintains deaf adulthood and competence, he also makes that competence depend on whether deaf people embrace his plan. "I pray God that the deaf and dumb may prove worthy of the name of men," he wrote; "if mutes *cannot* do this they are justly held as inferior and *useless* in the world" (43, 44). In Flournoy's terms, the success of the state becomes a test of deaf masculinity, a way for deaf Americans dramatically to prove their equality and capability. More controversially, he valued the deaf filial bond over the biological connection with hearing family members to the point where he would allow no hearing relatives in the state: hearing children would live elsewhere and could not inherit property in the deaf commonwealth. As Flournoy pointed out, at the time hearing parents often sent their deaf children off to residential schools for years, so he was simply inverting the dynamic. He did not address deaf-hearing marriages, but we can infer hearing spouses would also be banned. Notably, to Flournoy it did not matter if hearing people could sign; his criteria for membership in the state was not linguistic but biological, based on the inability to hear, since that was why deaf people were stigmatized.[18] In his formulation, deafness drew deaf people into kinship and made a hearing person an outsider, indeed a "foreigner" in the proposed state (124). With this boundary, this unshakable hearing line, Flournoy endeavored to maximize the deaf filial relationship apart from hearing involvement, to purify deaf identity and free it from its double self. Yet Flournoy's fixed vision of deaf separatism resembles nationalist consciousness in colonial resistance movements that, as Said puts it, "can very easily lead to frozen rigidity . . . chauvinism and xenophobia" (*Culture* 214). Moreover, if

Flournoy sought empowerment of all deaf people, he was particularly interested in empowering himself. In an early letter he unabashedly proclaimed, "I am to lead—and can only lead where deaf capacity be widely acknowledged" (123), paralleling the way the nationalist bourgeoisie in postcolonial situations sometimes became mere mimic men, in V. S. Naipaul's phrase, who replicated imperial conditions for personal gain after the colonizers had left.

Not surprisingly, these ideas provoked a strong response, with readers like Edmund Booth and John Burnet writing in to the *Annals* to contest them. A former student and teacher at the American Asylum who was now a newspaper editor in Iowa, Booth emerged as the chief detractor. While he was deeply committed to the deaf community, traveling to meet families with deaf members whenever they moved into his region, Booth drew upon his experience living on the western frontier to point out practical problems with the proposed state, including its size, location, and the difficulty of maintaining a deaf population. "I think the wiser course is, to let the mutes remain as they are—scattered and in one sense lost—among their hearing associates," he maintained, even as he offered advice about the best places to settle (41). Noting that some groups of deaf friends were already planning to live near each other, he thought this preferable to Flournoy's grandiose plan. "Mr. Flournoy's idea of distinction in the world appears to be political elevation alone," he wrote, expressing dismay at Flournoy's yearning for office (73). Burnet, who decades before had sought to foster greater hearing-deaf understanding with *Tales of the Deaf and Dumb*, also critiqued the self-aggrandizing aspects of the idea, sarcastically proposing that a separate deaf nation be established instead. "Will not *President* Flournoy sound better than *Governor* Flournoy?" he asked, and expressed the hope that he would be named ambassador to France or England (90). Both men were married to deaf women and had hearing children, and both disapproved of Flournoy's treatment of deaf people's biological family. Dryly remarking that Flournoy must not have a family based on the way he wrote of "sundering ties of parent and child," Booth called such familial connections "instinctive in the human heart and universal," showing how he gave them precedence over the deaf filial connection (75). Burnet flippantly proposed that hearing children be allowed to reside in the state provided they "would consent, like Ulysses on the coast of the Syrens, to stop their ears with wax" (90). Through the absurdity of the idea, he strives to reveal the nonsense of Flournoy's reordering of filial connections and the entire plan. Moreover, Booth questioned Flournoy's basic thesis that deaf people were unhappy and discriminated against among hearing people. "Out of the three or four thousand who are educated, I am acquainted with at least one thousand; and I have not perceived that they are much unhappier than, or held inferior to, the masses around them," he wrote (77). Booth not only disputes the very notion upon which Flournoy based his call, but also only refers to educated deaf people, suggesting that he did not feel the same affinity with uneducated deaf Americans, whom Flournoy did not exclude from his proposal.

As this may suggest, even as they raised reasonable objections Booth and other dissenters occasionally betrayed an elitism that aligns them with the intelligentsia in colonial settings, the *compadre* that is educated and relatively privileged and therefore may be less inclined to struggle for cultural and political independence. For example, in his initial response Booth was rather condescending to deaf people in general. "A community of this class would be a mixture of a few well and many half-educated; and among them must be many non-readers and frivolous," he wrote (40). In contrast to Flournoy's insistent assertions of deaf capability, Booth expresses doubt in deaf abilities that arises partially because they are "non-readers" who struggle with English. He went on to argue that among hearing people deaf Americans would be more apt to practice their English skills, showing how he valued the dominant language over sign. John Carlin, who just a few years earlier had expressed such confidence in the most gifted deaf people's potential in his call for a national college, expressed this latent contempt for average deaf people even more clearly. In a private letter to Clerc that he later agreed to have published, he superciliously belittled deaf competence. "It is a well known fact that the majority of [deaf people] show little decision of purpose in any enterprise whatever," he wrote (89). "I am content with my being 'lost among the hearing persons,' whose superior knowledge of the English language benefits my mind far more than would the perpetual gestures of the thousands of the *bona fide* residents in GESTURIA." Although he did not speak vocally, was married to a deaf woman, and interacted with deaf people all his life, Carlin lived by dominant values so much that he denigrates his own community and language of signs (rarely in deaf writing is there such a negative take on ASL) in favor of hearing people and English. His words seem related to Fanon's observation about the valorization of French among colonized Algerians, which causes them to belittle their own language and cultural traditions in favor of the dominant group's. Such self-disparagement showed up again when Booth endeavored to explain why some people are deaf. Deafness, Booth wrote, "is a part of the punishment inflicted for violation of nature's laws, which violation—whether it comes from carelessness, design or ignorance—results in deafness, blindness, lameness, etc." (77). While Clerc in 1818 had viewed deafness as a mark of divine, natural human variation that could in fact be a blessing, Booth gives a negative interpretation: deafness is punishment for breaking "nature's laws." His comment not only hearkens back to the view of deafness as a punishment from God for licentious behavior, but also anticipates social Darwinism and beliefs that deafness is an undesirable abnormality to be weeded out. While such sentiment was common among hearing Americans, Booth is one of the few nineteenth-century deaf writers to express it. In arguing for assimilation, then, deaf intelligentsia like Booth and Carlin defended the dominant order that positioned themselves as inferior, even if elsewhere they sought to reform it.

As they wrote back and forth about the proposal, Booth and Flournoy revealed how much American deaf identity was imbricated with larger tensions over issues like slavery, which shaped the way they saw each other and imagined their community. Booth, a fervent abolitionist, pointed out that Flournoy was "one of the wealthy slave-holders of the South," a difference that colored much of their disagreement as the nation veered toward civil war (78).[19] Arguing that Flournoy misjudged deaf people's status in society because he lived in the South, where "education is almost unknown [and] an educated deaf-mute must necessarily be almost literally 'lost,'" Booth positioned the South as the locus of prejudice, subtly linking deaf oppression with slavery (75). "The remedy is to educate the hearing masses," he bitingly continued. "If Mr. Flournoy, instead of fretting away his life in complaints, would endeavor to remedy the evil, he will have lived to some purpose" (75). Although in 1858 more than half of the nation's twenty-two schools for deaf students were in southern states, Flournoy did not dispute that the South was less progressive toward deaf people.[20] However, having already seen the failure of his attempts to lobby the Georgia legislature in 1833 for a school for deaf students, and to contest an 1840 law allowing the state to appoint a legal guardian of deaf people if they were deemed incompetent, he was less sanguine than Booth about the prospects of reforming a discriminatory society from within. Turning to slavery to describe deaf people's disenfranchisement, he wrote that "the mass of us be made little better than slaves," moving himself from a member of the oppressor class to the oppressed (142). He went on to clarify that he visualized the state as being not only deaf, but also white. "For my part I can not intend it to be a slave territory, or even to admit free Negroes," he wrote, presumably excluding deaf black people in the bargain (151). If the debate reflected deep disagreements over African Americans and hearing people, the two agreed on matters of gender, as both Flournoy and Booth supported women's suffrage in the proposed state more than sixty years before it became legal in the United States. Yet H. M. Chamberlayne again illustrated the contestatory nature of the community, writing from Richmond to declare this idea "ridiculous" since women's "limited knowledge" would prevent them from voting wisely (159). Even as they acknowledge their common bond, these deaf white males imagined the shape and boundaries of their community in markedly different ways, while deaf women and deaf African Americans themselves did not participate in the written discussion, again showing how gender and race structured the hearing line.

Although Booth, Carlin, and Burnet roundly criticized Flournoy's proposal, other correspondents expressed support, indicating that Flournoy spoke for more deaf people than himself. A deaf farmer in Indiana named P. H. Confer offered $5,000—more than was raised a few years before for the Gallaudet monument—to help carry out the scheme. Buttressing Flournoy's claims of social ostracism, Confer wrote, "The deaf mutes would all be happy, as they can not now be, because they have nobody that can or will converse with them, and many people look on a deaf-mute as if he were a fool, because he can not talk. . . . They are in many cases despised by hearing men" (87). His testimony contradicts those who maintained that deaf people did not suffer from prejudice so much as natural limitations; by changing the social environment, Confer suggested, both discrimination and limitations would recede. An instructor at the Indiana Institution, P. A. Emery, was similarly enthusiastic, calling Flournoy's plan a "noble undertaking," while H. M. Chamberlayne pronounced it "brilliant" (158, 159). Saying that he always found that deaf people benefited from being together, William Chamberlain proposed a compromise where two or three hundred deaf people could form a small township in the West with hearing family and friends, a solution that allowed for the benefits of community without the grandiosity or rigid separation of Flournoy's plan, and which Chamberlain wrote could be a "*permanent* and *beneficial*" arrangement (84). Such responses show how the idea resonated with some deaf Americans and suggest that it may have found additional support among deaf people who did not participate in the written debate. Lower-class, less-educated deaf people, who made up the majority of deaf Americans, were less comfortable with written English than these correspondents and more reliant on sign language, and perhaps would have found the idea of a settlement of signers especially appealing. Yet like deaf women and people of color, they remained silent on the margins on this issue, their voices lost to us, reminding us once more of the paradoxes surrounding the deaf community as a well-defined entity.

Despite expressions of support, and although Flournoy revised his plan and appealed to common deaf American values, by the end of 1858 momentum for the idea faded. Responding to his critics, Flournoy wrote that he himself had no personal ambition and would not go to the new state, reduced the size of the proposed commonwealth to forty square miles, and expressed flexibility about the location. Trying to align his plan with the most revered figures in the community, he asserted that the state would be called "GALLAUDET" and, noting how Clerc in 1820 had favored setting aside a portion of a land grant to the American Asylum as a place where deaf people could settle, claimed that the commonwealth idea had not originated with him, but with "my venerable friend, Laurent Clerc" (144, 79). It was a shrewd rhetorical gambit, seeking to link the plan with the most famous deaf man in America. Yet at the Convention of the New England Gallaudet Association of Deaf-Mutes in September 1858, Clerc himself addressed the controversy and disagreed with Flournoy's plan, saying (according to the minutes of the meeting) that it was too exclusive and impractical, and that it was convenient to have hearing people nearby in case of emergencies like sickness and fire. When he inquired if deaf attendees wanted to form a separate deaf community, "the general answer was, that they had rather live mixed with those who hear and speak" (Chamberlain, "Proceedings" 215). After that, the written deliberation over the commonwealth plan subsided. Like African Americans who assembled at the first National Negro Convention in 1830 in Philadelphia to discuss whether free blacks should emigrate to Canada to escape white discrimination, deaf attendees seemed to agree that it was best to stay and combat injustice from within.

The debate over a deaf state was not only the most spontaneous and revealing deaf American writing of the nineteenth century, but also part of a larger pattern of resistance literature by minorities and colonized groups. When Flournoy attacked hearing prejudice, he was participating in the tradition of black and Native American authors who inveighed against white oppression, and of women such as Margaret Fuller, who the decade before had written that "we would have every arbitrary barrier thrown down. We would have every path laid open to woman as freely as to man" (1629). Like these other early resistance writers, Flournoy was fervent and combative, and like many of their efforts, his attempt was doomed, but it did not just disappear. Terence Ranger has pointed out that early efforts at African resistance, though usually unsuccessful, "shaped the environments in which later politics developed" (439). However radical and even outrageous Flournoy's proposal was, he and his supporters contributed to a shift in consciousness that had long-lasting effects. In 1884 Alexander Graham Bell warned that the idea of a separate deaf state "is still favored by individual deaf-mutes, and may therefore be revived in organized shape at any time" (45). The idea of forming a settlement of deaf people where sign language would be the norm never entirely vanished, lingering on as a somewhat wistful utopian vision of escaping feelings of subjugation and two-ness. Ironically and yet appropriately, the entire written debate took place in a journal edited by a hearing person, Samuel Porter, who selected and cut letters to publish. That

Porter allocated so much space to the issue shows his respect for deaf people and their views, but even as they argued back and forth about achieving independence of their own, their written voices were subject to hearing surveillance and control.[21] Unlike native groups who had lived independently before colonization, deaf Americans never lived apart from hearing people, and had indeed come together because of hearing involvement. In his nationalist vision, Flournoy sought to reinscribe the abject space hearing authors created for deaf Americans and to create something altogether new.

PROGRESS . . . AND OBSTRUCTION

In 1864, Laurent Clerc traveled to Washington, D.C., to take part in the official opening of a National Deaf-Mute College. For the seventy-eight-year-old Clerc, it must have been a gratifying event to witness. When he had arrived in the United States almost a half-century before, the nation had no deaf education at all, and now, in 1864, there were not only twenty-six residential schools for the deaf, but also a new college, the first of its kind in the world, making the United States the most progressive nation for deaf people. The college confirmed everything Clerc had worked for during his long career. Authorized by Congress and President Lincoln, it served as a tacit refutation of Flournoy's claims of insurmountable prejudice, marking a high point in deaf-hearing collaboration and demonstrating that some influential hearing Americans had come to endorse Clerc's belief in the intellectual potential of deaf people.

In their written presentations at the inauguration, Clerc and Carlin agreed that the college marked an exciting time of increased opportunity and possibility, what Carlin called a "bright epoch in deaf-mute history," but they differed on what deaf scholars would accomplish ("Oration" 45). Clerc struck a cautionary note, calling attention to biological limitations on deaf people. "On account of their misfortune," he wrote, "[deaf people] cannot become masters of music, and perhaps can never be entitled to receive the degree of Doctor in Divinity, in Physic, or in Law" ("Address" 43). The younger Carlin was more optimistic: "Is it likely that colleges for deaf-mutes will ever produce mute statesmen, lawyers, and ministers of religion, orators, poets, and authors?" he asked. "The answer is: They will, in numbers, like angels' visits, few and far between" (47–48). He noted that deaf people could be public speakers in the courtroom, the pulpit, and the forum using precisely the method he was using then: by having hearing people read their addresses out loud, a point that Flournoy had made eight years before and that Clerc had demonstrated in 1816. Writing again serves as a way to find a voice and potentially overcome the hearing line, and Carlin, like several earlier deaf authors, indicated how changing social conditions would enable deaf people to gain a more equitable and productive place in society.

Despite the hope and buoyant spirits surrounding the inauguration, deaf writers subsequently continued to testify to debilitating discrimination in American society. In 1869, Carlin, who had scoffed at Flournoy's plan, disconsolately acknowledged that even deaf college graduates could not secure suitable employment because of bigotry. In an address to the Empire State Association of Deaf-Mutes convention, he wrote:

> What is the true obstruction in their way? Prejudice? I am sorry to say that it is. This spirit is common among even the most intelligent —the most benevolent men [and is] . . . as illogical as it is cruel. . . . Cruel, because it crushes the budding hopes in the applicant's mind. . . . But this Prejudice comes rather from ignorance than malice. . . . I presume that the prejudice will cease to exist where the true merits of the case are more properly understood. ("Oration" 265–66)

Locating prejudice even among the kindest and best-informed business leaders, Carlin confirms the endemic audism against deaf people in hearing society that Flournoy had fervently decried a decade earlier. Unable to imagine a life apart from hearing people, Carlin only dispiritedly holds out the hope for greater understanding in the future since, he writes, deaf people are completely dependent on their hearing counterparts for "all things necessary to our livelihood" ("Oration" 268).

These words were all too true for Adele Jewel, who came to rely on hearing strangers for her and her mother's maintenance. In her autobiographical pamphlet, she recounts the circumstances that reduced her to penury: to her regret, she was forced to leave the Michigan School for the Deaf due to serious illness, and since her mother was

The National Deaf-Mute College class of 1870.
(Photograph by Mathew B. Brady.)
Courtesy of Gallaudet University Archives.

now an invalid, the two had trouble supporting themselves and became homeless. In these critical circumstances, disempowered by both her deafness and gender, Jewel hit upon the idea of writing her story and selling it to the public. The narrative was published for her by the father of a deaf friend (indicating an interesting convergence of filial connections), and she apparently offered it on the streets to passersby in hopes of securing support, with modest success. "It is still a great trial for me to offer my book for sale, for though on one hand I meet with sympathy and kindness, on the other, coldness, slight, and discouragement chill me," Jewel writes, illustrating how the very lives of deaf people sometimes turned on the majority's attitudes (24). In the absence of a husband, father, or social services to support her, Jewel becomes utterly dependent on hearing people.

Even the person who was arguably the most successful deaf writer in America during the century, Laura Redden Searing, dealt with discrimination. Although she crafted a successful career as poet and journalist, interviewing members of Congress through writing, publishing in mainstream newspapers and magazines, and composing a lyric that Missouri Union soldiers sang during the Civil War, in a simple allegorical fable she bore witness to the stigma she endured. In "The Realm of Singing" (ca. 1872) a bird with a lame wing serves as a figure for Searing, the deaf poet. Lonely, overlooked, and laughed at for her attempts at songs, the bird notes that her lameness does not affect her ability to sing. "I suspect that there was still some prejudice against the songs of crippled birds," the narrator says, just as Searing evidently felt that hearing critics' stereotypes about her deafness kept her poetry from finding a broader audience (209). When the lame bird compares herself with other birds, she feels "mingled envy and resentment," emotions similar to Flournoy's, for "they were so free; she was so abject" (211). In the end she finds an appreciative audience of "the sick, the sad, the maimed, the feeble" to sing for, and comes to embrace her low place among these fellow outcasts (212). Although she was ostensibly an achiever in society, in the fable Searing finds satisfaction and comfort only in the company of similarly stigmatized and downtrodden beings, implicitly pointing to the connections deaf people had with disabled and other groups and testifying to the abiding need she felt for a community of appreciative peers.

Laura Redden Searing, ca. 1870.
Courtesy of the Portsmouth Athenæum,
Isles of Shoals Collection.

Would Searing, Jewel, and the jobless college graduates have fared better in Flournoy's deaf commonwealth? It is an interesting and of course unanswerable question. Deaf authors never quite escape their two consciousnesses: one as members of a hearing-dominated system, one as deaf people oppressed by it. As they sought to write their individual and collective identity, they revealed how difficult it was to escape this persistent double consciousness and find a place where they could be truly valued and whole.

Playing with the Hearing Line

DEAFNESS, PASSING, AND LAUGHTER

The duke . . . made all sorts of signs with his hands
and said "Goo-goo—goo-goo-goo," all the time,
like a baby that can't talk.
Mark Twain, *Adventures of Huckleberry Finn* (1885)

Both the process and discourse of passing
interrogate the ontology of identity categories
and their construction.
Elaine K. Ginsberg (1996)

In *The Autobiography of Mark Twain*, dictated near the end of his life, Twain recalls a childhood friend, Tom Nash, who suddenly became deaf at the age of fifteen: "He couldn't hear himself talk. When he supposed he was talking low and confidentially, you could hear him in Illinois" (37). Twain's whimsical exaggeration turns Nash's loud voice —and his attempt to behave like a hearing person—into caricature and illustrates a final aspect of the deaf presence in literature by hearing authors: deafness as a source of laughter.

Although writers since the ancient Greeks have used deafness for comic purposes,[1] in nineteenth-century America deafness became a more prominent vehicle for humor. Especially in the latter half of the century, as traditional forms of burlesque entertainment grew more popular in the United States, hearing authors such as Joel Chandler Harris, Horatio Alger, and especially Twain began to produce comical send-ups of deaf and hearing people interacting with or impersonating each other. Like other elements of the deaf presence, these episodes test the boundary of the hearing line, probing the nature of deaf and hearing identities. Such comedy implicitly undermines some of the pious sentimentality that we saw earlier. It also returns us to the ways gender and deaf representation intersect; while, as we saw in chapter 3, most serious literary renditions of deaf people tend to be of deaf women and children, in these comic episodes the characters are almost always men. The humor invariably revolves around individuals who attempt to pass across the hearing line: authors depict a few deaf people trying to act hearing and, more frequently, hearing people trying to act deaf. Although scholars have given increasing attention to passing across racial, gender, and class boundaries in American literature and culture,[2] they have left unremarked these instances of auditory passing, as well as what they reveal about power relations and identity formation. In this chapter I pay particular attention to the works of Twain, whose life intersected with deaf people in intriguing ways and whose work regularly touches on the comedy of deafness. Shelley Fisher Fishkin, Eric Lott, and others have elucidated Twain's complicated relation to African American vernacular, blackface minstrelsy, and related racial issues. Using their work and passing theory as a starting point, I investigate Twain and other hearing writers' comic treatment of the hearing line. Although these episodes regularly deride deaf people, affirming boundaries and the superiority of hearingness, they also point to deaf people's humanity. Simultaneously challenging and reinforcing stereotypes about deaf Americans, they occasionally indicate an in-between space where polar identities recede and respectful exchange might occur.

If many hearing Americans felt wonder and uneasiness at the emergence of deaf people in public during the first part of the nineteenth century, during the latter decades they encountered still more confusing images of deafness. As we have seen, through the residential schools for deaf students, the National Deaf-Mute College, and deaf social organizations, thousands of educated deaf signers appeared in society. Yet after the Civil War a movement known as oralism, which sought to instruct deaf people to speak vocally and to lipread, gained traction in deaf education. Baynton has persuasively shown that while hearing advocates of sign language in antebellum America like Thomas Hopkins Gallaudet were primarily concerned with teaching deaf people the gospel, oralists after the Civil War chiefly sought to make deaf people blend into mainstream America. In this time of immigration and the melting pot, forging a national identity around one language—became paramount: people who were different, whether because of national origin or deafness, were pressured to assimilate. Alexander Graham Bell, the most famous leader of the oralists, wrote of deaf students in 1884: "We should try ourselves to forget that they are deaf. We should teach *them* to forget that they are deaf" (qtd. in Lane, *When* 340). In other words, oralists' ideal deaf person would learn to pass as hearing. With this goal, oralists sought to counteract the new social visibility of deaf people by making them less apparent. To many deaf people's dismay, oralist schools were opened in New York (1864) and Massachusetts (1867) that forbade sign language, and a seismic shift gradually began to occur in many schools for deaf students where administrators discouraged sign and did not hire deaf teachers, challenging the shape of American deaf identity.

Also complicating matters was the continued presence of liminal deaf figures who did not fit neatly into binary categories, including those who became deaf later in life or who had considerable amounts of hearing. Like light-skinned people who, because of their "one drop of black blood," were legally black in the segregationist logic of late-

An articulation class. From "History of the Illinois Institution for the Education of the Deaf and Dumb," in Histories of American Schools for the Deaf, 1817–1893, *vol. 1, ed. Edward Allen Fay (Washington, D.C.: Volta Bureau, 1893).*

nineteenth-century America, these so-called "semi-deaf" people faced perplexing questions of social status and were the most likely to seek to pass, to blend in with the majority. While many Americans after the Civil War felt what Laura Browder calls "anxiety over racial and ethnic identity and its slipperiness," they experienced uneasiness about the parameters of deafness and hearingness too (6). If some deaf people were attempting to act hearing, how should the hearing line be conceived?

Through their comic treatments of deafness, hearing authors took on such questions and fears. These episodes were part of an increasingly popular form of humor marked by theatricality and exaggeration that confronted troubling matters, including the issue of how to relate to those who are different.[3] Writing about the impact of such humor on women, Alan Trachtenberg says that "burlesque took wicked fun in reversing roles, shattering polite expectations, [and] brazenly challenging notions of the approved ways women might display their bodies and speak in public" (xii). We could say something similar about African Americans (through blackface minstrelsy) and deaf people (through deaf-related comedy). Such modes emphasized spectacle and outward performance over inner spirituality. Perhaps no one better epitomized this burlesque than Phineas T. Barnum, the showman who knew precisely how to amuse sensation-hungry ticket buyers. Barnum's American Museum in New York City regularly featured freak shows, Indians, confidence men, and blackface minstrel routines, serving as an engrossing place where white, hearing, able-bodied Americans could judge authenticity.

By playfully testing the boundaries of identity, such entertainment allowed the public to release their anxieties through laughter. Bakhtin acknowledges this sense of comic relief when he notes that "laughter liberates not only from external censorship but first of all from the great internal censor; it liberates from the fear that developed in man during thousands of years: fear of the sacred, fear of the prohibitions, of the past, of power" (94). In previous chapters, I touched on many fears that hearing authors projected onto the deaf during the nineteenth century, including perceptions that deaf people were walking manifestations of sin, evil, death, brutishness, obliviousness, and insanity. As noted above, oral deaf and "semi-deaf" people may have caused uneasiness about auditory categories among hearing Americans. Moreover, deaf individuals probably raised discomfort in hearing people about how communication could occur, and reminded them of the frightening possibility of becoming deaf themselves. Through their comic treatments of deafness, hearing writers sometimes sought to divert such fears into the realm of laughter, where they were under more containment. As David Reynolds observes, "the best popular humor . . . frankly confronted dark forces in human nature and in American society but sought to control them by rechanneling them into the arena of linguistic play" (*Beneath* 442). Like the American burlesque of which it is a part, deaf-related humor by hearing authors confronted the disturbing emergence of different bodies in American culture and sought to bring them under restraint.

As critics have noted, the ability to pass over identity boundaries reveals the instability of seemingly straightforward categories, interrogating the convoluted relationship between biological and cultural aspects of difference. Such transgressions can uncover the flimsiness of the idea that identity is solely rooted in the body. Elaine K. Ginsberg asserts that "passing challenge[s] the essentialism that is often the foundation of identity politics, a challenge that may be seen as either threatening or liberating but in either instance discloses the truth that identities are not singularly true or false but multiple and contingent" (4). These multiple and contingent factors show up in auditory passing, where people do not need to alter their appearance but rather their behavior: they perform deafness or hearingness in the communicative realm, by responding to, misunderstanding, or ignoring speech, using sign language, or talking vocally. Yet if these episodes point to the degree that deafness and hearingness are performed, they nonetheless remind us of the recalcitrant material fact of audition, for deaf-as-hearing passers, even if successful temporarily, are invariably exposed, while hearing-as-deaf passers do manage to dupe other hearing people. In these episodes biological deafness cannot quite be acted away. In this manner, auditory passing reveals a continuous interplay between social behavior and biological status. If, as Samira Kawash has argued, racial passing plays on the color line, "exposing racial difference as a continually emerging distinction," we can say something similar about auditory passing (63). By testing the borders of the hearing line and breaching its boundaries, people repeatedly seek to name and define auditory status. These works offer a site where the conceptual intricacies of such identities can be displayed and worked out.

Like other forms of passing, these episodes reveal a system of power relationships. First, people seek to pass to escape the confinements of one identity and gain the privileges and status of another. Deaf people act like they are hearing to appear normal, fit into hearing society, elude oppression, and prove themselves capable workers; conversely, hearing people pretend to be deaf for fun, for financial gain, to avoid detection, and even, in the case of Ellen Craft in *Running a Thousand Miles to Freedom*, to escape from slavery. These episodes invariably have a triangulated structure, which Freud sees as a basic part of jokes. The hearing author and reader are positioned as an understanding "we," seeing the foolishness or incongruity of the unsophisticated deaf character or the gullible hearing person duped by a deaf impostor. Politically speaking, these episodes turn on whether the passers are members of the majority or minority group. The hearing-as-deaf passer typically appears as a daring figure of theatricality, even if his or her transgression contains a certain threat. In Browder's words, "there is an audacity inherent in [impersonators'] choices, a refusal to accept essentialist rules of race for themselves that has the transgressive quality of an outrageous joke" (11). Yet when passers try to move from the minority to the majority, the dynamic changes. Deaf-as-hearing passers are generally presented as self-deluded and pathetic, and the humor often reinforces stereotypes and reassures hearing readers that deaf people cannot escape their side of the line. These cases resemble ethnic humor that makes fun of an alien group to confirm cultural boundaries and bolster one's own sense of superiority, what Thomas Hobbes has in mind when he writes that laughter reveals a "sudden glory arising from sudden conception of some eminency in ourselves, by comparison with the infirmity of others" (54–55). While hearing passers have power in these accounts, deaf passers rarely do.

If these episodes affirm the priority of hearingness in hegemonic ideology, they also regularly humanize deaf people. As we will see, the humor of deaf characters arises from the incongruity of their actions; the sudden appearance of deafness can make a seemingly normal person appear not only terrifying or inspiring, but also ridiculous. As

Blaise Pascal puts it, "Nothing produces laughter more than a surprising disproportion between that which one expects and that which one sees" (qtd. in Ludovici 27). Furthermore, deaf characters (and hearing characters acting deaf) in these episodes frequently have a childish naivete, reacting nonsensically or performing absurd antics that allow hearing writers and readers to indulge in childlike pleasure. In *Jokes and Their Relation to the Unconscious*, Freud asserts that jokes, comedy, and humor are all ways to recover the "the mood of our childhood, when we were ignorant of the comic, when we were incapable of jokes and when we had no need of humour to make us feel happy in our life" (236). He seems to envision a rupture between adult reason and moral codes on the one hand and childlike happiness on the other. Like Rousseau before him, Freud believes that intellectual maturity causes humans to lose some freedom and energy. Through laughter, we recover our childhood spontaneity and pleasure. In deaf-related comedy, deaf characters, those figures of *infans*, serve as childlike jesters, making possible hearing people's delighted immersion in a childish world of play, where reason, language, and logos are less central.

I have been arguing that hearing writers' comical takes on deafness can relieve fears and desires, reify hearing superiority, and delight in incongruity, allowing hearing people—and sometimes deaf as well—to reexperience childlike joy. Henri Bergson adds an interesting corollary: for something to be funny, he posits, it must be human. Animals and objects are humorous to the extent that they remind us of something human; conversely, we might say that human subjects are sometimes funny to the degree that they resemble inanimate matter (Provine 17). Deaf characters in hearing texts occasionally amuse because they resemble posts, stones, doorknobs, and other objects. These insights show that when hearing writers and readers laugh at these deaf episodes, even if they mock, even if they express surprise, even if they reveal anxieties, they are implicitly acknowledging that the objects of their laughter, deaf people, are human too.

Twain's own ambivalent response to deaf issues was shaped by his contact with deaf people throughout his life. As noted, his boyhood friend Tom Nash became deaf at age fifteen. A pilot Twain worked with on a Mississippi steamboat, identified in *Life on the Mississippi* only as Brown, was deaf. While Twain lived in Washington, D.C., following the Civil War, he likely encountered deaf students from the newly opened National Deaf-Mute College. He knew the president of the college, Edward Miner Gallaudet (the youngest son of Thomas Hopkins Gallaudet), who was a leading figure in deaf education in the late nineteenth century.[4] When Twain moved to Hartford in 1871, he settled not far from the American Asylum for the Deaf, which Clerc and Thomas Hopkins Gallaudet had founded over fifty years before and which had several hundred deaf pupils and teachers. He could well have seen them around town.[5] Twain corresponded with the deaf author Laura Redden Searing and met the fourteen-year-old Helen Keller in the mid-1890s, forming a friendship with her.[6] He later became a financial supporter of Keller and called her "the most marvelous person of her sex that has existed on this earth since Joan of Arc" (*Speeches* 179). For her part, Keller included an affectionate chapter on him in her autobiography, *Midstream: My Later Life* (1929). She writes that Twain "knew with keen and sure intuition many things about me . . . things that others learned slowly or not at all" (48). These personal interactions probably prompted Twain not only to include deaf characters in his fiction, but also to play with some of the popular stereotypes that surrounded deaf people.

If these encounters with deafness made Twain more knowledgeable and sympathetic, they may also have made him fearful of becoming deaf himself, especially since he had a close brush with becoming deaf as a boy. In his autobiography, he recounts how he and Nash went ice skating on the Mississippi River one night. When the ice began to break, the boys desperately leapt from ice cake to ice cake to make it back to shore. Nash, just ahead of Twain, miscalculated one jump and fell into the frigid water. As a result, he fell ill with a succession of diseases, the last being scarlet fever (the same disease that deafens Jim's daughter 'Lizabeth in *Huckleberry Finn*), which left him completely deaf. "Within a year or two speech departed, of course," Twain says. "But some years later he was taught to talk, after a fashion—one couldn't always make out what it was he was trying to say" (*The Autobiography* 37). Twain probably realized how easily it could have been he, and not Nash, who plunged through the ice. For the man who achieved so much through speech and sound—by listening to

Helen Keller and Mark Twain, 1902. (Photograph by E. C. Kopp.)
From Helen Keller, The Story of My Life *(New York: Doubleday,*
Page & Co., 1904).

frontier tales, by becoming famous as a public speaker, conversationalist, and writer in the oral vernacular—such a possibility must have been disturbing. With his deaf characters, Twain/Clemens thus reveals another aspect of his lifelong fascination with doubles, twins, opposites, and impostors (Blount 70), for they resemble doppelgängers, living identities that could have been his own. He made the possibility of being deaf explicit in a 1900 speech, when, after commenting on how Keller acquired so much knowledge without distractions, he ironically concluded that "if I could have been deaf, dumb, and blind I also might have arrived at something" (*Speeches* 100). By writing comically about deafness, Twain likely confronts fears and attempts to convert them into mirth.

Twain's encounters with deaf people may have prompted yet another reaction: fascination and envy. While in his encounters with Nash and Brown, Twain saw isolated deaf people who were trying and largely failing to fit into a hearing world, in Washington and Hartford he found a different sort of deaf person. Hearing observers of signing deaf people were often struck by how they radiated happiness. For example, observing a deaf wedding in 1869, a reporter for the *New York Sun* wrote: "But a more happy appearing and satisfied company is seldom seen together. Many were the jokes passed in silence, and great the badinage enjoyed by these speechless beaux and belles, their faces and fingers conveying to each other thoughts and expressions with a degree of rapidity that speech could hardly excel" ("Pantomimic" 333). Such deaf people did not fit the public's construction of deafness. They did not look like victims of social isolation, and their cheerfulness probably caught many hearing viewers off guard. As the anonymous author of "The Deaf Girl" put it in 1836: "There is . . . a hilarity in the smile of the deaf that seems to ask amusement, not sympathy" (276–77). The unexpected "smile of the deaf" invites levity, it seems so incongruous. To Twain and the other hearing authors who chanced to see them, their apparent happiness must have sometimes seemed so illogical, so at odds with the presumed calamity of their condition, that it appeared the stuff of comedy.

In these episodes of auditory passing, hearing characters who act deaf sometimes pretend to sign, while physically deaf characters do not employ sign language, trying instead to fit into a hearing society of speech and sound. The result is a sometimes hilarious, sometimes pathetic game of identity shifting, where characters strive to be what they are not and constantly bumble and parody one another and themselves. Through such comedy, Twain and other hearing writers explore the ontology of deaf and hearing identities and further attempt to demarcate the elusive hearing line.

SHOUTING ACROSS THE HEARING LINE

Hearing authors' humorous depictions of physically deaf characters usually involve shouting, whether by deaf characters themselves or by the hearing individuals trying to communicate with them. The shouter tests and reveals the boundary that separates deaf and hearing people and in the process breaks conventional social mores of polite discourse. To begin with a modest example: in a brief scene in Louisa May Alcott's *Little Women* (1869), the professor inhabits the shouter role. We learn that, during a dinner party, "at the very bottom of the table was the Professor, shouting answers to the questions of a very inquisitive, deaf old gentleman on the one side, and talking philosophy with a Frenchman on the other" (118). Through his persistent questions, the imperceptive deaf gentleman adds absurdity to the hearing professor's situation, causing the latter to yell replies in the midst of his abstract conversation while consuming prodigious amounts of food. We do not know if this nameless deaf man understands the professor's answers or how well he himself speaks, whereas we are told that the professor has "a splendid big voice that does one's ears good" (116). We might guess that the gentleman became deaf in his old age and still behaves like the hearing person he once was, although we cannot say for sure. Having served his comic purpose of helping to define the jovial professor, the elderly deaf gentleman vanishes from the narrative.

In Twain's shouter episodes, the deaf characters assume a larger role. Tom Nash is one such screamer. As we have seen, Twain pokes fun at his boyhood friend's loud voice by drawing out the humorous gap between Nash's intention to speak softly and his yelling; part of the joke is that Nash does not realize what he is doing. The episode points to the comedy implicit in a deaf person trying to communicate through vocal speech at all. Nash somewhat resembles James Weldon Johnson's Ex-Colored Man or other examples of racial passing in literature. Just as the Ex-Colored Man looks white, so Nash appears to be a normal hearing person; he can pass as hearing until his shouting reveals his auditory status. Because he became deaf at age fifteen, his loud voice testifies not just to his current deafness, but also to the fact that he once was on the other side of the line.

In this way, Nash and probably Alcott's deaf gentleman reveal how auditory passing can be more complex than most other forms of passing, for unlike typical passers, they seek to hold onto an identity they once had. They resemble some people with other acquired disabilities who seek to hide their differences from the norm.[7] While passing for white has sometimes been perceived as a kind of self-hatred or betrayal—what Gayle Ward summarizes as "narrowly self-interested and complicit with structures of racial expression and domination" (16)—we cannot quite read Nash's performance in that manner. It is not just that he, as Kathleen Pfeiffer suggestively argues of black passers, "values individualism [and] may be idiosyncratic, self-determining, or inclined toward improvisation" (2). In trying to communicate vocally, Nash is being true to who he once was and is striving to retain the connection he had with hearing people like Twain. We do not know if he had exposure to sign language or other deaf people, or the opportunity to embrace his deafness. Even as Twain uses him to define both deafness and hearingness, Nash's comical efforts at vocal conversation evince his own negotiations of his deafened identity.

If Nash has a complex relation to the hearing line, so does Brown, the crusty steamboat pilot in *Life on the Mississippi*. Twain tells us that Brown "was deaf (although he always pretended he wasn't)" (350). However, Brown appears to have a good deal of hearing. He seems to have no trouble understanding face-to-face conversation; he successfully passes as hearing until a faraway shouter reveals his deafness. Here, the screamer is Twain's brother Henry, who yells to Brown an order from the captain to stop at a landing. "I very much doubted if he had heard the order," Twain says. "If I had had two heads, I would have spoken; but as I had only one, it seemed judicious to take care of it; so I kept still" (350). Sure enough, Brown sails by the landing and later denies that Henry had said anything. Young Twain stands up for his brother, and he and Brown wind up fighting as the steamboat plunges ahead with no one at the wheel. The comedy stems not so much from

Brown's deafness as from his foolish denial of it. The episode has a certain pathos, for Brown is ashamed of his deafness; he would rather fight than admit he is deaf. Perhaps he feels compelled to pass as hearing to keep his job, since discrimination against deaf people was common. At any rate, Henry's shouting explodes his charade, and the captain, who obviously does not like Brown, laughingly excuses Twain for his crime of fighting with a pilot. When Brown demands that either he or Twain go ashore, the captain tells him to leave the ship. Brown, the belligerent deaf grouch, is vanquished, and the chapter ends with Twain relishing his ability to hear. "I listened to George Ealer's flute; or to his reading from his two bibles, that is to say, Goldsmith and Shakespeare," he says (353). The account does not express sympathy for Brown. Twain chooses not to help him when he suspects he has not heard and gets pleasure out of casting the surly pilot from his position of power. It is a victory of youth over age, truth over falsehood, laughter over bitterness, and hearing over deafness.

Twain turns to more slapstick forms in some of his later comical treatments of deafness, employing rather generalized deaf figures to make a jest. In the sketch "How the Author was Sold in Newark" (1893), he plays the role of shouter and the joke is on him. When Twain comes to Newark to give a lecture, a young man mournfully informs him that his uncle is "permanently bereft of all emotions" (103). Touched, Twain urges him to bring his uncle to the lecture and resolves to get a response from the man. That night, after the young man seats his uncle in the second row, Twain makes every effort to get a reaction. "I fumed and sweated and charged and ranted till I was hoarse and sick, and frantic and furious; but I never moved him once—I never started a smile or a tear!" Twain says. "I was astounded" (104). Disconcerted and exhausted, he gives up, only to learn afterward that the old man is "deaf and dumb, and as blind as a badger!" (105). As in Melville's "Fragments" and Bierce's "Chickamauga," deafness emerges unexpectedly, but here the surprise amuses: Twain presents himself as ridiculous for being hoodwinked. This deaf, dumb, and blind man is hardly a character at all, hardly human at all, more like a statue than a conscious person. Twain wrote this episode before he befriended Helen Keller, who humanized deaf, dumb, and blind people for him. Deafness in this case appears as a trope for hearing authors' concerns of not communicating effectively, of their audiences not understanding them.[8]

We also get an exaggerated take on the hearing line in the essay "A Little Note to M. Paul Bourget" (1897), where Twain facetiously accuses Bourget, a French critic with whom he disagrees, of using the rules for a conversation between a shouter and a deaf person. The main characteristics of such interactions, Twain says, are "irrelevancy and persistent desertion of the topic at hand" (168). He goes on to give the following example:

> SHOUTER. Did you say his name is WETHERBY?
>
> DEAF PERSON. Change? Yes, I think it will. Though if it should clear off I—
>
> SHOUTER. It's his NAME I want—his NAME.
>
> DEAF PERSON. Maybe so, maybe so; but it will only be a shower, I think.
>
> SHOUTER. No, no, no!—you have quite misunderstood me. If—
>
> DEAF PERSON. Ah! GOOD morning; I am sorry you must go. (169)

This imagined exchange replicates clichés about deaf people, leading to a comedy of errors where little actual communication takes place. The shouter and deaf person are vague types rather than breathing individuals; we cannot even ascertain their genders or ages. Twain's main purpose is to illustrate the irrelevance of Bourget's argument rather than cast new light on deaf-hearing interactions. Still, we again see a shouter unable to surpass the hearing line. The deaf person's incongruous replies are amusing in their departure from expected norms. The shouter's loud voice adds to the humor, for, like the professor's and Nash's yelling, it breaks social conventions and seems ridiculous in its ineffectiveness. Perhaps the most laughable aspect of the exchange is the deaf person's own obliviousness to his errors. Like Nash and Brown, he displays ignorance, becoming an object of derision to superior hearing readers. In his earnest, well-meaning manner, he seems to believe that he can cross the hearing line and behave like a hearing person; he rather resembles a child trying to act like an adult. His failure serves to reinforce the hearing line and to demonstrate anew the gap that separates deaf and hearing people.

With these shouter episodes, Twain illustrates the immensity of the hearing line. If he occasionally humanizes deaf people somewhat, showing them to have emotions and foibles like everyone else, he also reinforces stereotypes about them. The shouter episodes reveal Twain's own firm stance on the hearing side of the line. With the possible exception of the wooden deaf, dumb, and blind man, we do not see any congenitally deaf people, or "deaf-mutes," as they were called, in these scenes. The deaf person is "semi-deaf": late deafened, like Tom Nash, or hard-of-hearing, like Brown. Such people have a more complex relation to sound and their deafness, since they often seem stuck between the hearing and deaf worlds, perched uncomfortably on the hearing line. It would be as if, in treating the color line, Twain wrote solely about light-skinned African Americans trying to fit into white society. None of his deaf characters uses sign language, although Twain clearly knew about the power of sign. In a story that he wrote in 1876, "A Murder, a Mystery, and a Marriage," Twain has a hearing stranger speak French, German, and other languages in an effort to communicate with a befuddled Missouri farmer. When he is not understood, the stranger finally produces "a succession of graceful but complex signs drawn from the deaf and dumb language" (56). Here, in a quick aside, Twain gives the most positive portrayal of American Sign Language in nineteenth-century fiction by a hearing writer (even if the stranger's signs only "undermine . . . [the farmer's] already tottering reason").[9] He tacitly equates sign language with spoken foreign languages, and his adjectives—"graceful" and "complex"—show his respect for deaf people's sign. Yet he does not allow any of his deaf characters to use this eloquent language, perhaps because having them sign would not be funny. Speech and sound are the norm. In this oral world, deaf people are isolated, different. The deaf individual tries but inevitably fails to negotiate the world of sound, and the gap, while humorous, buttresses the view of insiders (hearing people) as superior and outsiders (deaf citizens) as pitiable, self-deluded, bitter, or just ridiculous.

Perhaps we can best see these operative assumptions by quickly comparing Twain's shouter episodes with anecdotes by deaf Americans themselves. Such writers also found the hearing line funny, and their journals and newspapers contain humorous observations about deaf-hearing interaction. For example, William Swett reported the following encounter with a hearing man at a lodge in the late 1860s:

My signs and gestures and my little slate, of which I made free use in talking with my companions, soon attracted the attention of the company, to most of whom a deaf-mute was evidently a new thing. One man in particular, an Irishman . . . after eyeing me intently for some time, approached me, laid a hand on my shoulder, looked me in the face, and then, making the sign of the cross, he nodded, went back to his seat and resumed his pipe, apparently satisfied that it was all right. I could not help smiling at his behavior. (5)

Here the tables are reversed. The hearing person's actions are comical and unexpected, while Swett inhabits the role of the amused observer. The man responds to Swett's signs with a sign of his own, but his sign of the cross is rather absurd in its portentousness and pity, as out of place as Nash's yelling voice may have seemed to Twain. The perspective is from the deaf side of the hearing line, where deafness and visual communication are the norm. Swett, a deaf man from a deaf family, is secure and comfortable with his deaf identity. He does not try to hide it, like Brown, or to speak, like Nash.[10]

Deaf writers also poke fun at semi-deaf trickster figures who flirt with both sides of the hearing line, but again, the underlying paradigm is different. *American Annals of the Deaf and Dumb* contains an account of William Chamberlain, a "semi-mute" who tried to pass as hearing to serve in the Civil War. He enlists in the Union army, and "was never detected until I attempted to pass the guard line one day, when my inability to hear the sentinel led to the discovery of my deafness" ("A Deaf Soldier" 54). Once again, a shouter reveals a person's deafness, but here, the comedy lies not in his detection so much as in his temporary success at duping the hearing. He manages to reenlist and pass an exam by a doctor, "whose questions I readily comprehended from his lips, and who never suspected that I could not hear a sound." He is eventually caught and, like Brown, cast out: "I was very much annoyed, as I really desired to serve my country," Chamberlain writes (54).[11] The comedy primarily resides in just how close Chamberlain comes to putting one over on hearing people. His temporary passing is empowering, a source of amusement and fascination to his deaf friends. Even his eventual failure is humorous rather than pathetic, since it serves as a reassuring confirmation of his membership in the deaf community (and the limitations of oralism). Chamberlain, like most deaf people, faces discrimination by the hearing world. Such stories served to reinforce the group's identity, to pull deaf people together through shared experiences. The power balance and humor have shifted based solely on the identity of the narrator and the audience. If Twain's shouter episodes ultimately confirm hearing values, so Swett and Chamberlain's narratives reinforce deaf people's identity and their secure place on the deaf side of the line. All humans, no matter what their ethnic group, seem to have a need to erect certain boundaries, to determine who is "us" and who is "them."

PLAYING "DEEF AND DUMB"

In *Roughing It* (1871), when Twain breaks a long silence and says something to a woman sitting near him, she responds with surprise. "Danged if I didn't begin to think you fellers was deef and dumb," she says (27). Twain was not pretending to be deaf, but sometimes his characters, as well as those of other hearing authors, do. In creating such episodes, hearing writers were likely affected by the burgeoning deaf community. Not only did deaf people increasingly sign with each other in public, but sometimes hearing relatives, coworkers, and friends signed with them as well. A hearing person who signs proficiently may appear deaf. To an outsider, there is often an implicit incongruity in a hearing person silently communicating through sign and becoming seemingly indistinguishable from deaf signers: reliable markers of identity difference become destabilized. Moreover, pantomime has been associated with humor at least since Roscius, the celebrated Roman actor, through more modern visual comics such as Charlie Chaplin, Lucille Ball, and Jim Carrey.

Acting deaf for personal gain was not uncommon in nineteenth-century America. When Kentucky opened its school for the deaf in 1823, its first teacher proved to be a hearing person who faked deafness; he was fired as incompetent (Gannon 2). Newspapers for deaf Americans sometimes reported cases of deaf impostors. One account in *The Deaf-Mutes' Friend* describes a man acting deaf to convince others to give him money; another tells of a boy pretending not to hear to gain advantage over a stingy landlord (52, 358).[12] Such items may have bemused deaf readers by showing that what the public usually saw as a deprivation could sometimes be an advantage. They also may have served as a warning, as some readers were probably bothered by the equation of deafness with begging or malingering. Similarly, the abolitionist newspaper *Liberator* carried dozens of stories cautioning about impostors who pretended to be fugitive slaves to gain contributions from sympathetic people. During the Civil War, some hearing people acted deaf to avoid conscription. In 1862, the *Charleston Mercury* wryly noted that "some of the ablest-bodied men in town . . . have suddenly gone deaf," providing an interesting contrast to Chamberlain's effort to pass as hearing so he could serve ("Richmond" 1). People frequently used the phrase "deaf as a post" to describe someone acting deaf. For example, when an elderly southern man refused to give the Union forces information during the war, a *New York Herald* reporter wrote that he "might as well have played the part of 'deaf as a post'" ("Important"). The deaf-as-a-post figure has a certain magnetism and inexplicable allure, as the master showman Barnum well knew. Once, when Barnum wanted to attract more customers to his American Museum, he recruited a beggar to act deaf. He instructed him to walk back and forth in front of the museum, systematically picking up and putting down bricks. "To assist me properly you must seem to be as deaf as a post," Barnum told him. "Wear a serious countenance; answer no questions; pay no attention to any one; but attend faithfully to the work" (qtd. in Benton 119). The routine was successful, as the deaf charlatan soon had a crowd of at least five hundred people watching him curiously. After he entered the museum, some bought tickets and followed him, just as Barnum had hoped. By pretending deafness, impostors gained a certain power, winning the interest, pity, and money of a gullible public.

The empowering aspects of such performances become especially evident in William Craft's true account of fleeing slavery with his wife, Ellen, in *Running a Thousand Miles for Freedom* (1860). As they made their daring escape in 1848, Ellen Craft engaged in what we might call quadruple passing to avoid detection: she crossed not just racial, gender, and class boundaries as she pretended to be a genteel white male slaveowner, but also the hearing line. When Mr. Cray, an old friend of her master's, boarded the train, she "resolved to feign deafness as the only means of self-defence" against his recognizing her voice (29). As William Craft recounts it, referring to his disguised wife as "my master":

> After a little while, Mr. Cray said to my master, "It is a very fine morning, sir." The latter took no notice, but kept looking out of the window. Mr. Cray soon repeated his remark, in a little louder tone, but my master remained as before. This indifference attracted the attention of the passengers near, one of whom laughed out. This, I suppose, annoyed the old gentleman, as he said, "I will make him hear," and in a loud tone of voice repeated, "It is a very fine morning, sir."
>
> My master turned his head, and with a polite bow said, "Yes," and commenced looking out of the window again.
>
> One of the gentleman remarked that it was a very great deprivation to be deaf. "Yes," replied Mr. Cray, "and I shall not trouble that fellow any more." (29–30)

Although the scene must have been quite tense at the time, readers of Craft's account know they will escape and Ellen's auditory passing becomes a vehicle for humor. She performs deafness as obliviousness; she can speak, but she acts unaware. In the triangulated structure here, the Crafts and the reader are in on the joke, while the white southern supporter of slavery, Mr. Cray, is weakened and appears foolish. The ruse works, and even though Craft says Ellen had no ambition to don a disguise, it is precisely her performance that allows her and her husband to win freedom for themselves as hearing black Americans.

If hearing people acted deaf to gain certain privileges, they also sometimes did so just for the pleasure of it. While some of the enjoyment typically came from fooling others, some came from the act of pretending to be deaf (so long as it was temporary) itself. In an 1886 novel by Kate Douglas Wiggin, *The Birds' Christmas Carol*, we are informed that the children "play 'Deaf and Dumb School' all afternoon" (30). To act deaf, to enter a silent world where vocal talking is forbidden and all communication must come visually, through gestures and facial expressions, is an exciting game, taking us back to what Freud describes as the realm of childhood play where logos is no longer dominant. We can discern similar pleasure in a blackface minstrel routine, *Not as Deaf as He Seems*, which was performed in San Francisco in 1865. Orpheus, a young man pretending to be deaf, goes to Plato for music lessons.

> PLATO. Well, can you sing?
> (Orpheus looking vacantly before him)
> PLATO. (Impatiently, nearly knocks Orpheus over with a shove.) I
>   ask you, can you—oh, put up that trumpet ag'in! (Orpheus
>   takes horn from bag, and applies it to his ear.) Can you sing?
> ORPHEUS. Yes.
> PLATO. Ah, that's better. Where's your voice, high or low?
> ORPHEUS. Yes, I've brought my banjo. (2)

The routine creates what Lott has called "a doubled structure of looking" (152), where the "deaf" figure on stage becomes the object of fascination both for the hearing character and for the hearing audience. The farcical exchange is more ridiculous than any of Twain's shouter episodes, for both characters are hearing. Spectators know that Orpheus is a hearing actor pretending to be deaf; they can laugh simultaneously at his burlesque of deaf people and his duping of the hapless music teacher. The sketch simultaneously blurs the color line (through blackface) and the hearing line (by featuring deaf impostors), yet it remains the product of white hearing fantasies and fears.

Performing in blackface and acting deaf parallel each other in many ways. While minstrelsy showed whites grappling with the color line, deaf impostors helped hearing people negotiate the hearing line. In both cases, the white, hearing performers assume the role of dreaded, fascinating others. Their enactments automatically contain double meaning (another of the techniques that Freud identifies for jokes), for performing on the other side of the hearing or color line is perforce two-faced and ironical. We can never quite forget that the performance is an impersonation, which actually contributes to the humor, to the sense of incongruity and dangerously liberating transgression. While David Roediger argues that "blackface minstrels were the first self-consciously *white* entertainers in the world" (117), we might claim similar awareness of being hearing among those who performed deafness. Through their absurd burlesques, minstrels and deaf impostors infantilize African Americans and deaf people and reveal their delight in nonlogical ways of being. As I have suggested, both modes offer ways to relieve the anxieties of a young republic through laughter and by placing deaf or black men under representational restraint. Lott's words about the blackface minstrel mask apply equally to performances of deafness: they "offered a way to play with collective fears of a degraded and threatening—and male—Other while at the same time maintaining some symbolic control over them" (*Love* 25). If, as Lott contends, blackface was underwritten by fear and attraction, so was acting deaf. The engagement with the color and hearing lines both reinforced differences (by asserting the superiority of white hearing people through derision) and provided the opportunity to erase them (by paying tribute to and acknowledging the humanity of black or deaf others). Building on the work of John Szwed, Lott maintains that "at the very least, symbolic crossings of . . . boundaries—through dialect, gesture, and so on—paradoxically engage and absorb the culture being mocked or mimicked" (29).[13] Even ridicule, then, offers the possibility of increased awareness and understanding. At any rate, the popularity of the *Not as Deaf as He Seems* skit—it was republished at least once— and other episodes of auditory crossing demonstrate the pleasure many nineteenth-century Americans felt at vicariously breaching the hearing line.

These lessons must not have been lost on Twain and his peers, who absorbed this culture of blackface minstrelsy (Twain called blackface a "glad and stunning surprise" [*The Autobiography* 59]) and burlesque humor. On at least one occasion, Twain acted deaf in person, going onstage before an audience and just standing there, expressionless, as if he did not even know he was supposed to be the speaker. As Roy Blount Jr. tells it, Twain "realized that he could hold people silent on the edges of their seats for about as long as he wanted to without uttering a word" (49). No surprise, then, that humorous depictions of hearing people feigning deafness began appearing in literature around midcentury. In *Paul Prescott's Charge* (1865), Horatio Alger's mischievous boy Ben pretends to be deaf to have fun with a traveler. We get an exchange as foolish as those in *Not as Deaf as He Seems* or Twain's "A Little Note to M. Paul Bourget." Alger's scene begins with the stranger asking directions.

"Will you tell me whether this is the road to Sparta?"

Ben put his hand to his ear, and seemed to listen very attentively. Then he slowly shook his head, and said, "Would you be kind enough to speak a little louder, sir?"

"The boy is deaf, after all," said the driver to himself. "IS THIS THE ROAD TO SPARTA?"

"Yes, sir, this is Wrenville," said Ben, politely.

"Plague take it! he don't hear me yet. IS THIS THE ROAD TO SPARTA?"

"Just a little louder, if you please," said Ben, keeping his hand to his ear, and appearing anxious to hear.

"Deaf as a post!" muttered the driver. "I couldn't scream any louder, if I should try. Go along."

"Poor man! I hope he hasn't injured his voice," thought Ben, his eyes dancing with fun. "By gracious!" he continued a moment later, bursting into a laugh, "if he isn't going to ask the way of old Tom Haven. He's as deaf as I pretended to be." (160–61)

Ben's deaf performance segues into the real thing with Tom Haven. When the traveler approaches the deaf man, the inane exchange repeats itself, and Haven naively suggests that the traveler talk to Ben. Disgusted, the stranger drives his horse away rapidly, muttering, "I believe you're all deaf in this town. I'll get out of it as soon as possible" (162). The seeming failure of speech and logic disturbs the traveler. While his departure baffles Tom Haven, it amuses Ben and us readers, for we can indulge in the pleasure of being in on the joke.

Joel Chandler Harris also lets readers vicariously experience the delight of transgressing the hearing line in his Uncle Remus trickster tales. In "The Fate of Mr. Jack Sparrow," Brer Fox pretends not to hear the gossipy Jack Sparrow, who wants to tell him some news. " 'Git on my tail, little Jack Sparrer,' sez Brer Fox, sezee, 'kaze I'm deaf in one year, en I can't hear out'n de udder' " (64). Brer Fox repeats this line to induce the bird to hop onto his back, his head, and finally his tooth, whereupon he eats him. Once again, pretending to be deaf gives a character strength, and the overly talkative sparrow loses in the process. Similarly, in the more famous "The Wonderful Tar-Baby Story"

(1881), Brer Rabbit assumes that Brer Fox's tar-baby cannot hear when it does not respond to his salutation. " 'Is you deaf?' sez Brer Rabbit, sezee. 'Kaze if you is, I kin holler louder,' sezee" (7). Becoming angry at the tar-baby's unresponsiveness, Brer Rabbit hits him and becomes stuck. Brer Fox's cunning use of the "deaf" tar-baby reveals Brer Rabbit's aggressive and superior attitude and makes him pay for it. In all these cases, acting deaf gives hearing characters power. Such performances lampoon deaf people, but they also indirectly empathize with them by revealing the pride, impatience, loquaciousness, aggression, and other shortcomings of the hearing.

For the most sophisticated treatment of deaf impostors, we must return to Twain. He experiments with a hearing character acting deaf in *The Adventures of Tom Sawyer* (1876) and then, in *Huckleberry Finn*, produces an entire episode around a deaf fraud. Ironically, when his hearing characters try to pass as deaf, they appear more deaf than his deaf characters. They do not speak and sometimes even pretend to use sign language, whereas none of Twain's deaf characters sign. The people who act deaf in Twain's work are villains. Their attempts to cross the hearing line are quite comical, but such routines also contain an implicit threat: they almost allow unscrupulous characters to take advantage of innocent people. In *Tom Sawyer*, Injun Joe pretends to be an "old deaf and dumb Spaniard" after Tom identifies him as a murderer (140). To appear like an old Spaniard, he dons a clownish outfit, including cape and goggles. To act deaf, he presumably does not talk or respond to sound, although Twain never shows this directly. The disguise allows Injun Joe to elude capture despite a massive search. Apparently no one thinks a deaf foreigner could be of any significance, although the deaf Spaniard shows up in town shortly after Injun Joe disappears.[14] The fugitive uses his deaf role to spy and plot his revenge. We learn his true identity when Huck and Tom overhear him speak:

> "Dangerous!" grunted the "deaf and dumb" Spaniard, to the vast surprise of the boys. "Milksop!"
> The voice made the boys gasp and quake. It was Injun Joe's! (140)

Once again, a voice indicates to which side of the hearing line a person belongs. While Nash's shouting reveals his deafness, here Injun Joe's normal-sounding voice demonstrates he is hearing. This unexpected regularity, for all its humor, is frightening. The boys "gasp and quake," for if Injun Joe detects them, he could well kill them too. Yet the menace is never severe, for we know that in this boy's adventure story, Tom and Huck will prevail. When the townspeople discover Injun Joe's corpse, the comic threat of his charade vanishes. Still, Twain's villainizing of the transgression hints at the dangers of a person pretending to be what he is not.

In *Huckleberry Finn*, Twain provides his longest and most ingenious treatment of the hearing line. Like Injun Joe, the duke acts deaf to try to take advantage of other people. When he and the king learn of Peter Wilks's death, they pretend to be his brothers from England to claim the estate. Since one brother, William, is deaf, the duke becomes a deaf impostor, which he says will be easy since he "had played a deef and dumb person on the histrionic boards" (160). Histrionic is the proper term here, for the duke's rendition of deafness is highly theatrical, a burlesque of the deaf people that Twain may have seen around Hartford. "The duke . . . made all sorts of signs with his hands and said 'Goo-goo—goo-goo-goo,' all the time, like a baby that can't talk," Huck tells us (163). The duke's inane goos parody some deaf people's attempts at speech. Huck's colorful similes heighten the comedy; he likens the duke's voice not only to a baby's, but also to "a jug that's googling out buttermilk" (187). We see the nonsense of the duke's goos even more clearly when he skips back and forth over the hearing line; he talks quietly to the king in private and at one point even sends the king a note correcting *his* speech (the king was saying "orgies" when he meant "obsequies"). It is a brilliant twist, the seemingly deaf person correcting the hearing person's speaking ability, and one of several masterful touches in the whole exaggerated episode. In addition to spoofing deaf people's voices, the duke travesties sign language, concocting meaningless signs as he goes along. The king participates in this signplay as well, for he acts like the duke's interpreter. When they arrive, he makes "a lot of idiotic signs to the duke on his hands" (161). The two frauds treat this mock signing seriously, for it is the key to their performance. At one point in Huck's description, when the king makes his ludicrous signs, the duke watches him "stupid and leatherheaded for a while, then, all of a sudden he seems to catch his meaning, and jumps for the king, goo-gooing with all his might for joy" (165). The duke's hyperbolic reactions are a caricature of deaf people who communicate effectively through sign; his antics are as grotesque a representation as that of white men in blackface, singing outlandish versions of what they claim are Negro songs.

Perhaps the most striking aspect of the Wilks episode is that no one questions the duke's deafness. While the doctor and townspeople suspect the two are impostors, they never shout at the duke to test his hearing, as happens in so many other Twain scenes. They do not eavesdrop outside the king and duke's room and overhear them talking, as Huck and Jim do with Injun Joe. They do not even think to wonder about the duke's signing ability, although the doctor immediately doubts the king's British accent. These oversights become especially visible when the second set of would-be brothers arrives. The new deaf William has his arm in a sling, which means, his ostensible brother explains, that he "can't even make signs to amount to much, now 't he's only got one hand to work them with" (188). Anyone who has been around signing deaf people knows this statement is ridiculous; deaf people are perfectly capable of holding whole conversations with one hand, whether they are carrying a baby or have a broken arm. If Twain was unaware of this fact, it would be another example of the limitations of his representations of deaf people. Yet the sling could mean that the second Wilks brothers are impostors as well. The king points out that the sling is "very convenient, too, for a fraud that's got to make signs, and hain't learnt how" (188). One might wish that Twain had pushed the sign language aspect further and had the townspeople, in their inquisition in the tavern, test the two deaf Williams' ability to understand signs from their brothers. One somehow wants the duke's charade to be exploded, just as Nash's and Brown's efforts to pass as hearing are inevitably exposed.

Why did Twain not have the townspeople discover the duke's charade? When Huck pretends to be a girl earlier in the novel, the woman he visits does test and detect his true gender. However, no physically deaf character (unless the second William is who he claims to be) is present to reveal the absurdity of the king and duke's mock signing. In addition, like many of the later portions of the novel, the Wilks epi-

"ALAS, OUR POOR BROTHER."

The artist Edward W. Kemble produced 174 illustrations for the original edition of Adventures of Huckleberry Finn *(1885), but none of the king and duke signing. This drawing of the two men pretending to mourn their dead "brother" softens Twain's exaggerated burlesque. Courtesy of the Clifton Waller Barrett Library of American Literature, Special Collections, University of Virginia Library.*

sode has an acerbic undertone. This harsher feeling may be a product not just of Twain's satire, but also of his state of mind when he took up writing the novel again in 1879 or 1880, after a hiatus of several years and the collapse of the promises of Reconstruction. Then again, when the king pretends to be a born-again pirate at the camp meeting, his act is not uncovered and that does not seem particularly bothersome. As Matterson points out, there is a peculiarly American delight in confidence men, an admiration for their cleverness and initiative (xvi). Through their tricks, confidence men reveal the trust of the people they dupe. Against the king and duke's treachery, Mary Jane and the townspeople appear even more innocent, a quality that Twain often tacitly celebrates throughout his writing (including with Jim's deaf daughter 'Lizabeth). In some ways, Twain the author resembles a confidence man. The humorous storyteller's strategy, Twain once wrote, is to fake innocence in order to take advantage of the audience's (Blount 73), much as the king, duke, Huck, and even Jim do in *Huckleberry Finn*.

While we are at it, we could also wish that Twain, to complete his exploration of the hearing line, had written about a strong deaf person like William Swett: someone who was confident in his deaf side of the hearing line, in his ability to communicate through sign language and writing, and in avoiding the pitfalls of speech. We do get a caricature of someone like Swett in the duke's comical charade, but we never get the real thing. Twain does not satisfy these desires, just as he never quite provides a strong black character who is free of what Ralph Ellison calls the minstrel mask (*Shadow* 50). For all the suggestiveness of his deaf episodes, Twain finally keeps his portrayals in the relatively harmless realm of comedy. Just as he had a profoundly ambivalent attitude toward African Americans, so he seems to have been simultaneously convinced of deaf people's humanity and disturbed by their difference. Perhaps we can take this ambivalence as another reminder of how, despite his vision, Twain was a product of his times.

All these comic episodes by hearing authors have a triangulated structure that relies on a bond between hearing author and hearing reader. Especially in the case of deaf characters, the laughter of hearing readers is the laughter of reassurance; while much of the pleasure stems from seeing the hearing line transgressed, boundaries and identities challenged, and the social order disrupted, by the end of each episode order—and hearingness—seems to have been restored. Deaf impostors, especially in the case of Twain, prove a more discomforting threat, and yet in these cases, too, the heroes prevail, permitting relieved amusement. We might compare such episodes to the one in *The Confidence-Man*, where Melville presents a deaf stranger who could well be a fraud, although we cannot tell for sure. We do not laugh at this potential impostor because, unlike the duke or Brer Fox or Ben, we do not know what he is. Melville leaves us in the position of the passengers on the boat, which is named *Fidèle* and yet has a sign prominently displayed saying "NO TRUST" (10). Should we have faith in the deaf man—or, for that matter, the narrator himself—or not? Melville leaves it up to us to decide, and the mystery, while piquing curiosity, is not quite funny. Because we cannot fully trust the author, we do not know if the correct response is compassion or laughter.

This deaf-related comedy also reveals the hearingness of the authors. Significantly, we never witness meaningful communication between deaf and hearing characters in nineteenth-century American literature by hearing writers. In these fictions, the hearing line is never erased, as the gap always exists and deaf characters frequently come out as deficient. As we have seen, when hearing characters transgress the hearing line, they may appear silly, but they invariably wind up with more power. Conversely, when deaf characters try to act hearing, they always seem oblivious, childlike, and foolish; they lose power. In writing about deaf characters, these authors are performing a sort of deaf impostor act of their own. They are ventriloquizing their hearing attitudes through deaf bodies. We have to look to writing by deaf authors to see how eloquently nineteenth-century deaf Americans could communicate, and how unique and accomplished as individuals they were.

If Twain and other hearing authors did not push their treatment of the hearing line as far as they might have, they still produced some of the most illuminating and humorous considerations of deafness in their time. Their deaf-related comedy helped nineteenth-century Americans to negotiate the arrival of deaf people in society. Through their humorous treatments of deafness, hearing authors began to make it more familiar and less threatening to the reading public. They addressed hearing people's anxieties and began to compress and release some of those fears. While they sometimes ridiculed the deaf as inferior individuals with childlike naivete, they nevertheless pointed to deaf people's basic humanity, opening the way for more understanding.

Twain managed to preserve his comic vision of deafness to the end. Fittingly, one of his last recorded encounters with deafness was with the first deaf person in his life, Tom Nash. Twain recounts how he returned to Hannibal fifty-five years after their skating misadventure and met Nash again. One can imagine that it was a powerful moment: Twain, the famous author and speaker, returning in his white suit to his hometown and encountering a boyhood friend whose deafness could easily have been his own. To Twain, Nash may have resembled something of a doppelgänger, a "there but for the grace of God go I" figure. He writes that he saw his old friend approaching "across a vacant space," which perhaps is a fitting metaphor for the gap that separates deaf and hearing people (*The Autobiography* 37). He went to meet him, which we might read as an indication of how hearing people need to be flexible and willing to meet deaf people halfway in communicating. Twain concludes: "He came up to me, made a trumpet of his hands at my ear, nodded his head toward the citizens and said confidentially—in a yell like a fog horn—'Same damned fools, Sam' " (37). It is a perfectly told anecdote. Once again, Nash's shouting voice, made more comical by his confidential manner and the fog horn simile, becomes a source of mirth. However, Twain humanizes his friend even as he ridicules him. Nash appears not obtuse but genial and sarcastic, calling the citizens (and perhaps also himself and Twain) "damn fools." Nash might even intend for the townspeople to hear what he says; he could be exploiting his own deafness by transgressing rules of appropriate conversation. Again, we see a three-part structure, where the citizens are derided as lesser than Nash and Twain, if also kin to them. By calling Mark Twain "Sam," Nash establishes a personal and nontheatrical relationship with his old friend, bringing them closer together. The presentation gently mocks and empathizes at the same time, as much of Twain's most effective humor does, inviting readers to laugh and realize anew how full of human foibles we all are.

Twain manages to begin bridging the "vacant space" that separates him and Nash, and to bring deaf and hearing people closer together through comedy. In confronting the formidable hearing line that so often separates the deaf and hearing, he seems to say, the best way to try to achieve connection is with empathy and laughter.

(((EPILOGUE)))

I have examined the contradictory roles that writing played in shaping
not just the emergence and reception of deaf people, but also ideologies of hearingness and deafness in nineteenth-century America.
From Laurent Clerc's first answers upon the chalkboard in 1816 to the
charged debate over John J. Flournoy's idea of a deaf commonwealth,
from the ambiguous silences in Washington Irving's tales to the appearance of deaf characters in fiction by Herman Melville, Mark
Twain, and Ambrose Bierce, writing was a primary means that Americans used to try to work out the meanings of deafness and hearingness
and to define their identities. In 1884 Alexander Graham Bell noted
that hearing Americans' "information concerning [deaf people] is
chiefly derived from books and periodicals" (43), while in 1869 John
Burnet upheld reading literature by Cooper, Irving, and others as
"nearly an equivalent to listening to the conversation of the witty, the
good, the wise, which our misfortune otherwise makes unattainable
to us" ("Fiction"). The cultural spaces of these texts gave deaf and
hearing Americans a place where they could explore auditory difference. As we have seen, in this literature the hearing line is a ceaselessly
emerging boundary, perpetually being inscribed, erased, and reimagined, but never quite definitively resolved. How did the issues
that these authors grappled with continue after their time?

If, as I observed at the outset, nineteenth-century deaf writers provided a test of whether writing could completely supplant vocal
speech, the clear answer seems to be no. For all the power of writing to
give marginalized people a voice in public discourse, for all the significant changes in deaf education and life that authors like Clerc and
Burnet were able to effect through their pens, writing by itself did not
replace hearing people's esteem for vocal speech as a distinguishing
attribute of humanness. Even near the beginning of deaf education in
America, in 1819, the hearing poet Moses Scott held out hope that deaf
people would learn to speak vocally:

Far, far more interest attracts us then,
When voice succeeds the language of the pen.
And is that silent tongue no more the same!
And may those lips their gratitude proclaim! (15–16)

Scott presents vocal speech as a higher and more desirable form of communication than writing, bearing out Jacques Derrida's argument in *Writing and Difference* that a logocentric society privileges vocal speech for its closeness to the source of utterance. Writing seems to split words and utterance, since signifiers are no longer connected to their signifieds, so it does not quite have the clout of the literal human voice. This attitude contributed to discrimination against deaf signers; in one glaring example, *The Deaf-Mutes' Friend* disapprovingly reported of a Chicago judge who had imprisoned a deaf man because he could not speak vocally. "He said the Constitution guaranteed to every man the right of speech, and this witness must speak or go to jail. The Justice certainly lacked brains as much as the witness lacked hearing and speech; and the Justice was, to our mind, the more unfortunate of the two" (281). In this way, study of the hearing line provides a useful corrective to Henry Louis Gates's assertions of the primacy of writing in humanizing oppressed groups for the majority in nineteenth-century America. It reveals that both writing and vocal speech played essential roles, and both were necessary to gain respect and acceptance in the larger society.

The valuation of vocal speech appeared in deaf education in the decades after the Civil War, as the use of sign language in schools gradually gave way to oralism, the method that sought to eradicate sign and teach deaf students to speak and speechread. As scholars like Lane and Baynton have shown, a growing distrust of foreigners and difference, a belief in scientific progress, and Alexander Graham Bell's charismatic leadership helped oral methods to gain popularity among hearing educators.[1] Drawing on the nativist and eugenicist spirit of the times, in *Memoir upon the Formation of a Deaf Variety of the Human Race* (1884) Bell expressed alarm over intermarriage between deaf people,[2] the rise of deaf associations, clubs, and publications, and the development of sign language, which were all leading to the "great calamity" of a separate "deaf variety of the human race" (41). The solution, Bell argued, was to stop residential deaf education, remove sign language from schools, fire deaf instructors, and teach deaf students to speak and speechread English. In these ways, Bell and his oralist colleagues attempted to address the hearing line in a new way by making deaf people essentially into hearing people who just could not hear. For Bell, the overriding purpose of deaf education was to achieve integration with the hearing majority; he wanted to remove all aspects of the distinct American deaf identity nurtured by Clerc and other deaf leaders. Like Flournoy, Bell acknowledged widespread prejudice and fear of deaf people, but whereas Flournoy wanted to create a separate deaf state to foster deaf solidarity and escape hearing oppression, Bell desired the exact opposite: assimilation and the suppression of deafness.[3] Under Bell's guidance, he and his hearing associates managed to transform deaf education. From the late nineteenth century until the 1970s, many schools for deaf students in the United States employed oral methods of instruction (the National Deaf-Mute College, or Gallaudet, as it became known in 1894, was a notable exception), as did most schools throughout Europe.

My study adds a new dimension to this narrative by foregrounding how both deaf and hearing writers likely contributed to the rise of oralism. Hearing authors from Sigourney to Twain effectively used deaf characters not just to prop up hearing identity, but also to raise awareness of a form of difference in American society that Bell and his colleagues would seek to minimize and eliminate. Paradoxically, deaf Americans' own writing also probably played a role. It is not just that a few early deaf authors, who invariably were deafened after they learned some vocal speech, expressed cautious support of oralism. Burnet, for one, included a few pages on teaching articulation in his *Tales of the Deaf and Dumb*, and William Chamberlain also commented positively about such methods. It is also not just that deaf authors sometimes express the wish to be able to speak. John Carlin's "The Mute's Lament" and other written anticipations of becoming hearing in heaven helped to set the stage for oralists, putting them in position to claim that they were enabling deaf people to achieve what they always wanted. It was the very success of deaf people's writing itself that upended traditional assumptions about their abilities and proved to hearing people that they could think and feel. Once hearing Americans accepted the pre-

Deaf students at Gallaudet College, 1896.
Courtesy of Gallaudet University Archives.

viously incredible notion that deaf people could write, it is not surprising that they wondered if deaf students could be taught to speak, so that the figurative voice of their pens could become a literal voice of the mouth, tongue, and larynx. To many hearing people, especially after Darwin, that doubtless seemed the logical next step in the story of scientific progress. As Frantz Fanon puts it, "To speak is to exist absolutely for the other" (17). Deaf people were almost too successful in their humanizing enterprise of writing, for they opened up the possibility in hearing people's eyes that they could exist even more absolutely as human beings by achieving the grail of vocal speech.

Deaf leaders strenuously protested the suppression of their sign language by hearing educators. In 1896 Robert P. McGregor wrote, "What heinous crime have the deaf been guilty of that their language should be proscribed?" (qtd. in Lane, *When* 338). He went on to call Bell the greatest enemy that deaf Americans had ever faced. Arguing that deaf people would never be able to communicate effectively through vocal speech, Olaf Hanson, a deaf architect, wrote in 1889 that "the deaf are foreigners among a people whose language they can never learn" (qtd. in Van Cleve and Crouch 134). Whereas seventy years before Clerc had called written English necessarily a foreign language to deaf people, one that could only be learned arduously, Hanson calls spoken English a foreign language that can never be learned: in contrast to sign, it is unnatural for deaf people. One motivation behind the formation of the National Association of the Deaf in 1880 was to have an organization to represent deaf Americans' interests on the national level. However, these deaf adults' written voices were given little heed, and the emphasis on vocal speech gained force.

The debates over the merits of speech versus sign language, assimilation versus segregation, prejudice and civil rights—over the hearing line—have continued to the present day. In recent decades, deaf people have seen great progress in their status in the United States. Their sign language gained new prominence and prestige when, in 1965, William Stokoe, Carl Croneberg, and Dorothy Casterline published a sign language dictionary. Based on linguistic principles, it showed that American Sign Language is a full human language with a grammar and morphology of its own, sparking a surge of interest in sign and deaf people as a linguistic group. Today large numbers of hearing college students take ASL as a foreign language, deaf actors regularly appear signing onstage and onscreen, and hearing parents are encouraged to communicate with their hearing babies through simple signs. Deaf people have also won more access and leadership positions in society. When, in 1988, I. King Jordan triumphantly became the first deaf president of Gallaudet University, he proclaimed that "deaf people can do anything but hear," a sentiment that directly echoes Flournoy's insistent claims of deaf capability one hundred and thirty years before. In 1990, the passage of the Americans with Disabilities Act guaranteed deaf and other disabled people "reasonable accommodations" like sign language interpreters and notetakers at schools, public events, and places of employment, making another of Flournoy's visions, which had seemed so quixotic, a reality. Thanks to such legal protection, as well as new technology like the worldwide web, electronic mail, video-relay service, and closed captioning, deaf people enjoy access in society that would stun their nineteenth-century counterparts. As deaf activist Greg Hlibok put it in 1994, "From the time God made earth until today, this is probably the best time to be deaf" (qtd. in Solomon 43).

Yet in other ways, deaf Americans still face daunting obstacles. Even as more hearing people study American Sign Language, the majority of deaf children in the United States are not exposed to ASL, instead being taught other manual communicative systems or the oral method. In November 2005, a deaf man even started a hunger strike to protest the lack of ASL in classrooms at the Michigan School for the Deaf. In recent decades most American deaf students have come to be mainstreamed in local public schools, often with an interpreter. This arrangement has allowed greater access and some deaf students have flourished, but it has isolated other deaf children who, without deaf peers or contact with other signers or deaf role models, can easily feel stigmatized and alone. Similarly, even as deaf people make gains in society, they remain one of the more underemployed groups in the nation, and evidence of persistent discrimination regularly appears. Deaf people still have a high rate of intermarriage (90 percent according to some estimates); Gallaudet University, the National Association of the Deaf, and other institutions for deaf people still thrive; and despite all the new technology and legal access, deaf people still regularly gather at association meetings, conferences, festivals, and social events, pointing to the strong filiation they still feel for one another, the ties of language and shared experience that do not easily go away. Tellingly, even Flournoy's plan for a deaf commonwealth has reappeared in revised form: plans are under way for a new town of signers, named Laurent for Clerc and located in South Dakota. Almost one hundred families, including deaf and hearing people, have already declared their intention to settle there (Davey A1). As I write this in 2006, many deaf students, faculty, staff, and alumni at Gallaudet are protesting the appointment of a new president, who happens to be congenitally deaf. They say she has poor leadership skills, that the search process was flawed, and some people question her sign language ability (she was raised orally) and capacity to represent deaf culture. If the 1850s commonwealth debate was the most public demonstration of the contestatory nature of the deaf community during the nineteenth century, the current turmoil is attracting international attention to deaf-versus-deaf disagreement today. Whatever the outcome of this protest, we can at least note that the participants are no longer simply deaf white men. Deaf women and people of color are taking a prominent role in the debate, and their voices—coming as they do in ASL and in written English over videos and blogs on the worldwide web—are no longer always policed by hearing editors. To return to Wsevolod S. Isajiw's insight: "Ethnicity is a matter of double boundary, a boundary from within, maintained by the socialization process, and a boundary from without established by the process of intergroup relations" (122). The hearing line emerges as something not purely disadvantageous or advantageous, but potentially stifling and beneficial, and continuously worked out.

We do not yet know precisely how literature by deaf and hearing authors from the beginning of the twentieth century to the present negotiates such concerns. We need more scholarship into how the deaf presence functions in literary works by Flannery O'Connor, Carson McCullers, and other hearing authors, and how twentieth-century deaf writers like Albert Ballin, Bernard Bragg, and Henry Kisor revise or expand on the deaf authors covered in this study. Popular treatments of the hearing line have extended beyond writing to include ambitious theatrical productions, television programs, motion pictures, and films of deaf signers performing original sign language narratives and poetry, a rich cultural form that only in the last few decades has begun to attract scholarly attention.[4] These modes add additional dimensions to the discourse over the hearing line in American culture and deserve more critical exploration.

Perhaps the most intriguing and crucial development relates to controversies over medical intervention with deaf people. The arrival of hearing aids, cochlear implants, and now genetic engineering technology blurs the hearing line in new ways, giving more control over who is on the hearing or deaf side of the line and raising convoluted new questions: Is it ethical for fertility doctors to use genetic tests to screen out embryos that carry a deaf gene, a non-life-threatening trait, as happened in Australia in 2003 (Weiss A6)? Should a lesbian deaf couple be able to increase their chances of having a deaf baby by choosing a deaf sperm donor from a deaf family, as happened in 2002 (Mundy 22)? What voices can or should deaf adults have in answering such questions? Even as ASL and deaf culture gain more respect and appreciation in society, many people struggle with their feelings about deafness. Between valuing diversity and enforcing normalcy, between the desire to respect difference and create sameness, more always remains to be said.

INTRODUCTION

1. The following seminal work on race and culture has proven especially important to this study: Gates, *Signifying Monkey* and his introductory essay to *"Race," Writing, and Difference*; Morrison, *Playing in the Dark*; the essays in Wonham, *Criticism and the Color Line*; Fanon, *Black Skin, White Masks*; Lott, *Love and Theft*; Hale, *Making Whiteness*; Said, *Culture and Imperialism*; Bhabha, *Location of Culture*; and Ashcroft, Griffiths, and Tiffin, *Empire Writes Back*.

2. I am thinking here of Baynton, *Forbidden Signs*; Padden and Humphries, *Deaf in America* and *Inside Deaf Culture*; Lane, *When the Mind Hears*, *Mask of Benevolence*, and, with Bahan and Hoffmeister, *Journey into the DEAF-WORLD*; Van Cleve and Crouch, *Place of Their Own*; Joyner, *From Pity to Pride*; Gannon, *Deaf Heritage*; Burch, *Signs of Resistance*; Buchanan, *Illusions of Equality*; the essays in Van Cleve, *Deaf History Unveiled*; and Winefield, *Never the Twain Shall Meet*.

3. Because new scholarship in this area is rapidly appearing, any listing must be partial and incomplete. See, for example, Garland-Thomson, *Extraordinary Bodies*; Davis, *Enforcing Normalcy* and *Bending over Backwards*; Mitchell and Snyder, *Narrative Prosthesis*; Brueggemann, *Lend Me Your Ear*; Linton, *Claiming Disability*; and the essays in the following collections: Snyder, Brueggemann, and Garland-Thomson, *Disability Studies*; Corker and Shakespeare, *Disability/Postmodernity*; Davis, *Disability Studies Reader*; Garland-Thomson, *Freakery*; Wilson and Lewiecki-Wilson, *Embodied Rhetorics*; and Mitchell and Snyder, *Body and Physical Difference*.

4. Several recent books do examine the impact of deaf people on American intellectual life in the nineteenth century. Baynton's *Forbidden Signs* astutely explores shifting attitudes toward sign language, while Lepore's *A Is for American* usefully places Thomas Hopkins Gallaudet and Alexander Graham Bell's thinking about sign language within the larger framework of language and letters in the United States. Elisabeth Gitter's *Imprisoned Guest* and Ernest Freeberg's *Education of Laura Bridgman* consider the deaf-blind woman Laura Bridgman (1832–89) in relation to nineteenth-century culture. Of these, Baynton's study is the most valuable, although he, like the others, chooses to focus

mainly on hearing people's attitudes, and more on cultural history than on how such issues play out in literature.

5. Of course such perceptions extend well beyond the United States. Deafness (and disability more generally) is typically perceived as marginal to identities and literatures around the world. In this study I have chosen to focus on deafness and writing in nineteenth-century America, but such an approach is surely transnational and could be applied to almost any nation, literature, period, and physical difference, as scholars in deaf and disability studies have begun to demonstrate.

6. Toward the end of the century, some southern states did implement education for deaf African Americans, but these schools were always segregated and typically in poorer condition than the schools for white deaf students.

7. It was not until the twentieth century that deaf African Americans, often victims of both racism and audism (discrimination based on hearing status), began to make their identity felt on a national scale. Recently the chairman of Gallaudet University's board of trustees was a black deaf man, Glenn Anderson, and today organizations such as the National Black Deaf Advocates represent black deaf interests, although much work remains to be done. For more on the black deaf community, begin with Hairston and Smith, *Black and Deaf in America*; Dunn, "Education, Culture and Community"; Burch, *Signs of Resistance*; and Padden and Humphries, *Inside Deaf Culture*.

8. Brenda Jo Brueggemann points out that there are telling analogies between gay and deaf people. Both have been considered savage, repulsive, and perhaps insane, both frequently are compelled to pass as "normal" (heterosexual or hearing), both usually have to go outside the family and home to find others like themselves, and both often employ coming out narratives. Brueggemann's work suggests the way that deaf experience parallels that of many other groups. See *Lend Me Your Ear* 152–54.

9. Interestingly, in recent years deaf Americans who use sign language have dealt with a similar dynamic with regard to other disabled groups. In the last several decades, deaf people and their advocates have won recognition from linguists that American Sign Language is a complex human language and also recognition from anthropologists of their unique cultural forms, including folklore, common values, institutions, and behavioral norms, all leading to acknowledgment of a "deaf culture" with ASL at its center. When other disabled groups recently began to talk about a "disability culture" (see, for example, Mitchell and Snyder's documentary film *Vital Signs*), some signing deaf people

might have understandably felt that other disabled people were trying to minimize differences and take advantage of their hard-won gains. After all, other disabled groups do not have a distinct language. Deaf people and other disabled groups have both important similarities and crucial differences, just as white deaf Americans and hearing African Americans had in the nineteenth century. The challenge for scholars is to explore similarities while attending to differences, thereby uncovering both commonalities and uniqueness in the array of American minority experience.

10. In recent years deaf Americans have increasingly acknowledged similarities with black Americans. For example, in the early 1990s Fred Beam, who is both black and deaf, explained to a hearing audience that, just as the black community has people with a variety of skin tones, from quite black to quite light, so the deaf community includes individuals whose audiological status ranges from profoundly deaf to those who hear well enough to use the telephone. On a more political level, during the successful protest for a deaf president of Gallaudet University in 1988, demonstrators repeatedly invoked blacks' civil rights rhetoric. At one point they marched the mile from Gallaudet to the U.S. Capitol behind a large banner that read, in reference to Martin Luther King Jr., "We Still Have a Dream." For scholarly considerations of the parallel, see Humphries, "Of Deaf-Mutes," and Lane, *Mask of Benevolence*.

11. Edwards, "Deaf and Dumb in Ancient Greece," and Winzer, "Disability and Society," give useful overviews of attitudes toward deaf people in ancient Greece and Rome. For a discussion of Aristotle's supposed comment on deafness, see Lane, *When the Mind Hears* 427n88.

12. Other colleges for blacks were founded before or about the same time, including Lincoln University (1854), Wilberforce University (1854), and Fisk University (1867). Howard was the first black institution to establish undergraduate, graduate, and professional schools. See Smith, *Black Firsts* 98–100, and Christian, *Black Saga* 219–20. Like the National Deaf-Mute College, Howard was chartered by Congress, and both continue to receive an annual federal appropriation today. For over a century after their founding, the schools graduated a high percentage of the nation's deaf and black leaders.

13. See especially Baynton, *Forbidden Signs*.

14. In this study I do not pay a great deal of attention to writing by hearing educators of deaf students such as Thomas Hopkins Gallaudet. Baynton ably considers such texts in *Forbidden Signs*.

CHAPTER ONE

1. Clerc, "Further." This statement and much of the other deaf writing discussed in this study has been republished in my collection *A Mighty Change*.

2. Padden and Humphries's insightful analysis of what they call "the problem of voice" for twentieth-century deaf Americans helped to inspire my ideas here. In *Inside Deaf Culture*, they discuss the many ways that twentieth-century deaf people sought to make themselves heard, including through films of signers, writing, dramatic productions with both sign language and voiced English interpretation, and recent advancements like telephone relay operators. Such developments have produced both benefits and losses for culturally deaf Americans, Padden and Humphries reveal. I seek to extend their analysis by exploring the factors that shaped the emergence of deaf voices in nineteenth-century America.

3. For more on this privileging of vocal speech and its relation to deaf people, see Brueggemann, *Lend Me Your Ear* 11.

4. Here is a moment when study of the hearing line potentially offers back to our understanding of the color line, for it calls attention to the likelihood that spoken black vernacular includes gestural forms that are seldom remarked and do not show up in written English. It also implicitly points again to the existence of deaf African Americans during the period, who, though largely absent from the written historical record, probably used some system of signs within their larger oral communities.

5. For more on the empowering aspects of hybridity and ambivalence, see, for example, Bhabba, *Location of Culture* (especially chapter 6), and Young, *Colonial Desire*.

6. I am indebted here to Grace Elizabeth Hale, who makes a similar point about African Americans' efforts to assert their identity after winning freedom from slavery. See *Making Whiteness* 15.

7. Drawing on impressive research, Lane gives a colorful description of these exhibitions in *When the Mind Hears* 30–41. However, because Lane, a hearing author, chooses to write from Clerc's point of view, issues of representation and voice are problematic. Often his late-twentieth-century hearing perspective seems to shape his presentation of Clerc. For nineteenth-century reports of Sicard's popular exhibitions, see "Account of the Institution in Paris" and Ladebat, *Collection of the Most Remarkable Definitions*.

8. The story of how Gallaudet and Clerc met and returned to America together to found deaf education became something of a creation story for

culturally deaf Americans, repeatedly told in both print and sign language through the years. Today, the story is still performed at many schools for deaf students each December on Gallaudet's birthday. For more detailed discussion of the Gallaudet-Clerc tale, see my *A Mighty Change*, especially xiii–xvi, 22–31, 142–47; Van Cleve and Crouch, *Place of Their Own* 29–46; Lane, *When the Mind Hears* 155–205; and Baynton, *Forbidden Signs* 3, 7.

9. See "Account of the Institution in Paris" 234 and Lane, *When the Mind Hears* 34.

10. Despite his success as a painter, Brewster felt a keen desire for formal education. When the American Asylum opened in 1817, Brewster, then fifty-one years old, put his career on hold and enrolled in the first class alongside deaf children. He remained at the school for three years, studying English and learning the sign language brought to America by Clerc. For more on Brewster, see Lane, *Deaf Artist in Early America*.

11. One of the first recorded teachers of deaf people, Pedro Ponce de Leon, was a priest in sixteenth-century Spain. Another Spanish priest, Juan Pablo Bonet, published one of the first books on educating deaf people. In France in the eighteenth century, a priest named the Abbé Charles-Michel de l'Epée helped to popularize deaf education, publishing numerous treatises and founding the Royal National Institute for the Deaf, which Laurent Clerc later attended. Sicard, Epée's successor, was also a Catholic priest, while Thomas Hopkins Gallaudet was a Congregationalist minister. For more on the intertwining of religion and deaf education, see Lane, *When the Mind Hears* 204, 229; Baynton, *Forbidden Signs* 15–22; and Brueggemann, *Lend Me Your Ear* 158–59.

12. Despite such extreme language, Gallaudet was by all accounts a kind and gentle man who formed a relationship of equals with Clerc and who married a deaf woman, Sophia Fowler, one of his former students. For a discerning consideration of Gallaudet's "benevolent paternalism" and the impact of his religious beliefs on his views of deaf people, see Phyllis Valentin, "Thomas Hopkins Gallaudet."

13. Initially called the Connecticut Asylum for the Education and Instruction of Deaf and Dumb Persons, the new school's name was soon changed to the American Asylum in recognition of its national character. It took on its current name, the American School for the Deaf, in the 1890s. For an overview of deaf schools in the United States and the chronology in which they were founded, see Gannon, *Deaf Heritage* 16–58.

14. Harlan Lane makes a related postcolonial critique of hearing society's

treatment of deaf people in the twentieth century, arguing that the civilizing forces of "hearing paternalism" seek to make deaf people conform to hearing norms, much as colonizers in Africa tried "to supplant native languages, religions, and institutions with those of the European mother country" (*Mask* 37, 45). See Lane, *Mask of Benevolence* 31–66. For more on hearing people's control of deaf people through the schools, see Padden and Humphries, *Inside Deaf Culture* 11–36; Berger, "Uncommon Schools"; and Valentin, "Thomas Hopkins Gallaudet."

15. This is another way that nineteenth-century deaf people differ from other disabled groups, who frequently saw segregated institutionalization as more negative and oppressive.

16. Although they have diverged considerably over the years, ASL still resembles French Sign Language more closely than any other signed language. See Woodward, "Historical Bases of American Sign Language" 333–48, and Valli and Lucas, *Linguistics of American Sign Language* 15.

17. Baynton provides an insightful consideration of antebellum claims that sign language is universal. See *Forbidden Signs* 108–15.

18. It is true that when deaf people from different countries meet, they are often able to communicate through a mixture of gesture, mime, and teaching each other their signs. Used to visual communication, they typically seem to have an easier time than two hearing people who speak different vocal languages, although it would be misleading to suggest that meaningful communication is easy. I have experienced this in my own travels and at international deaf conferences like the Deaf Way II Conference in Washington, D.C., in 2002.

19. In 1998, researchers noted that deaf children in the United States and Taiwan who developed gesture systems on their own used an ergative structure, where a direct object is treated as syntactically analogous to the subject of an intransitive verb and where the object is placed before the verb. Such order appears more common in signed languages than in spoken languages; neither English nor Mandarin Chinese use an ergative structure. See DuBoff, "New Study" 1.

20. Lane presents this early group identity in terms of "we-who-use-this-language" (*A Deaf Artist* 71), although I would add that the consciousness included the experience of being audiologically deaf as well.

21. "Laurent Clerc" 110; "Trial for the Robbery of a Mute" 72; "Marriage of a Deaf and Dumb Person" 308.

22. If anyone wants to claim, with Jacques Derrida, that writing predates

speech and hearing, I would ask them to explain the difficulty that congenitally deaf people often have in learning written English. In 1995–96, the average eighteen-year-old deaf student did not read above the fourth-grade level (Johnson, "Educational" 164). The reasons for this poor performance are formidable, and persist despite such promising educational innovations as the Bilingual-Bicultural approach and Cued Speech. In addition to the obvious factor of deaf children not hearing English, Ronnie Wilbur identifies three causes: "(1) among deaf children of hearing parents, reduced language input in the early years; (2) inadequate methods of teaching written language to deaf children, in part due to the controversy concerning modality (sign or speech) and in part due to a failure to understand the complexities of the language acquisition process; and (3) reading instruction that narrowly focuses on one aspect of reading" but ignores others (146). For more on this issue, see Johnson, "Educational Reform," and the essays in Brueggemann, *Literacy and Deaf People*.

23. While Burnet's general point is valid, his example of Chinese is probably not the best, since written Chinese is not tied to specific pronunciations and is more visual. It may actually be easier to learn without hearing the spoken form of the language than written English.

24. Davis elides this distinction when he suggests that reading and writing are a kind of sign language, since "to read requires muteness and attention to nonverbal signs" (*Enforcing* 62). Even on the printed page, the differences between deaf and hearing people often cannot be completely erased.

25. Another obstacle was that deaf children typically did not arrive at the schools until they were age eight or older, which we now know is after the peak years of language acquisition had passed. Also, in the early years of deaf education, students stayed in the schools five to seven years, much less than the typical child today.

26. I am indebted here to Henry Louis Gates Jr. and Claude McKay's thoughtful introduction to Wheatley, in *Norton* 166–67.

27. As mentioned earlier, Burnet gives in to exaggerated rhetoric of savages and heathens elsewhere himself. Even when writers knew better, the hyperbolic imagery of uneducated deaf people often persisted.

28. We might fruitfully compare Burnet's assertion to Douglass arguing that the problem was not that African Americans were black, but that they were enslaved, or Fuller asserting the barrier was not that women were female, but that society offered them few career opportunities. By turning attention from essentialist features of bodily difference to the way society was organized against

their groups, these minority authors held out the hope of achieving positive change.

29. Despite the development of glosses and other systems for representing ASL on paper, Burnet's observation still holds largely true today. It was not until the advent of motion picture technology in the early twentieth century that signed lectures and performances began to be recorded and preserved.

30. Clerc also no doubt conveyed a great deal to spectators just through his gentlemanly demeanor and confident physical presence. In a study of nonverbal communication, anthropologist Albert Mehrabian reports that, in face-to-face encounters, as much as 55 percent of communication takes place nonverbally, through facial expression. See *Silent Messages* 44.

31. The manual alphabet is a system for indicating each letter of the alphabet with one hand. By changing handshapes, signers can spell out English words letter by letter. A part of American Sign Language, the manual alphabet is used to convey proper names and other select words.

32. For an insightful discussion of the current meanings of DEAF, see Padden and Humphries, *Deaf in America* 17, 39, 43.

33. It is interesting to note that Burnet, who so celebrates the visual aspects of the deaf community, could only see out of one eye; he lost most of the vision in the other to the same disease that caused his deafness at age eight (Peet 71). This loss probably made him even more aware of the primacy of vision in deaf people's lives, and added to his interest in deaf-blind people, about whom he included a section in *Tales*. Writing before the education of Laura Dewey Bridgman (1829–89) and Helen Keller (1880–1968), Burnet describes the situation of deaf-blind people as "well nigh irremediable," although he acknowledges some progress could be made (44). Here again we see how deafness intersects with other disabilities in complex fashion.

34. I take these terms from Dorothy J. Hale, who uses them in her penetrating explication of Du Bois's passage about double consciousness. See "Bakhtin" 449.

CHAPTER TWO

1. For example, in the early eighteenth century, Eliza Haywood and perhaps Daniel Defoe wrote about Duncan Campbell, a purportedly deaf seer who attracted much attention in London. Defoe probably helped to write the most influential book about him, *The History of the Life and Adventures of Mr. Duncan Campbell* (1720). Steele and Addison mentioned him quite a few times in *The Tatler* and *The Spectator*; Haywood wrote two accounts of him, *A Spy on the*

Conjuror (1724) and *The Dumb Projector* (1725); and three other volumes about him were published. As such, Campbell is the first deaf main character in English literature. Whether the real Campbell was actually deaf, and whether these books constitute novels, remains debatable. For more on Campbell and what he reveals about interpretations of deafness, see my article, "Duncan Campbell."

2. As scholars in disability studies are demonstrating, blindness and many other disabilities map as well onto larger philosophical questions and issues of civil rights. However, in early-nineteenth-century America, deafness seems to have been a particularly popular and flexible trope for the larger metaphysical concerns of the nation.

3. Following Morrison's call, in the 1990s scholars such as Robert Stepto, Shelley Fisher Fishkin, Eric Lott, David Roediger, Grace Hale, and many others produced a wave of penetrating criticism that examines the ways in which canonical literature formulates whiteness. For a helpful overview of such theoretical work, see Fishkin, "Interrogating 'Whiteness.' "

4. All poems are reprinted in Hodgson, *Facts, Anecdotes and Poetry*.

5. In an intriguing example of how prominent nineteenth-century people often appear in American deaf history, Irving and Gallaudet spent a month together on the ship *Mexico* crossing the Atlantic from New York to Liverpool. Irving, thirty-two years of age, had achieved moderate success as a writer; Gallaudet, twenty-seven, had graduated from Yale, embarked on a career as a minister, and now was headed to Europe to learn methods of deaf education (he would return with Laurent Clerc the following year). We do not have any record of their interactions, but it seems likely that they met and Irving learned the details of Gallaudet's mission.

6. Such views have a direct correlation with Thomas Alva Edison's comment that he appreciated his deafness because it helped him to concentrate. Edison, who lost much of his hearing at age twelve, often cultivated silence. At Edison's winter estate in Fort Myers, he would sometimes sit with his fishing pole for hours on a pier. However, he did not use a hook on his line, for he no more wanted to disturb the fish than he wanted to be bothered by others. See Lang, *Deaf Persons* 109.

7. We could even question whether silence exists beyond the interpretations of the perceivers; the "silences" in these texts are sometimes not literal absences of sound, but rather absences of expected or potential sounds, while other sounds continue.

8. Thomas Philbrick is the only scholar that I could locate who calls attention to Cooper's "extraordinary" emphasis on sound. While his article provides a useful starting point, Philbrick does not explore the sound imagery in detail or make a connection with deafness. See his "*Last of the Mohicans* and the Sounds of Discord."

9. Again, the hearing line offers back to our understanding of minority cultures, in this case by subtly calling attention to the existence of deaf Native Americans. We have little written documentation of them during the nineteenth century, although accounts of the 1890 massacre at Wounded Knee usually say that it began when a young deaf warrior named Black Coyote refused to give up his rifle (see, for example, Brown, *Bury My Heart at Wounded Knee* 442). Like their deaf black counterparts, deaf Native Americans no doubt found distinctive ways to live and communicate in their larger cultures. Today an organization called the Intertribal Deaf Council advocates for deaf American Indians, Alaska Natives, and First Nations. For a useful overview of scholarship on deaf Native Americans, see Kelley, "History of the American Indian Deaf." For recent accounts of deaf Native American life, see Paris and Wood, *Step into the Circle*.

10. Although he did not have significant contact with Native Americans himself, Cooper apparently got his facts right about their esteem for silence. Europeans first encountering Native Americans in the seventeenth century frequently noted their quietude. In 1671 John Ogilby wrote of the Tuscarora and Catawba tribes of Carolina: "After their Salutation they sit down; and it is usual with them to sit still almost a quarter of an hour before they speak, which is not an effect of stupidity or sullenness, but the accustom'd Gravity of their Countrey" (qtd. in Smith 316). Observing a similar phenomenon, in 1643 Roger Williams wrote:

> Their manner is upon any tidings to sit round double or treble or more, as their numbers be; I have seene neer a thousand in a round, where *English* could not well neere halfe so many sitten: Every man hath his pipe of their *Tobacco*, and a deepe silence they make, an attention give to him that speaketh. (qtd. in Smith 315–16)

Such accounts of Native American silence give credence to Cooper's depictions. His Indian characters resemble deaf people in that they have a markedly different attitude toward speech and sound than the white hearing outsiders.

11. Cooper's depictions again seem generally on the mark; Native Americans did possess a system of gestures that they used to communicate, which caused some nineteenth-century Americans to link them with deaf people. When the

deaf editor Edwin Mann gathered materials for his *The Deaf and Dumb: or, a Collection of Articles Relating to the Condition of Deaf Mutes* (1836), he included an essay by Major Stephen F. Long on the "Indian Language of Signs." Long, who traveled to the Rocky Mountains in 1819, reports that various tribes in the west were not able to communicate with each other by spoken language, but that "this difficulty is overcome by their having adopted a language of signs, which they all understand, and by means of which, the different tribes hold converse, without speaking" (183). In the remainder of the essay, Long describes Indian signs for such concepts as truth, house, eat, moon, pretty, and good, and compares these to signs used by deaf Americans. Long makes explicit what is implicit throughout much of *The Last of the Mohicans*: that Native Americans have some striking commonalities with deaf people. For more recent studies of Native American sign languages, see Davis and Supalla, "Sociolinguistic Description," and McKay-Cody, "Plains Indian Sign Language."

12. Cooper once more appears accurately to represent Native American attitudes. The merchant William Wood reported in 1634: "Garrulitie is much condemned of them, for they utter not many words, speake seldome, and then with such gravitie as is pleasing to the eare" (qtd. in Smith 314).

13. For a thoughtful consideration of Emerson's fear that "the corruption of man is followed by the corruption of language," and the relation of these ideas to deaf people's signs, see Baynton 122–23.

14. A good example is Gallaudet's popular 1824 sermon, "The Duty and Advantages of Affording Instruction to the Deaf and Dumb," in which he calls uneducated deaf people "heathen" and worse off than "the wild and untutored savage," but also praises "the almost magical facility" of Clerc's sign language (217, 230, 226).

CHAPTER THREE

1. Quoted in Winzer, "Disability and Society" 91. Interestingly, elsewhere St. Augustine makes positive mention of deaf people's sign language, noting that they could "use gestures to talk and answer questions, to teach and to make known to each other their wishes" (qtd. in Rée 120n7). Apparently Augustine did not see sign as a way to impart the gospel, however.

2. Foucault, *Madness and Civilization* 107. Perhaps not surprisingly, people conflated deafness and madness for centuries since both prompt otherwise "normal"-appearing individuals to behave in abnormal ways.

3. Along the same lines, in *Revolution in Poetic Language* (1984), Kristeva

privileges the semiotic, pre-Oedipal—that primary, anarchic raw material of signification—as the source of poetic language.

4. Nack had entered the New York Institution the year before. Scott subsequently wrote of his visit to the school: "I have never witnessed a more interesting spectacle than was there exhibited" (20n7).

5. Sigourney's introduction to deaf people came in 1814, when she taught eight-year-old Alice Cogswell (the deaf daughter of prominent Hartford surgeon Mason Cogswell) as best she could in a class with hearing students. Alice deeply affected Sigourney, who later called her "a child of genius" and "the darling of all" (*Letters* 251, 253). Sigourney went on to become one of the American Asylum's most important benefactors. When Alice fell mortally ill at age twenty-five, Sigourney, along with Gallaudet and Catherine Beecher (sister of Harriet Beecher Stowe), visited and tried in vain to engage her. In the early 1840s, when two educated deaf-blind women, Julia Brace and Laura Bridgman, met for the first time, Sigourney was there to witness the event. At a memorial service for Gallaudet in the early 1850s, she read a poem of tribute. For more on Sigourney and the deaf community, see Lane, *When the Mind Hears* 178–81.

6. Gallaudet met the eight-year-old Alice in the spring of 1814 and succeeded in teaching her the written English word "hat." This encounter set in motion the events that led to Gallaudet going to Europe to learn methods of deaf education and returning with Laurent Clerc the following year. For more on the Gallaudet-Clerc story, see chapter 1, note 8.

7. Brace was the first deaf-blind American to receive an education. After losing her hearing and sight to a fever when she was five, she received some instruction, and at age eighteen moved to the American Asylum for the Deaf, where she lived from 1825 until 1860. She captured the attention of educators and curious civic leaders. Visitors would sometimes test her memory and perception "by giving her their watches and employing her to restore them to the right owner," which she apparently always did correctly (Burnet, *Tales* 139). In Brace, Samuel Gridley Howe found encouragement to pursue education of the deaf-blind girl Laura Bridgman, who would receive more fame.

8. "Phebe P. Hammond," a biographical sketch perhaps written by Sigourney, provides an illuminating glimpse into how one deaf girl thought about herself in heaven. While enduring her final illness at home in Massachusetts in 1829, the twelve-year-old Phebe repeatedly had conversations in sign language with her cousin, assuring her that she knew and accepted the gospel. When Gallaudet wrote her a letter reminding her of her faith, she signed, "I do trust in

Jesus Christ. . . . I shall go to Heaven. I desire to see all the deaf and dumb there" (303). Phebe's last remark shows how, when she imagined the bliss of heaven, she immediately thought of the pleasure of seeing other deaf people. That seems more important to her than hearing. It is unclear if Phebe expected to become hearing, but either way, her comment reveals that in her vision her deaf identity would not be effaced in heaven, but still be part of her.

9. Notably, here Sigourney does not portray deaf people becoming hearing in heaven. In contrast to "Alice," which she had published ten years before, she seems to imagine deaf and hearing both transcending the limits of their silence and speech to find bliss. In this way, we can see how Sigourney's imaginative conception of heaven moved beyond Isaiah's prophecy and the strictly doctrinal, and how her understanding of deafness and hearingness became more ambivalent and complex.

10. Stillness is a fundamental part of all the world's religions. Hesychasm, the tradition of achieving communion with God through inner quietude, dates back at least until the fourth century. The Trappist order and Quakers make silence an especially central part of their worship. It can hint at the inexpressible, suggesting larger truths incapable of being put into mere words. For an overview of this topic, see McCumsey, "Silence."

11. Although not always the case, as "The Deaf Girl" reminds us (the officer cites Marianne's speechlessness as the reason he cannot marry her), in other instances the appeal of deaf women to hearing men seems clearly related to their muteness and perceived helplessness. This attitude shows up in some later-nineteenth-century comical verse by anonymous hearing poets. In "A Model Woman," the admired title character never gossips, never demands things, never chastises her husband when he stays out late, and "never talks of women's rights" because "The woman's deaf and dumb" (Hodgson 224). "A Mute Suggestion" flippantly expresses the attraction of deaf female speechlessness more succinctly:

> Noise and strife
>> Would never come,
> If my wife
>> Were deaf and dumb. (Hodgson 225)

However, these poems seem more of a reaction to assertive hearing women than a genuine desire for deaf wives, and present deaf femininity more as passive blankness than as three-dimensional humanity.

12. First coined by Tom Humphries in 1975, "audism" has come to signify,

according to Dirksen Bauman, "1. The notion that one is superior based on one's ability to hear. . . . 2. A system of advantage based on hearing ability. 3. A metaphysical orientation that links human identity with speech" (245). For a helpful overview of the concept and its use, see Bauman's "Audism: Exploring the Metaphysics of Oppression."

13. These literary episodes also partake of the sublime, of Freud's *unheimlich*, and of Barthes's concept of *jouissance*, where horror is transformed into libidinal gratification.

14. Extending Said's theory of Orientalism, we might even speculate that such characterizations of deafness as Bierce's potentially contributed to the formation of American national identity as *hearing* in the late nineteenth century.

CHAPTER FOUR

1. I say "mostly lost" because short films made in the early twentieth century of older signers give us a fairly good idea of what late-nineteenth-century sign language looked like. We have a 1902 film made by Thomas Edison of a deaf woman signing "The Star-Spangled Banner," and quite a few short films from the 1910s made by the National Association of the Deaf in an effort to preserve sign language.

2. In 1854, the hearing superintendent of the Ohio Institution, Collins Stone, lamented that despite progress, deaf students seldom attained "the free and accurate use" of written English. "The results of education which are attained in our Institutions, are to so great an extent incomplete and partial," he wrote (4). See his *On Difficulties Encountered by the Deaf and Dumb in Learning Language*, where "language" of course refers to English rather than sign.

3. To give a small example of such usage: When I taught English composition at Gallaudet University in the early 1990s, some of my students wrote "big different," presumably because that is how the concept "very different" is often signed in ASL.

4. In her autobiographical pamphlet, Adele Jewel mentions a private school for "poor colored children" who were deaf or blind near Niagara Falls, indicating that such institutions did exist at midcentury (20). For more on deaf African Americans, see introduction, note 7.

5. Adele Jewel and Laura Redden Searing both married, but they did the bulk of their writing while single. After publishing her unusual pamphlet, Jewel wed and had three children, but the union soon ended unhappily, whereupon she revised the pamphlet and again started selling it on the streets. Searing married

in 1876 at the age of thirty-six, after her reputation as a journalist and poet was well established.

6. However, this did not prevent Searing from writing forcefully about women's right to vote. See Jones, "On Signing an Appeal."

7. Deaf Americans celebrated such moments of deaf-hearing collaboration, which both on Martha's Vineyard and with Gallaudet include hearing people learning their language of signs, something unusual in the nineteenth century that almost always caused deaf people to feel respected and valued.

8. The deaf leader John Carlin was moved to comment on this marital trend in an 1869 address: "This condition [deafness] is so controlling that male mutes *naturally* prefer female mutes for wives and females the males for husbands" (my emphasis, "Oration" 268).

9. The editor also admiringly compared a person born deaf producing respectable poetry with "all the niceties of accent, measure, and rhythm," like Carlin, to a congenitally blind person painting a landscape.

10. Baynton makes a similar point in his useful examination of silence as a metaphor for deaf experience in the nineteenth century in *Forbidden Signs* 22–25. For more general considerations of silence and deafness, see Padden and Humphries, *Deaf in America* 91–109; Brueggemann, *Lend Me Your Ear* 223–26; and Davis, *Enforcing Normalcy* 108–25.

11. Although the state legislature authorized the Michigan school in 1848, it was not opened until six years later, in 1854, when Jewel was close to twenty years old. The school initially occupied a rented house in Flint. For a brief history of the school, see Gannon, *Deaf Heritage* 30–31.

12. Spofford was the lone presenter at the 1850 event who did not write his address in advance. His signs were spontaneously translated into voiced English by Gallaudet's oldest son, Thomas, and a transcription made and subsequently published in the *Annals*. Spofford, presumably chosen to be orator because he was an eloquent signer, thus was another of the few deaf Americans who made it into print without writing themselves.

13. For example, Jesus says that "unless you change and become like children, you will never enter the kingdom of heaven" (Matthew 18:3).

14. Deaf people like Clerc did serve in supervisory positions, and some deaf graduates of the first schools founded schools on their own, including the Indiana School for the Deaf (William Willard, 1843) and the Kansas School for the Deaf (Philip A. Emery, 1861), but these deaf leaders apparently were not called fathers. The term seems to have been reserved for hearing benefactors.

For his part, in his 1850 address Clerc referred to deaf attendees as "dear friends" (Rae, "Testimonial" 200).

15. Adding to the irony was that Gallaudet had taught at the American Asylum for thirteen years, resigning in 1830, while Clerc continued to teach at the school from its inception until 1858, retiring at age seventy-three. Clerc no doubt contributed to deaf people's veneration of Gallaudet by consistently praising his friend. He concluded his address in 1854 by writing, "Neither greatness, nor favor, nor rank, could seduce or dazzle him. [He was] benevolent, obliging and kind to everybody. No wonder, therefore, that he was beloved by all the deaf and dumb" (Rae, "Ceremonies" 26).

16. In 1815 Clerc wrote in French, "The deaf and dumb, who never heard nor spoke, have never lost either hearing or speech, therefore cannot lament either the one or the other. And he who has nothing to lament cannot be unhappy, consequently the deaf and dumb are not unhappy. Besides it is a great consolation for them to be able to replace hearing by writing, and speech by signs" (Ladebat 93).

17. After losing his hearing, the disoriented Flournoy withdrew from the University of Georgia, visited the American Asylum in Hartford, where he witnessed the flourishing deaf community there, and then voluntarily committed himself to the Lunatic Asylum in South Carolina for a short time. Returning to Georgia, he was seen as something of a crazy figure: he apparently rode about on a donkey, rarely cut his hair, and wore a raincoat in all weather. Taking an active interest in public affairs, in 1833 he unsuccessfully lobbied the state legislature for a school for deaf students in Georgia, and in 1835 argued that every African American should be expulsed from America. Flournoy did have an older brother, Marcus, who was deaf, so he was exposed to deaf issues his entire life and presumably knew at least a home sign. His father's attempts to disinherit Marcus may have provided Flournoy with an early glimpse of discrimination against deaf people. Hannah Joyner provides an excellent overview of Flournoy's career in *From Pity to Pride* 107–19. For more on Flournoy, see Coulter, *John Jacobus Flournoy*. For historical interpretations of the commonwealth debate, see Lepore, *A Is for American* 107–10; my anthology, *A Mighty Change* 161–211; Van Cleve and Crouch, *Place of Their Own* 60–69; and Padden and Humphries, *Deaf in America* 112–14.

18. Deaf organizations that started forming around midcentury were "of the deaf," also based on hearing status rather than language use. However, while voting members of these organizations were deaf people, they rarely if ever

explicitly banned hearing involvement. For example, it is difficult to imagine the New England Gallaudet Association of the Deaf preventing deaf members from bringing their hearing children to functions, and hearing adults who signed sometimes attended and presented at meetings. Flournoy's attempt at exclusion made his plan more radical.

19. According to the federal census, Flournoy owned fourteen slaves in 1860: seven male and seven female, ranging in age from two to sixty-five years old.

20. Schools for deaf students were founded in the South in Kentucky (1823), Virginia (1839), Tennessee (1845), North Carolina (1845), Georgia (1846), South Carolina (1849), Arkansas (1850), Missouri (1851), Louisiana (1852), Mississippi (1854), Texas (1857), and Alabama (1858). See Gannon, *Deaf Heritage* 20–34.

21. Porter also occasionally added notes that commented on deaf correspondents' claims. In response to P. H. Confer's statement that deaf people were frequently despised by hearing people, Porter asserted that "such a feeling [had] no foundation for it in fact" (Confer 87).

CHAPTER FIVE

1. For example, Aristophanes, in his play *Knights*, has one character call another deaf, apparently to emphasize the latter's clownish nature; Chaucer, in *The Canterbury Tales*, makes his exuberant, playful Wife of Bath somewhat deaf; Shakespeare has one of his most popular comic characters, Falstaff, briefly act deaf in *Henry IV Part Two*, and so forth. However, in these works actual deafness has a decidedly minor role, and profoundly deaf characters are almost entirely absent.

2. See, for instance, Ginsberg, *Passing and the Fictions of Identity*; Wald, *Crossing the Line*; Browder, *Slippery Characters*; and Pfeiffer, *Race Passing*.

3. For more on this American burlesque tradition, see Allen, *Horrible Prettiness*; Reynolds, *Beneath the American Renaissance*; Lott, *Love and Theft*; and Browder, *Slippery Characters*.

4. Edward Miner Gallaudet (1837–1917) mentions Twain a number of times in his journals. When Gallaudet resided in Hartford during the years 1887–89, he lived not far from Twain. At one point Gallaudet agreed to raise funds to buy a home for a minister, Joseph Twichell, who was retiring. Because Twichell was a close friend of Twain's, Gallaudet asked for Twain's support. "He was favorable to the plan," wrote Gallaudet, "but did not want to put his name down." The next day Gallaudet sent his son to Twain's house with a note in a sealed envelope. Twain read it and promptly wrote a check for $1,500. Unfortunately, we do not

know what this note said. Yet Twain's relationship with Gallaudet adds another dimension to the way his personal life seems repeatedly to have converged with deafness. See Boatner, *Voice of the Deaf* 117–19.

·5. Although I have not located evidence that Twain visited the American Asylum, he did apparently have a positive opinion of the education such institutions offered. In *Following the Equator* (1897), he writes that "the methods used in the asylums are rational" because instructors gradually develop children's capacity without jumping ahead in lessons, as teachers in public schools do (597). Twain concludes that "it is a pity that we can't educate all the children in the asylums" (605). However, he appears to base these claims on the example of Helen Keller, who was not educated at an asylum (although her teacher, Anne Sullivan, was a graduate of the Perkins School for the Blind, where she had shared a cottage with the deaf-blind woman Laura Bridgman for several years), raising questions of just how familiar Twain was with deaf and deaf-blind education.

6. Twain met Keller on March 31, 1895. He gives a memorable description of the encounter in his autobiography, describing how the girl could follow a long story he told by placing her hand on his lips; how when a name was difficult, Anne Sullivan would fingerspell it swiftly upon Keller's hand; and how she recognized him as he patted her lightly on the head as he left—a feat that baffled Twain at the time. In his biography, Albert Bigelow Paine reports that later, Keller dispelled the mystery by telling Twain that she had identified him by the smell of his hand. See the 1924 version of Twain's autobiography, 2:297–303, and Paine, *Mark Twain* 1273–75.

7. For a consideration of people with disabilities passing as able-bodied, see Siebers, "Disability as Masquerade."

8. A related anecdote exists about Charles Dickens, who, when lecturing in the west, was said to be struck by an intelligent-looking lady who watched him intently. Afterward he asked about her and was informed that "she is a deaf-mute, but she has read all your books, and she was very anxious to see you, although she could hear nothing you said" (Hodgson 59–60).

9. It is a bit lamentable that the most adult representation of a deaf person by a nineteenth-century hearing American shows up in Melville's mediocre *The Confidence-Man*, while the most flattering depiction of ASL appears in this substandard tale. Perhaps this dynamic just underscores the difficulties surrounding a hearing author writing a deaf character accurately and well.

10. We could compare Swett's anecdote to other narratives of encounters

with a dominant group, like Equiano's description of meeting white slave trad-
ers in Africa, that position what the majority usually sees as different and
inferior (blackness, deafness) as comforting and human instead.

11. While Chamberlain was not allowed to serve, several deaf and hard-of-
hearing Americans did fight in the Civil War. William Simpson, a hard-of-
hearing man from St. Louis, went to New York, pretended to be hearing, and
enlisted there. Another account tells of a deaf Confederate prisoner whose guard
was also deaf; they supposedly carried on lively conversations in sign language.
Two other deaf men, Hartwell Chamberlayne and William M. Berkeley, served in
the Confederate army, which may have been more willing to let deaf men fight
due to its pressing need for soldiers. See Gannon, *Deaf Heritage* 10.

12. Stories of deaf imposters and identity confusion showed up in mainstream newspapers too. For examples, see Hodgson, *Anecdotes* 60–94.

13. Lott develops this point about blackface quite compellingly in his *Love
and Theft*. In writing this section, I drew especially on his chapter "Racial
Pleasure and Class Formation in the 1840s" (136–68) and his essay on Twain,
"Mr. Clemens and Jim Crow: Twain, Race, and Blackface."

14. Although the people in *Tom Sawyer* do not suspect Injun Joe's masquerade, in nineteenth-century America deaf individuals were sometimes accused of
being frauds with evil intentions. When Edmund Booth was traveling in the mid-
west in 1839, he was stopped by citizens who thought he resembled a murderer on
a handbill. They believed he pretended to be deaf, and only after inspecting his
luggage did they let him go. See Edmund Booth, *Forty-Niner* 2. Similarly, during
the Civil War, Union soldiers refused to believe that an eighteen-year-old southern boy, Joshua Davis, was deaf, thinking him a spy instead. Finally an officer who
knew the manual alphabet fingerspelled to him, "Are you deaf?" Joshua responded in signs, and the officer ordered him to be released. See Gannon 9.

EPILOGUE

1. In *Forbidden Signs*, Baynton gives an excellent account of cultural factors
that contributed to the rise of sign language in the first part of the century and
of oralism in the later decades. He shows that while manualists like Thomas
Hopkins Gallaudet were primarily evangelical Christians interested in securing
religious redemption for deaf people, later oralists saw themselves as progres-
sives who were raising deaf people from an antiquated system and helping them
to assimilate into society. Both groups believed their approaches were beneficial
and displayed patronizing attitudes toward deaf Americans. Lane gives a helpful

look at Alexander Graham Bell in *When the Mind Hears*. For more on oralism, see Van Cleve and Crouch, *Place of Their Own*, and Winefield, *Never the Twain Shall Meet*.

2. Bell argued against deaf intermarriage out of the belief that it would increase the number of deaf people. He himself had a deaf mother and wife and, in contrast to attitudes we saw earlier, was unperturbed by the idea of deaf-hearing sexual unions.

3. Again, it is instructive to compare deaf people's situation with racial issues. Just as Bell viewed deafness as a blemish on humanity to be removed, so he and other eugenicists interpreted blackness as a sign of inferiority. "English, Irish, Scottish, German, Scandinavian, and Russian blood seems to mingle beneficially with the Anglo-Saxon American, apparently producing increased vigor in offspring," he wrote at one point (qtd. in Lane, *When the Mind Hears* 355). Bell's crusade was part of the larger eugenics movement that would later lead to sterilization laws, racial restrictions on immigration, and Bell's own warnings that America was committing race suicide. In these ways, Bell, like many of his contemporaries, championed hearingness and whiteness against the abjecting foreignness of deafness and color.

4. For examples of such scholarship, start with Padden and Humphries, *Deaf in America* and *Inside Deaf Culture*; Peters, *Deaf American Literature*; the essays in Bauman, Nelson, and Rose, *Signing the Body Poetic*; and Schuchman, *Hollywood Speaks*.

(((BIBLIOGRAPHY)))

"An Account of the Institution in Paris for the Education of the Deaf and Dumb." Rpt. in *The Deaf and Dumb, or, a Collection of Articles Relating to the Condition of Deaf Mutes.* Ed. Edwin John Mann. Boston: D. K. Hitchcock, 1836. 232–41.

Alcott, Louisa May. *Little Women, or, Meg, Jo, Beth & Amy* [1869]. New York: Thomas Y. Crowell Co., 1926.

Alger, Horatio. *Paul Prescott's Charge: A Story for Boys.* Boston: Loring, 1865.

Allen, Robert C. *Horrible Prettiness: Burlesque and American Culture.* Chapel Hill: University of North Carolina Press, 1991.

Anderson, Benedict. *Imagined Communities: Reflections on the Origin and Spread of Nationalism.* London: Verso, 1983.

"An Appeal to the Ladies." *The Deaf-Mutes' Friend* 1 (Sept. 1869): 30–31.

Ashcroft, Bill. "Is That the Congo? Language as Metonymy in the Post-Colonial Text." *World Literatures Written in English* 29:2 (Autumn 1989): 3–10.

Ashcroft, Bill, Gareth Griffiths, and Helen Tiffin. *The Empire Writes Back: Theory and Practice in Post-Colonial Literatures.* London: Routledge, 1989.

Bakhtin, Mikhail. *Rabelais and His World* [1965]. Trans. Helene Iswolsky. Bloomington: Indiana University Press, 1984.

Baldwin, James. "If Black English Isn't a Language, Then Tell Me, What Is?" [1979]. *Ten on Ten: Major Essayists on Recurring Themes.* Ed. Robert Atwan. Boston: Bedford, 1992. 321–24.

Ballin, Albert. *The Deaf Mute Howls* [1930]. Washington, D.C.: Gallaudet University Press, 1998.

Barber, Karin, and P. F. de Moraes Farias. *Discourse and Its Disguises: The Interpretation of African Oral Texts.* Birmingham, England: Centre of West African Studies, University of Birmingham, 1989.

Barnard, Frederick A. P. *Observations on the Education of the Deaf and Dumb.* Boston: J. H. Low, 1834.

Barnard, Henry. *Tribute to Gallaudet. A Discourse in Commemoration of the Life, Character, and Services of the Rev. Thomas H. Gallaudet, with an Appendix* [1852]. 2nd ed. Hartford: Hutchinson & Ballard, 1859.

Batson, Trent, and Eugene Bergman, eds. *Angels and Outcasts: An Anthology of*

Deaf Characters in Literature [1973]. Washington, D.C.: Gallaudet University Press, 1987.

Bauman, H.-Dirksen L. "Audism: Exploring the Metaphysics of Oppression." *Journal of Deaf Studies and Deaf Education* 9:2 (2004): 239–46.

Bauman, H.-Dirksen L., Jennifer L. Nelson, and Heidi M. Rose, eds. *Signing the Body Poetic: Essays on American Sign Language Literature*. Berkeley: University of California Press, 2006.

Baynton, Douglas C. *Forbidden Signs: American Culture and the Campaign against Sign Language*. Chicago: University of Chicago Press, 1996.

Bell, Alexander Graham. *Memoir upon the Formation of a Deaf Variety of the Human Race*. Washington, D.C.: Government Printing Office, 1884.

Benton, Joel. *Life of Hon. Phineas T. Barnum*. Philadelphia: Edgewood, 1891.

Ben-Ze'ev, Aaron. "Envy and Pity." *International Philosophical Quarterly* 33 (1993): 3–19.

Berger, Jane. "Uncommon Schools: Institutionalizing Deafness in Early-Nineteenth-Century America." *Foucault and the Government of Disability*. Ed. Shelley Tremain. Ann Arbor: University of Michigan Press, 2005. 153–71.

Bergson, Henri. *Time and Free Will: An Essay on the Immediate Data of Consciousness*. Trans. F. L. Pogson. London: George Allen & Unwin, 1910.

Bérubé, Michael. "Afterword." *Disability Studies: Enabling the Humanities*. Ed. Sharon L. Snyder, Brenda Jo Brueggemann, and Rosemarie Garland-Thomson. New York: Modern Language Association, 2002. 337–43.

Bhabha, Homi K. *The Location of Culture*. London: Routledge, 1994.

Bierce, Ambrose. "Chickamauga" [1889]. *The Collected Works of Ambrose Bierce*. Vol. 2. New York: Neale Publishing Co., 1909. 46–57.

Bloom, Harold. *Agon: Towards a Theory of Revisionism*. New York: Oxford University Press, 1982.

Blount, Roy, Jr. "Mark Twain's 'Skeleton Novelette'" and "Mark Twain's Reconstruction." *Atlantic Monthly* 288 (July–Aug. 2001): 49–51, 67–81.

Boatner, Maxine Tull. *Voice of the Deaf: A Biography of Edward Miner Gallaudet*. Washington, D.C.: Public Affairs Press, 1959.

Booth, Edmund. *Edmund Booth, Forty-Niner: The Life Story of a Deaf Pioneer*. Stockton: San Joaquin Pioneer and Historical Society, 1953.

——. [Letters on the proposal for a deaf commonwealth]. *American Annals of the Deaf and Dumb* 10 (1858): 40–42, 72–79, 151–54.

Bragg, Bernard. *Lessons in Laughter: The Autobiography of a Deaf Actor*. As

signed to Eugene Bergman. Washington, D.C.: Gallaudet University Press,
1989.

Browder, Laura. *Slippery Characters: Ethnic Impersonators and American
Identities*. Chapel Hill: University of North Carolina Press, 2000.

Brown, Dee. *Bury My Heart at Wounded Knee: An Indian History of the
American West*. New York: Holt, Rinehart & Winston, 1970.

Brueggemann, Brenda Jo. *Lend Me Your Ear: Rhetorical Constructions of
Deafness*. Washington, D.C.: Gallaudet University Press, 1999.

——, ed. *Literacy and Deaf People: Cultural and Contextual Perspectives*.
Washington, D.C.: Gallaudet University Press, 2004.

Buchanan, Robert M. *Illusions of Equality: Deaf Americans in School and
Factory 1850–1950*. Washington, D.C.: Gallaudet University Press, 2002.

Burch, Susan. *Signs of Resistance: American Deaf Cultural History, 1900 to World
War II*. New York: New York University Press, 2002.

Burnet, John R. "Annual Examination at the New York Institution." *The Deaf-
Mutes' Friend* 1 (Aug. 1869): 232–34.

——. "Fiction as Reading for Deaf-Mutes." *The Deaf-Mutes' Friend* 1 (May
1869): 188.

——. "Letters from New York." *The Deaf-Mutes' Friend* 1 (May 1869): 157–58.

——. [On the proposal for a deaf commonwealth]. *American Annals of the Deaf
and Dumb* 10 (1858): 89–90.

——. *Tales of the Deaf and Dumb, with Miscellaneous Poems*. Newark, N.J.:
Benjamin Olds, 1835.

Carlin, John. "Advantages and Disadvantages of the Use of Signs." *American
Annals of the Deaf and Dumb* 4 (1852): 49–57.

——. Letter to Laurent Clerc. 1858. Rpt. in *American Annals of the Deaf and
Dumb* 10 (1858): 88–89.

——. "The Mute's Lament." *American Annals of the Deaf and Dumb* 1 (1847): 15–16.

——. "The National College for Mutes." *American Annals of the Deaf and Dumb*
6 (1854): 175–83.

——. "Oration" [at Empire State Association of Deaf-Mutes convention]. *The
Deaf-Mutes' Friend* 1:9 (Sept. 1969): 262–70.

——. "Oration." *Inauguration of the College for the Deaf and Dumb, at
Washington, District of Columbia*. Washington, D.C.: Gideon and Pearson,
1864. 45–55.

——. [Reminiscences on the Life of Laurent Clerc]. 1885. Clerc Papers no. 34a,
Manuscripts and Archives, Yale University Library.

Cawelti, John G. "Cooper and the Frontier Myth and Anti-Myth." *James Fenimore Cooper: New Historical and Literary Contexts*. Ed. W. M. Verhoeven. Amsterdam and Atlanta: Rodopi, 1993. 151–59.

Chamberlain, William. *In Memoriam: A Tribute to the Memory of Thomas Brown*. Flint: Michigan School for the Deaf, 1888.

——. [On calls for a national deaf convention]. *The Deaf-Mutes' Friend* 1 (Aug. 1869): 241–42.

——. [On deaf people hearing sounds]. *The Deaf-Mutes' Friend* 1 (Mar. 1869): 67.

——. [On the proposal for a deaf commonwealth]. *American Annals of the Deaf and Dumb* 10 (1858): 84–87.

——. "Proceedings of the Third Convention of the New England Gallaudet Association of Deaf-Mutes." *American Annals of the Deaf and Dumb* 10 (1858): 205–15.

——. "Salutatory." *The Deaf-Mutes' Friend* 1 (Jan. 1869): 18.

Chamberlayne, H. M. [On the proposal for a deaf commonwealth]. *American Annals of the Deaf and Dumb* 10 (1858): 159–60.

"The Children of Silence." *American Annals of the Deaf and Dumb* 1 (July 1848): 209.

Chivers, T. H. "The Beautiful Silence: Composed on Seeing a Beautiful Deaf Mute Lady." *Virginalia; or Songs of My Summer Nights. A Gift of Love for the Beautiful*. Philadelphia: Lippincott, Grambo & Co., 1853. 19–21.

Christian, Charles M. *Black Saga: The African American Experience*. New York: Houghton Mifflin, 1995.

Clerc, Laurent. "Address." *Inauguration of the College for the Deaf and Dumb, at Washington, District of Columbia*. Washington, D.C.: Gideon and Pearson, 1864. 41–43.

——. *An address written by Mr. Clerc: and read by his request at a public examination of the pupils in the Connecticut Asylum, before the governour and both houses of the legislature, 28th May, 1818*. Hartford, Conn.: Hudson & Co., Printers, 1818.

——. [Answers to questions]. Transcribed by Clerc from *Albany Daily Advertiser*, Nov. 12, 1816. Clerc Papers no. 69, Manuscripts and Archives, Yale University Library.

——. *The Diary of Laurent Clerc's Voyage from France to America in 1816*. Hartford: American School for the Deaf, 1952. Rpt. from Clerc Papers no. 68, Manuscripts and Archives, Yale University Library.

——. [Further answers to questions]. Transcribed by Clerc from *Philadelphia Gazette & Daily Advertiser*, Dec. 11, 1816. Clerc Papers no. 69, Manuscripts and Archives, Yale University Library.

——. "Laurent Clerc." *Tribute to Gallaudet: A Discourse in Commemoration of the Life, Character, and Services, of the Rev. Thomas H. Gallaudet, with an Appendix* [1852]. 2nd ed. Hartford: Hutchinson & Bullard, 1859. 102–12.

——. Letter to Frederick A. P. Barnard [1835]. Clerc Papers no. 38, Manuscripts and Archives, Yale University Library.

Cohen, Jeffrey Jerome. "Preface: In a Time of Monsters." *Monster Theory: Reading Culture*. Ed. Jeffrey Jerome Cohen. Minneapolis: University of Minnesota Press, 1996. vii–xiii.

Confer, P. H. [On the proposal for a deaf commonwealth]. *American Annals of the Deaf and Dumb* 10 (1858): 87–88.

Cooper, James Fenimore. *The Last of the Mohicans* [1826]. New York: Viking Penguin, 1986.

Corker, Mairian, and Tom Shakespeare, eds. *Disability / Postmodernity: Embodying Disability Theory*. London: Continuum, 2002.

Coulter, E. Merton. *John Jacobus Flournoy: Champion of the Common Man in the Antebellum South*. Savannah: Georgia Historical Society, 1942.

Craft, William. *Running a Thousand Miles for Freedom* [1860]. Athens: University of Georgia Press, 1999.

Davey, Monica. "As Town for Deaf Takes Shape, Debate on Isolation Re-emerges." *New York Times* (Mar. 21, 2005): A1, A12.

Davis, Jeffrey, and Sam Supalla. "A Sociolinguistic Description of Sign Language Use in a Navajo Family." *Sociolinguistics in Deaf Communities*. Ed. Ceil Lucas. Washington, D.C.: Gallaudet University Press, 1995. 77–106.

Davis, Lennard J. *Bending over Backwards: Disability, Dismodernism, and Other Difficult Positions*. New York: New York University Press, 2002.

——, ed. *The Disability Studies Reader*. New York: Routledge, 1997.

——. *Enforcing Normalcy: Deafness, Disability, and the Body*. New York: Verso, 1995.

"The Deaf and Dumb." *Connecticut Mirror* (Jan. 27, 1817). Rpt. in *Facts, Anecdotes and Poetry Relating to the Deaf and Dumb*. Ed. Edwin Allan Hodgson. New York: Deaf-Mutes' Journal Print, 1891. 95–97.

"The Deaf Girl." *The Deaf and Dumb, or, a Collection of Articles Relating to the Condition of Deaf Mutes*. Ed. Edwin John Mann. Boston: D. K. Hitchcock, 1836. 275–83.

"The Deaf-Mute College: Commencement Exercises at the National Capital."
Washington Correspondence Boston Advertiser. Rpt. in *The Deaf-Mutes'
Friend* 1 (July 1869): 194–97.

"Deaf Mutes." *Encyclopedia Americana*. Rpt. in *The Deaf and Dumb, or, a
Collection of Articles Relating to the Condition of Deaf Mutes*. Ed. Edwin
John Mann. Boston: D. K. Hitchcock, 1836. 20–44.

The Deaf-Mutes' Friend 1. Henniker, N.H.: Swett and Chamberlain, publishers,
1869.

"A Deaf Soldier." *American Annals of the Deaf and Dumb* 20 (1875): 54.

Derrida, Jacques. "Racism's Last Word." *"Race," Writing, and Difference*. Ed.
Henry Louis Gates Jr. Chicago: University of Chicago Press, 1986. 329–38.

——. *Writing and Difference* [1967]. Trans. Alan Bass. Chicago: University of
Chicago Press, 1978.

Douglas, Mary. *Purity and Danger: An Analysis of Concepts of Pollution and
Taboo*. London: Routledge, 1966.

DuBoff, Rob. "New Study Shows Children have Innate Ability to
Communicate." *Chicago Maroon* 109 (Jan. 27, 1998): 1.

Du Bois, W. E. B. *The Souls of Black Folk* [1903]. New York: W. W. Norton, 1999.

——. "The Talented Tenth." *The Negro Problem: A Series of Articles by
Representative Negroes of Today*. New York: J. Pott & Company, 1903. 31–75.

Dunn, Lindsay. "Education, Culture and Community: The Black Deaf
Experience." *Deafness: Life and Culture II: A Deaf American Monograph*. Ed.
Mervin Garretson. Silver Spring, Md.: National Association of the Deaf,
1995. 37–41.

Edmundson, Mark. *Nightmare on Main Street: Angels, Sadomasochism, and the
Culture of the Gothic*. Cambridge, Mass.: Harvard University Press, 1997.

"Education of the Deaf and Dumb." *American Annals of Education*. Series 3
(1834): 53. Rpt. in *The Deaf and Dumb, or, a Collection of Articles Relating to
the Condition of Deaf Mutes*. Ed. Edwin John Mann. Boston: D. K.
Hitchcock, 1836. 2–19.

Edwards, Martha L. "Deaf and Dumb in Ancient Greece." *The Disability
Studies Reader*. Ed. Lennard J. Davis. New York: Routledge, 1997. 29–51.

Ellison, Ralph. *Going to the Territory*. New York: Random House, 1986.

——. *Shadow and Act* [1964]. New York: Vintage, 1995.

Emerson, Ralph Waldo. *The Conduct of Life* [1856]. Boston: Ticknor and Fields,
1861.

——. *Nature* [1836]. *Selections from Ralph Waldo Emerson*. Ed. Stephen E. Whicher. Boston: Houghton Mifflin, 1960.

Emery. P. A. [On the proposal for a deaf commonwealth]. *American Annals of the Deaf and Dumb* 10 (1858): 154–59.

"Empire State Association of Deaf-Mutes: Proceedings of the Third Biennial Convention." *The Deaf-Mutes' Friend* 1 (Sept. 1869): 257–69.

Equiano, Olaudah. "The Interesting Narrative of the Life of Olaudah Equiano, or Gustavas Vassa, the African" [1789]. *My Soul Has Grown Deep: Classics of the Early African-American Literature*. Ed. John Edgar Wideman. New York: Ballantine, 2001. 176–352.

Fanon, Frantz. *Black Skin, White Masks* [1952]. New York: Grove, 1967.

Faux, William. *Memorable Days in America: Being a Journal of a Tour to the United States*. London: W. Simpkin and R. Marshall, 1823.

Fiedler, Leslie. *The Return of the Vanishing Native*. New York: Stein and Day, 1968.

Finnegan, Ruth. *Orality and Literacy*. Oxford: Basil Blackwell, 1988.

Fishkin, Shelley Fisher. "Interrogating 'Whiteness,' Complicating 'Blackness': Remapping American Culture." *Criticism and the Color Line: Desegregating American Literary Studies*. Ed. Henry B. Wonham. New Brunswick, N.J.: Rutgers University Press, 1996.

——. *Was Huck Black? Mark Twain and African-American Voices*. New York: Oxford University Press, 1993.

Flournoy, John Jacobus. [Letters advocating a deaf commonwealth]. *American Annals of the Deaf and Dumb* 8 (1856): 120–25; 10 (1858): 42–45, 79–83, 140–51.

Foucault, Michel. *Madness and Civilization: A History of Insanity in the Age of Reason* [1965]. Trans. Richard Howard. New York: Vintage, 1988.

Freeberg, Ernest. *The Education of Laura Bridgman: First Deaf and Blind Person to Learn Language*. Cambridge, Mass.: Harvard University Press, 2002.

Freud, Sigmund. *Jokes and Their Relation to the Unconscious* [1905]. Trans. James Strachey. New York: W. W. Norton, 1960.

——. *Three Essays on Sexuality* [1905]. *The Standard Edition of the Complete Psychological Works of Sigmund Freud*. Trans. and ed. James Strachey. Vol. 7. London: Hogarth Press and the Institute of Psycho-Analysis, 1978. 125–245.

——. "The 'Uncanny' " [1919]. *The Standard Edition of the Complete Psychological Works of Sigmund Freud*. Trans. and ed. James Strachey. Vol.

17. London: Hogarth Press and the Institute of Psycho-Analysis, 1978. 217–56.

Fuller, Margaret. "The Great Lawsuit: Man Versus Men. Woman Versus Women" [1843]. *The Norton Anthology of American Literature*. 6th ed. Ed. Nina Baym. New York: W. W. Norton, 2003. 1620–54.

Gallaudet, Edward Miner. *Life of Thomas Hopkins Gallaudet: Founder of Deaf-Mute Instruction in America*. New York: Henry Holt, 1888.

Gallaudet, Thomas Hopkins. "The Duty and Advantages of Affording Instruction to the Deaf and Dumb" [1824]. *The Deaf and Dumb, or, a Collection of Articles Relating to the Condition of Deaf Mutes*. Ed. Edwin John Mann. Boston: D. K. Hitchcock, 1836. 217–31.

——. "On the Natural Language of Signs; and Its Value and Uses in the Instruction of the Deaf and Dumb." *American Annals of the Deaf and Dumb* 1 (Oct. 1847): 55–60; (Jan. 1848): 79–93.

Gannon, Jack R. *Deaf Heritage: A Narrative History of Deaf America*. Silver Spring, Md.: National Association of the Deaf, 1981.

Garland-Thomson, Rosemarie. *Extraordinary Bodies: Figuring Physical Disability in American Culture and Literature*. New York: Columbia University Press, 1997.

——, ed. *Freakery: Cultural Spectacles of the Extraordinary Body*. New York: Columbia University Press, 1997.

Gates, Henry Louis, Jr., ed. *"Race," Writing, and Difference*. Chicago: University of Chicago Press, 1986.

——. *The Signifying Monkey: A Theory of African-American Literary Criticism*. New York: Oxford University Press, 1988.

Gates, Henry Louis, Jr., and Nellie Y. McKay, eds. "Phillis Wheatley." *The Norton Anthology of African American Literature*. New York: W. W. Norton, 1997. 164–67.

Gee, James Paul, and Walter J. Ong. "An Exchange on American Sign Language and Deaf Culture." *Language and Style: An International Journal* 16 (1983): 234–37.

Gibson, Nigel C. *Fanon: The Postcolonial Imagination*. Cambridge: Polity Press, 2003.

Gilbert, Sandra M., and Susan Gubar. *The Madwoman in the Attic: The Woman Writer and the Nineteenth-Century Literary Imagination*. New Haven, Conn.: Yale University Press, 1984.

Ginsberg, Elaine K., ed. *Passing and the Fictions of Identity*. Durham, N.C.: Duke University Press, 1996.

(((BIBLIOGRAPHY)))

Girard, René. *The Scapegoat*. Trans. Yvonne Freccero. Baltimore: Johns
    Hopkins University Press, 1988.

Gitter, Elisabeth. *The Imprisoned Guest: Samuel Howe and Laura Bridgman, the
    Original Deaf-Blind Girl*. New York: Farrar, Straus and Giroux, 2001.

Gramsci, Antonio. *Selections from the Prison Notebooks*. Ed. and trans. by
    Quintin Hoare and Geoffrey Nowell-Smith. New York: International
    Publishers, 1971.

Groce, Nora Ellen. *Everyone Here Spoke Sign Language: Hereditary Deafness on
    Martha's Vineyard*. Cambridge, Mass.: Harvard University Press, 1985.

Gutwirth, Marcel. *Laughing Matter: An Essay on the Comic*. Ithaca, N.Y.:
    Cornell University Press, 1993.

Hairston, Ernest, and Linwood Smith. *Black and Deaf in America: Are We That
    Different?* Silver Spring, Md.: T. J. Publishers, 1983.

Hale, Dorothy J. "Bakhtin in African American Literary Theory." *ELH* 61:2
    (1994): 445–71.

Hale, Grace Elizabeth. *Making Whiteness: The Culture of Segregation in the
    South, 1890–1940*. New York: Vintage, 1998.

Harris, Joel Chandler. "The Fate of Mr. Jack Sparrow" [1880]. *The Complete
    Tales of Uncle Remus*. Boston: Houghton Mifflin, 1955. 19–65.

——. "The Wonderful Tar-Baby Story" [1881]. *The Complete Tales of Uncle
    Remus*. Boston: Houghton Mifflin, 1955. 6–8.

Hawthorne, Nathaniel. *The English Notebooks 1856–1860*. Ed. Thomas
    Woodson and Bill Ellis. Columbus: Ohio State University Press, 1997.

Hobbes, Thomas. *Human Nature* [1650]. *Human Nature and Decopore Politico*.
    Oxford: Oxford University Press, 1999.

Hodgson, Edwin Allan, ed. *Facts, Anecdotes and Poetry, Relating to the Deaf and
    Dumb*. New York: Deaf-Mutes' Journal Print, 1891.

Humphries, Tom. "Of Deaf-Mutes, the *Strange*, and the Modern Deaf Self."
    Deaf World: A Historical Reader and Primary Sourcebook. Ed. Lois Bragg.
    New York: New York University Press, 2001. 348–64.

"Important from Dix's Department." *New York Herald* (June 30, 1863): item
    #7687.

Irving, Washington. *The Sketch-Book of Geoffrey Crayon, Gent.* [1819–20]. New
    York: Oxford University Press, 1998.

Isajiw, Wsevolod W. "Definitions of Ethnicity." *Ethnicity* 1 (1974): 111–24.

Jameson, Frederic. "Pleasure: A Political Issue." *The Ideologies of Theory, 1971–
    86*. Vol. 2. Minneapolis: University of Minnesota Press, 1988.

Jankowski, Katherine A. *Deaf Empowerment: Emergence, Struggle, and Rhetoric.* Washington, D.C.: Gallaudet University Press, 1997.

Jewel, Adele M. *A Brief Narrative of the Life of Mrs. Adele M. Jewel (Being Deaf and Dumb).* Jackson, Mich.: Daily Citizen Steam Printing House, ca. 1860.

Johnson, James Weldon. *The Autobiography of an Ex-Coloured Man* [1912]. New York: Vintage, 1989.

Johnson, Robert Clover. "Educational Reform Meets Deaf Education at a National Conference." *Sign Language Studies* 4:2 (Winter 2004): 99–117.

Jones, Judy Yaeger. "On Signing an Appeal." *Deafness: Life and Culture II: A Deaf American Monograph.* Vol. 45 (1995). Ed. Mervin D. Garretson. Silver Spring, Md.: National Association of the Deaf, 1995. 63–66.

Jones, Judy Yaeger, and Jane E. Vallier, eds. *Sweet Bells Jangled: Laura Redden Searing: A Deaf Poet Restored.* Washington, D.C.: Gallaudet University Press, 2003.

Joyner, Hannah. *From Pity to Pride: Growing Up Deaf in the Old South.* Washington, D.C.: Gallaudet University Press, 2004.

Kawash, Samira. "*The Autobiography of an Ex-Coloured Man*: (Passing for) Black Passing for White." *Passing and the Fictions of Identity.* Ed. Elaine K. Ginsberg. Durham, N.C.: Duke University Press, 1996. 59–74.

Keller, Helen. "Our Mark Twain." *Midstream: My Later Life.* Garden City, N.Y.: Doubleday, Doran & Co., 1929. 47–69.

Kelley, Walter P. "History of the American Indian Deaf." *Deaf Studies Today: A Kaleidoscope of Knowledge, Learning and Understanding.* Ed. Bryan K. Eldredge, Doug Stringham, and Minnie Mae Wilding-Diaz. Orem, Utah: Deaf Studies Today, 2005. 217–23.

Key, Francis Scott. "Lines Given to William Darlington, A Deaf and Dumb Boy." *Poems of the Late Francis S. Key, Esq.* New York: Robert Carter and Brothers, 1857. 134–35.

Kisor, Henry. *What's That Pig Outdoors? A Memoir of Deafness.* New York: Penguin, 1991.

Krentz, Christopher. "Duncan Campbell and the Discourses of Deafness." *Prose Studies* 27:1, 2 (Apr.–Aug. 2005): 39–52.

——, ed. *A Mighty Change: An Anthology of Deaf American Writing 1816–1864.* Washington, D.C.: Gallaudet University Press, 2000.

Kristeva, Julia. *Powers of Horror: An Essay on Abjection.* Trans. Leon S. Roudiez. 1980. Rpt., New York: Columbia University Press, 1982.

——. *Revolution in Poetic Language*. Trans. Margaret Waller. New York: Columbia University Press, 1984.

Ladd, Paddy. *Understanding Deaf Culture: In Search of Deafhood*. Clevedon, Buffalo, Toronto, and Sydney: Multilingual Matters Ltd., 2003.

Ladebat, M. Laffon de, ed. *A Collection of the Most Remarkable Definitions and Answers of Massieu and Clerc*. Trans. J. H. Sievrac. London: Cox and Baylis, 1815.

Lane, Harlan. *A Deaf Artist in Early America: The Worlds of John Brewster Jr.* Boston: Beacon, 2004.

——. *The Mask of Benevolence: Disabling the Deaf Community*. New York: Knopf, 1992.

——. *When the Mind Hears: A History of the Deaf*. New York: Vintage, 1984.

Lane, Harlan, Robert Hoffmeister, and Ben Bahan. *A Journey into the DEAF-WORLD*. San Diego: Dawn Sign Press, 1996.

Lane, Harlan, Richard C. Pillard, and Mary French. "Origins of the American Deaf-World: Assimilating and Differentiating Societies and Their Relation to Genetic Patterning." *Sign Language Studies* 1:1 (Fall 2000): 17–44.

Lang, Harry G. *Edmund Booth: Deaf Pioneer*. Washington, D.C.: Gallaudet University Press, 2004.

Lang, Harry G., and Bonnie Meath-Lang. *Deaf Persons in the Arts and Sciences: A Biographical Dictionary*. Westport, Conn.: Greenwood Press, 1995.

Lazarus, Emma. *The Poems of Emma Lazarus*. New York: Houghton Mifflin, 1889.

Lepore, Jill. *A Is for American: Letters and Other Characters in the Newly United States*. New York: Alfred A. Knopf, 2002.

Levine, Lawrence. *Black Culture and Black Consciousness: Afro-American Folk Thought from Slavery to Freedom*. New York: Oxford University Press, 1977.

Lewis, David Levering. *W. E. B. Du Bois: Biography of a Race 1868–1919*. New York: Henry Holt and Co., 1993.

Leyda, Jay. *The Melville Log: A Documentary Life of Herman Melville, 1819–1891*. Fairfield, Conn.: Gordian Press, 1969.

Linton, Simi. *Claiming Disability: Knowledge and Identity*. New York: New York University Press, 1998.

Lipsitz, George. "The Possessive Investment in Whiteness: Racialized Social Democracy and the 'White' Problem in American Studies." *American Quarterly* 47 (Sept. 1995): 369–87.

Long, Stephen F. "Indian Language of Signs." *The Deaf and Dumb; Or, a Collection of Articles Relating to the Condition of Deaf Mutes.* Ed. Edwin John Mann. Boston: D. K. Hitchcock, 1836. 182–91.

Lott, Eric. *Love and Theft: Blackface Minstrelsy and the American Working Class.* New York: Oxford University Press, 1993.

———. "Mr. Clemens and Jim Crow: Twain, Race, and Blackface." *Criticism and the Color Line: Desegregating American Literary Studies.* Ed. Henry B. Wonham. New Brunswick, N.J.: Rutgers University Press, 1996. 30–42.

Ludovici, Anthony. *The Secret of Laughter.* New York: Viking, 1933.

Mairs, Nancy. *Waist-High in the World: A Life among the Nondisabled.* Boston: Beacon, 1996.

"Marriage of a Deaf and Dumb Person." Rpt. in *The Deaf and Dumb.* Ed. Edwin John Mann. Boston: D. K. Hitchcock, 1836. 307–8.

Matterson, Stephen. "Introduction." *The Confidence-Man: His Masquerade.* By Herman Melville. New York: Penguin, 1990. vii–xxxvi.

McCarthy, Michael. *Dark Continent: Africa as Seen by Americans.* Westport, Conn.: Greenwood, 1983.

McCumsey, Elizabeth. "Silence." *The Encyclopedia of Religion.* Ed. Mircea Eliade. Vol. 13. New York: Macmillan, 1987. 321–24.

McKay-Cody, Melanie. "Plains Indian Sign Language: A Comparative Study of Alternate and Primary Signers." M.A. thesis, University of Arizona, 1996.

Mehrabian, Albert. *Silent Messages.* Belmont, Calif.: Wadsworth, 1971.

Melville, Herman. *The Confidence-Man: His Masquerade* [1857]. New York: Penguin, 1990.

———. "Fragments from a Writing Desk, No. 2" [1839]. *The Writings of Herman Melville,* Vol. 9: *The Piazza Tales and Other Prose Pieces 1839–1860.* Evanston, Ill.: Northwestern University Press, 1987. 197–204.

———. "Hawthorne and his Mosses" [1850]. *Moby-Dick, Billy Budd, and Other Writings.* New York: Library of America, 2000. 911–28.

———. *The Letters of Herman Melville.* Ed. Merrell R. Davies and William H. Gilman. New Haven, Conn.: Yale University Press, 1960.

———. *Moby-Dick, or, The Whale* [1851]. New York: Penguin, 1992.

———. *Redburn: His First Voyage* [1849]. Boston: The St. Botolph Society, 1924.

Mitchell, David T. "Narrative Prosthesis and the Materiality of Metaphor." *Disability Studies: Enabling the Humanities.* Ed. Sharon L. Snyder, Brenda Jo Brueggemann, and Rosemarie Garland-Thomson. New York: Modern Language Association, 2002. 15–30.

Mitchell, David T., and Sharon L. Snyder, eds. *The Body and Physical Difference: Discourses of Disability.* Ann Arbor: University of Michigan Press, 1997.

———. *Narrative Prosthesis: Disability and the Dependencies of Discourse.* Ann Arbor: University of Michigan Press, 2000.

———, dirs. *Vital Signs: Crip Culture Talks Back.* Brace Yourselves Productions, 1996.

Mitchell, Ross E., and Michael A. Karchmer. "Chasing the Mythical Ten Percent: Parental Hearing Status of Deaf and Hard of Hearing Students in the United States." *Sign Language Studies* 4:2 (Winter 2004): 138–63.

"A Model Woman." *Yonkers Statesman.* Rpt. in *Facts, Anecdotes and Poetry Relating to the Deaf and Dumb.* Ed. Edwin Allan Hodgson. New York: Deaf-Mutes' Journal Print, 1891. 224.

Montiglio, Silvia. *Silence in the Land of Logos.* Princeton, N.J.: Princeton University Press, 2000.

Morreall, John. *Taking Laughter Seriously.* Albany: State University of New York Press, 1983.

Morrison, Toni. *Playing in the Dark: Whiteness and the Literary Imagination.* Cambridge, Mass.: Harvard University Press, 1992.

———. "Unspeakable Things Unspoken: The Afro-American Presence in American Literature." *Michigan Quarterly Review* 28 (Winter 1989): 1–34.

Mundy, Liza. "A World of Their Own." *Washington Post Magazine* (Mar. 31, 2002): 22+.

"A Mute Suggestion." *Facts, Anecdotes and Poetry Relating to the Deaf and Dumb.* Ed. Edwin Allan Hodgson. New York: Deaf-Mutes' Journal Print, 1891. 225.

Nack, James. *The Legend of the Rocks, and Other Poems.* New York: E. Conrad, 1827.

Naipaul, V. S. *The Mimic Men* [1967]. New York: Vintage, 1995.

Nelson, Jennifer L., and Bradley S. Berens. "Spoken Daggers, Deaf Ears, and Silent Mouths: Fantasies of Deafness in Early Modern England." *The Disability Studies Reader.* Ed. Lennard J. Davis. New York: Routledge, 1997. 52–74.

Nietzsche, Friedrich. *On the Genealogy of Morals* [1887]. Trans. Walter Kaufman and R. J. Hollingdale. New York: Vintage, 1989.

Nooy, Juliana de. *Derrida, Kristeva, and the Dividing Line: An Articulation of Two Theories of Difference.* New York: Garland, 1998.

Not as Deaf as He Seems: An Ethiopean Farce. Clyde, Ohio: A. D. Ames, 1865.

Oliver, Kelly. *Reading Kristeva: Unraveling the Double-bind*. Bloomington: Indiana University Press, 1993.

Oring, Elliott. *Jokes and Their Relations*. Lexington: University Press of Kentucky, 1992.

Padden, Carol, and Tom Humphries. *Deaf in America: Voices from a Culture*. Cambridge, Mass.: Harvard University Press, 1988.

———. *Inside Deaf Culture*. Cambridge, Mass.: Harvard University Press, 2005.

Paine, Albert Bigelow. *Mark Twain: A Biography*. 3 vols. New York: Harper & Brothers, 1912.

"A Pantomimic Wedding." *New York Sun*. Rpt. in *The Deaf-Mutes' Friend* 1 (Nov. 1869): 333–34.

Paris, Damara Goff, and Sharon Kay Wood, eds. *Step into the Circle: The Heartbeat of American Indian, Alaskan Native, and First Nations Deaf Communities*. Salem, Ore.: AGO Publications, 2002.

Parker, Hershel. *Herman Melville: A Biography*. Vol. 2, 1851–1891. Baltimore: Johns Hopkins University Press, 2002.

Peet, Isaac Lewis. "John Robertson Burnet." *American Annals of the Deaf and Dumb* 20 (1875): 55–72.

Peters, Cynthia L. *Deaf American Literature: From Carnival to the Canon*. Washington, D.C.: Gallaudet University Press, 2000.

Pfeiffer, Kathleen. *Race Passing and American Individualism*. Amherst: University of Massachusetts Press, 2003.

"Phebe P. Hammond." *The Deaf and Dumb, or, a Collection of Articles Relating to the Condition of Deaf Mutes*. Ed. Edwin John Mann. Boston: D. K. Hitchcock, 1836. 295–306.

Philbrick, Thomas. "*The Last of the Mohicans* and the Sounds of Discord." *American Literature* 43 (1971): 25–41.

"The Poetry of the Deaf." *Harper's New Monthly Magazine* 68 (1884): 588–98.

Provine, Robert R. *Laughter: A Scientific Investigation*. New York: Viking, 2000.

Quarles, Benjamin. *Black Abolitionists*. New York: Oxford University Press, 1969.

Rae, Luzerne, ed. "Ceremonies at the Completion of the Gallaudet Monument." *American Annals for the Deaf and Dumb* 7 (1854): 19–54.

———, ed. "Testimonial of the Deaf Mutes of New England to Messrs. Gallaudet and Clerc." *American Annals for the Deaf and Dumb* 3 (1851): 41–64. Rpt. in *Tribute to Gallaudet: A Discourse in Commemoration of the Life, Character, and Services of the Rev. Thomas H. Gallaudet, with an Appendix* [1852]. 2nd ed. Hartford: Hutchinson & Bullard, 1859. 189–205.

Ranger, Terence. "Connexions between 'Primary Resistance' Movements and Modern Mass Nationalisms in East and Central Africa." *Journal of African History* 9:3 (1968): 437–54, 631–42.

Rée, Jonathan. *I See a Voice: Deafness, Language and the Senses—A Philosophical History*. New York: Henry Holt, 1999.

Reynolds, David S. *Beneath the American Renaissance: The Subversive Imagination in the Age of Emerson and Melville*. Cambridge, Mass.: Harvard University Press, 1988.

———. *Walt Whitman's America: A Cultural Biography*. New York: Knopf, 1995.

"Richmond News and Gossip." *Charleston Mercury* (Mar. 15, 1862): 1.

Roediger, David. *The Wages of Whiteness: Race and the Making of the American Working Class*. New York: Verso, 1991.

Rogin, Michael Paul. *Subversive Genealogy: The Politics and Art of Herman Melville*. Berkeley: University of California Press, 1985.

Rundle, Rhonda L. "Essential or Not, Push Is On to Check Infants for Hearing Problems." *Wall Street Journal* (Apr. 8, 1998): A1.

Rutherford, Susan. *A Study of Deaf American Folklore*. Burtonsville, Md.: Linstock, 1993.

Said, Edward W. *Culture and Imperialism*. New York: Vintage, 1993.

———. *Orientalism*. New York: Pantheon, 1978.

———. *The World, the Text, and the Critic*. Cambridge, Mass.: Harvard University Press, 1983.

Scheler, Max. *Ressentiment*. Trans. Lewis B. Coser and William W. Holdheim. Milwaukee: Marquette University Press, 1994.

Schuchman, John S. *Hollywood Speaks: Deafness and the Film Entertainment Industry*. Urbana: University of Illinois Press, 1999.

Scott, Moses Y. *The Deaf and Dumb; a Poem*. New York: Elam Bliss, 1819.

Searing, Laura Redden. "A Few Words about the Deaf and Dumb." *American Annals of the Deaf and Dumb* 10 (1858): 177–81.

———. "The Realm of Singing" [pub. as "Down Low" ca. 1872]. *Sweet Bells Jangled: Laura Redden Searing: A Deaf Poet Restored*. Ed. Judy Yaeger Jones and Jane E. Vallier. Washington, D.C.: Gallaudet University Press, 2003. 206–12.

Sedgwick, Eve Kosofsky. *Epistemology of the Closet*. Berkeley: University of California Press, 1990.

Seiss, Joseph A. *The Children of Silence; Or, The Story of the Deaf*. Philadelphia: Porter & Coates, 1887.

Siebers, Tobin. "Disability as Masquerade." *Literature and Medicine* 23.1 (2004): 1–22.

———. *The Subject and Other Subjects: On Ethical, Aesthetic, and Political Identity.* Ann Arbor: University of Michigan Press, 1998.

Sigourney, Lydia Huntley. *Letters to My Pupils: With Narrative and Biographical Sketches.* New York: Robert Carter & Brothers, 1853.

———. *Scenes in My Native Land.* Boston: James Munroe & Co. 1845.

———. *Select Poems.* 3rd ed. Philadelphia: Frederick W. Greenough, 1838.

———. *Select Poems.* Philadelphia: Carey & Hart, 1848.

"The Sign Language: Graphic Description of a Church Service Among the Deaf and Dumb." *The Deaf-Mutes' Friend* 1 (July 1869): 197–99.

Smith, Bruce R. *The Acoustic World of Early Modern England: Attending to the O-Factor.* Chicago: University of Chicago Press, 1999.

Smith, Jessie Carney, ed. *Black Firsts: 2,000 Years of Extraordinary Achievement.* Detroit and Washington, D.C.: Visible Ink, 1994.

Snyder, Sharon L., Brenda Jo Brueggemann, and Rosemarie Garland-Thomson, eds. *Disability Studies: Enabling the Humanities.* New York: Modern Language Association. 2002.

Solomon, Andrew. "Defiantly Deaf." *New York Times Magazine* (Aug. 28, 1994): 38+.

Sontag, Susan. "The Aesthetics of Silence." *A Susan Sontag Reader.* New York: Vintage, 1983. 182–204.

Southard, N. [Visit to American Asylum]. *Youth's Cabinet* 3 (Sept. 10, 1840): 146.

Spivak, Gayatri. "Can the Subaltern Speak? Speculations on Widow Sacrifice." *Marxism and the Interpretation of Culture.* Ed. Cary Nelson and Lawrence Grossberg. Urbana: University of Illinois Press, 1988. 271–313.

Stallybrass, Peter, and Allon White. *The Politics and Poetics of Transgression.* Ithaca, N.Y.: Cornell University Press, 1986.

Stanford, Raney. "The Romantic Hero and that Fatal Selfhood." *Centennial Review* 12:4 (Fall 1968): 440–43. Rpt. in *Ahab.* Ed. Harold Bloom. New York: Chelsea, 1991. 36–38.

Steiner, George. *Language and Silence: Essays on Language, Literature, and the Inhuman* [1958]. New York: Atheneum, 1982.

Steiner, Stan. *The New Indians.* New York: Harper & Row, 1968.

Stone, Collins. *On Difficulties Encountered by the Deaf and Dumb in Learning Language.* Columbus, Ohio: Statesman Steam Book and Job Press, 1854.

Stowe, Harriet Beecher. *Uncle Tom's Cabin, or Life Among the Lowly* [1852]. New York: Penguin, 1986.

Swett, William B. "Life and Adventures of William B. Swett." Trans. and ed. by William Chamberlain. *The Deaf-Mutes' Friend* 1 (Jan. 1869): 1–6.

Szwed, John F. "Race and the Embodiment of Culture." *Ethnicity* 2.1 (1975): 19–33.

"Thanksgiving at the Indiana Institute." *The Deaf-Mutes' Friend* 1 (Jan. 1869): 24–26.

Thoreau, Henry David. *Walden, or Life in the Woods* [1854]. New York: Signet, 1980.

———. *A Week on the Concord and Merrimack Rivers* [1849]. Boston: Houghton Mifflin, 1906.

Trachtenberg, Alan. "Foreword." *Horrible Prettiness: Burlesque and American Culture.* By Robert C. Allen. Chapel Hill: University of North Carolina Press, 1991. xi–xiv.

"Trial for the Robbery of a Mute." *N.Y. Com. Advertiser.* Rpt. in *The Deaf and Dumb: Or, a Collection of Articles Relating to the Condition of Deaf Mutes.* Ed. Edwin John Mann. Boston: D. K. Hitchcock, 1836. 72–75.

Turner, Frederick J. *The Frontier in American History.* Huntington, N.Y.: Krieger, 1976.

Turner, William W. Letter to John J. Flournoy. Dec. 6 1855. Rpt. in *American Annals of the Deaf and Dumb* 8 (1856): 118–20.

Twain, Mark. *Adventures of Huckleberry Finn* [1885]. Boston: Bedford, 1995.

———. *The Adventures of Tom Sawyer* [1876]. London: Octopus Books, 1978.

———. *The Autobiography of Mark Twain: Including Chapters Now Published for the First Time.* Ed. Charles Neider. New York: Harper & Brothers, 1959.

———. *Following the Equator: A Journey around the World* [1897]. New York: Dover Publications, 1989.

———. "How the Author was Sold in Newark." *Sketches New and Old.* Hartford: American, 1893. 103–5.

———. *Life on the Mississippi* [1875–83]. New York: Library of America, 1985.

———. "A Little Note to M. Paul Bourget" [1897]. *How to Tell a Story and Other Essays.* St. Clair Shores, Mich.: Scholarly Press, 1977.

———. *Mark Twain's Autobiography.* Ed. Albert Bigelow Paine. 2 vols. New York: Harper & Brothers, 1924.

———. *Mark Twain's Speeches.* New York: Harper & Brothers, 1910.

———. "A Murder, a Mystery, and a Marriage." *Atlantic Monthly* 288 (July–Aug. 2001): 54–64.

——. *Roughing It* [1871]. Hartford: American, 1891.

Valentin, Phyllis. "Thomas Hopkins Gallaudet: Benevolent Paternalism and the Origins of the American Asylum." *Deaf History Unveiled: Interpretations from the New Scholarship*. Ed. John Vickrey Van Cleve. Washington, D.C.: Gallaudet University Press, 1993. 53–73.

Valli, Clayton, and Ceil Lucas. *The Linguistics of American Sign Language*. Washington, D.C.: Gallaudet University Press, 1992.

Van Cleve, John Vickrey, ed. *Deaf History Unveiled: Interpretations from the New Scholarship*. Washington, D.C.: Gallaudet University Press, 1993.

Van Cleve, John Vickrey, and Barry A. Crouch. *A Place of Their Own: Creating the Deaf Community in America*. Washington, D.C.: Gallaudet University Press, 1989.

"Visit to the American Asylum." Rpt. in *The Deaf and Dumb, or, a Collection of Articles Relating to the Condition of Deaf Mutes*. Ed. Edwin John Mann. Boston: D. K. Hitchcock, 1836. 286–89.

Wald, Gayle. *Crossing the Line: Racial Passing and Twentieth-Century U.S. Literature and Culture*. Durham, N.C.: Duke University Press, 2000.

Weiss, Rick. "Screening Embryos for Deafness." *Washington Post* (July 14, 2003): A6.

Wheatley, Phillis. "On Being Brought from Africa to America." *The Norton Anthology of African American Literature*. Ed. Henry Louis Gates Jr. and Nellie Y. McKay. New York: W. W. Norton, 1997. 171.

Whitman, Walt. *Complete Poetry and Selected Prose*. Ed. James E. Miller Jr. Boston: Houghton Mifflin, 1959.

Whorf, Benjamin Lee. *Language, Thought, and Reality: Selected Writings*. Ed. John B. Carroll. Cambridge, Mass.: MIT Press, 1956.

Wiggin, Kate Douglas. *The Birds' Christmas Carol* [1886]. Boston: Houghton Mifflin, 1891.

Wilbur, Ronnie. "Language: Reading and Writing." *Gallaudet Encyclopedia of Deaf People and Deafness*. Ed. John V. Van Cleve. Vol. 2. New York: McGraw-Hill, 1987. 146–51.

Wilson, James C., and Cynthia Lewiecki-Wilson, eds. *Embodied Rhetorics: Disability in Language and Culture*. Carbondale: Southern Illinois University Press, 2001.

Winefield, Richard. *Never the Twain Shall Meet: Bell, Gallaudet, and the Communications Debate*. Washington, D.C.: Gallaudet University Press, 1987.

Winzer, Margaret A. "Disability and Society Before the Eighteenth Century: Dread and Despair." *The Disability Studies Reader*. Ed. Lennard J. Davis. New York: Routledge, 1997. 75–109.

Wonham, Henry B., ed. *Criticism and the Color Line: Desegregating American Literary Studies*. New Brunswick, N.J.: Rutgers University Press, 1996.

Woodward, James. "Historical Bases of American Sign Language." *Understanding Language through Sign Language Research*. Ed. Patricia Simple. New York: Academic Press, 1978. 333–48.

Wrigley, Owen. *The Politics of Deafness*. Washington, D.C.: Gallaudet University Press, 1996.

Young, Robert J. C. *Colonial Desire: Hybridity in Theory, Culture and Race*. London: Routledge, 1995.

(((INDEX)))

Abjection: in deaf authors' work, 141, 143, 167; of deaf characters by hearing authors, 34, 106, 107, 111, 112, 118, 125, 127, 129, 132, 164, 232 (n. 3); Kristeva's theory of, 17, 100, 104–6, 128

Affiliation, 14, 138–39, 147

African Americans, 14, 15–16, 64, 91, 163, 216 (n. 6), 219–20 (n. 28); and blackface minstrelsy, 76, 175, 191; and black vernacular English, 43, 55; deaf, 8, 161, 214 (nn. 6–7), 216 (n. 4), 226 (n. 4); differences from deaf Americans, 8–9, 48; and Flournoy, 161, 228 (n. 17); historical parallels with white deaf Americans, 2, 9–13, 35, 37, 100; and miscegenation, 119; and racism, 13, 54; and Twain, 172, 186, 198; and writing, 11, 23–24, 45, 50, 135. *See also* Black vernacular English; Color line; Slavery

African Free Schools, 12, 35

Alcott, Louisa May, 182, 183

Alger, Horatio, 172, 192–93

American Annals of the Deaf and Dumb, 133, 148, 152, 187, 227 (n. 12); and Carlin, 139, 142, 144; and deaf commonwealth debate, 153, 154, 157, 158

American Asylum for the Deaf and Dumb (Hartford, Conn.), 133, 217

(nn. 10, 13), 224 (n. 7), 228 (n. 15); and Booth, 137, 158; and Flournoy, 162, 228 (n. 17); founding of, 33, 34; Gallaudet and Clerc honored at (1850), 148–51; and Sigourney, 108, 114, 116, 224 (n. 5); and Twain, 179, 230 (n. 5)

American Museum, Barnum's, 175, 189

American Sign Language (ASL), 5, 42, 56, 57, 83, 132, 134, 152, 160, 226 (n. 3), 230 (n. 9); as binding deaf Americans together, 12, 43; emergence of, 2, 35, 41; and manual alphabet, 220 (n. 31); relationship to other sign languages, 42, 218 (n. 16); status today, 208–9, 210, 211; and Twain, 186; as unwritten, 24, 220 (n. 29). *See also* Sign language

Anderson, Benedict, 145

Apess, William, 22, 47

Appropriation, by deaf authors, 25, 45–46, 52, 57, 143

Aristotle, 10, 215 (n. 11)

Ashcroft, Bill, 25, 45, 56

Audism, 125, 165, 214 (n. 7), 225–26 (n. 12)

Bakhtin, Mikhail, 56, 57

Bannaker, Benjamin, 10

Barnard, F. A. P., 29, 49, 102

(n. 6), 227–28 (n. 14), 228 (n. 16);
address to Connecticut legislature
(1818), 40–45, 46–47, 160; and
deaf commonwealth debate, 159,
162, 163; at dedication of Gallaudet monument, 151, 228 (n. 15);
first addresses in America (1816),
22, 28–35, 39, 143; at inauguration
of college, 164–65; at tribute to
(1850), 150, 152

Cohen, Jeffrey Jerome, 106

Colonialism, 11, 14, 25, 37, 42, 48, 61,
131, 132, 217–18 (n. 14); and Clerc,
28, 37, 39, 46; and deaf commonwealth debate, 18, 154, 157, 158, 159,
160, 163, 164; Fanon on, 135–37,
138; and filiation, 138

Color line: and blackface minstrelsy,
191–92; and passing, 176, 186; and
power, 15–16; relationship to hearing line, 2, 8, 13, 15–16, 18, 24, 83,
104, 118, 191–92, 216 (n. 4)

Condillac, Etienne Bonnot de, 28, 41

Confer, P. H., 161–62, 229 (n. 21)

Connecticut Asylum for the Educa-
tion and Instruction of Deaf and
Dumb Persons. *See* American
Asylum for the Deaf and Dumb

Cooper, James Fenimore, 3, 64, 67, 75,
78, 88, 94, 101, 203, 222–23 (nn. 8,
10–12); *The Last of the Mohicans*,
63, 74, 78–88, 222 (n. 8)

Craft, Ellen, 5, 177, 189–90

Craft, William, 189–90; *Running a
Thousand Miles for Freedom*, 5,
189–90

Croneberg, Carl, 208

Davis, Lennard J., 16, 21, 23, 26, 68,
219 (n. 24)

Deaf community, 2, 7, 11, 16, 18, 52, 61,
146, 151–52; beginnings as intertwined with hearing people, 138,
146, 149, 150; and Booth, 158, 159;
and Carlin, 141, 145, 160; connection of, 60, 146, 147, 188; and deaf
associations, 151, 163; deaf people
finding way to, 49, 53, 58, 146, 147;
deaf people not part of, 148, 162;
and deaf periodicals, 133, 134, 151;
emergence of, through schools,
39, 40, 46, 47, 95, 145, 148, 151; and
gender, 134, 135, 161; heterogeneity
of, 49, 132, 154, 215 (n. 10); and
Martha's Vineyard, 29, 54, 138; and
race, 8, 134–35, 148, 160, 214 (n. 7);
role of writing in, 17, 132, 133–34,
135, 146; sign language at center of,
24, 57, 132–33; and Sigourney, 224
(n. 5); and Twain, 179

Deaf-Mutes' Friend, 134, 188, 204

Deaf presence, in literature, 13, 17,
18, 63, 64–67, 97, 100, 101, 172,
210; and Cooper, 80, 86, 88; and
Irving, 77, 78; and Melville, 88–
96

Deaf studies, 19

Derrida, Jacques, 44, 57, 204, 218–19
(n. 22)

Disability, 2, 3, 5, 14, 19, 100, 101, 209,
214 (n. 5), 221 (n. 2); and deaf
authors, 47, 155, 167, 220 (n. 33);
deafness perceived as, 37; and literary characters, 91, 116–17; and
passing, 183

Disability studies, 14, 19, 214 (n. 5), 221 (n. 2)

Disabled people, 6; deaf people's relation to, 14, 167, 218 (n. 15)

Double consciousness, 13, 35, 45, 132, 136, 169, 220 (n. 34)

Douglas, Mary, 103, 124

Douglass, Frederick, 23, 24, 32, 47, 219–20 (n. 28)

Du Bois, W. E. B., 65, 145; and color line, 2, 13; and double consciousness, 13, 35, 45, 132, 136, 220 (n. 34)

Edison, Thomas Alva, 4, 221 (n. 6), 226 (n. 1)

Edmundson, Mark, 112

Education, deaf, 2, 10, 11, 14, 47, 52, 62, 148, 164; and African Americans, 8, 34, 135, 214 (n. 6); and Brewster, 29, 217 (n. 10); and Burnet, 53, 58, 60, 203, 220 (n. 33); and Christian evangelicism, 16, 30, 103, 217 (n. 11); and Clerc, 26, 28–29, 31, 33–34, 39–41, 44–45, 203; and deaf-blind people, 220 (n. 33), 224 (n. 7); and English literacy, 44–45, 218–19 (n. 22), 219 (n. 25), 226 (n. 2); and Gallaudet-Clerc story, 33, 149, 216–17 (n. 8), 221 (n. 5), 224 (n. 6); and oralism, 16, 173, 204–5; and Twain, 230 (n. 5). *See also* Schools for deaf students

Ellison, Ralph, 1, 5, 65, 198

Emerson, Ralph Waldo, 81, 95, 223 (n. 13)

Emery, P. A., 162

Empire State Association of Deaf-Mutes, 165

English language
—spoken, 6, 83, 136, 205, 208, 216 (n. 2), 227 (n. 12). *See also* Black vernacular English; Oralism; Speech
—written, 13, 18, 28, 35, 49, 59, 133, 148, 216 (n. 4), 218–19 (nn. 22–23), 220 (n. 31), 220–21 (n. 1), 226 (nn. 2–3); and Americanization, 23, 173; appropriation of, by deaf authors, 25, 45–46, 52, 56–57, 143; as bridging gap between deaf and hearing, 43–44, 224 (n. 6); Burnet's efforts to convey sign with, 53, 55, 56; and deaf commonwealth debate, 154, 159–60, 162; and deaf expressions of inferiority, 152; as foreign language to deaf people, 24, 44, 133–34, 208; hearing authors' attitude toward, 88, 94; inability to convey sign language, 17, 55; inability to express deafness, 68; as language of power, 135; schools making more deaf people literate in, 2, 39, 40, 47, 58, 132, 217 (n. 10); as voice for deaf people, 22, 135

Epée, Abbé Charles-Michel de l', 11, 102, 217 (n. 11)

Ethnicity, 8, 15, 23, 48, 104, 175, 177, 188, 210; deaf signers as comprising, 14, 35, 61

Eugenics, 13, 232 (n. 3)

Fanon, Frantz, 131, 135–38, 141, 142, 147, 150, 153, 154, 160, 208

(((INDEX)))

Faux, William, 10

Filiation: in deaf commonwealth debate, 146, 157, 158–59; in deaf tributes, 146, 150–51; and Jewel, 147, 167; Said's theory of, 138–39

Finnegan, Ruth, 134

Fishkin, Shelley Fisher, 172

Flournoy, John Jacobus, 1, 5, 131, 146, 153–64, 165, 167, 169, 203, 205, 209, 210, 228–29 (nn. 17–19)

Foucault, Michel, 37, 40, 104, 147

Freud, Sigmund, 71, 74, 105, 106, 177, 178, 190, 191, 226 (n. 13)

Fuller, Margaret, 23, 135, 163, 219–20 (n. 28)

Gallaudet, Edward Miner, 7, 179, 229–30 (n. 4)

Gallaudet, Thomas Hopkins, 26, 28, 31, 33, 34, 37, 38, 39, 42, 55, 69, 83, 108, 138, 146, 148–51, 152, 156, 162, 173, 179, 215 (n. 14), 216–17 (n. 8), 217 (nn. 11–12), 221 (n. 5), 224 (nn. 5–6, 8), 227 (nn. 7, 12), 228 (n. 15), 231 (n. 1); "The Duty and Advantages of Affording Instruction to the Deaf and Dumb," 30, 47, 85, 103, 223 (n. 14); at tribute to (1850), 150

Gallaudet Guide and Deaf-Mutes' Companion, 151

Gallaudet monument, dedication of (1854), 148–51, 161

Gallaudet University, 4, 205, 209, 214 (n. 7), 215 (n. 10), 226 (n. 3). *See also* National Deaf-Mute College

Garland-Thomson, Rosemarie, 3, 100

Garrison, William Lloyd, 47, 96

Gates, Henry Louis, Jr., 13, 23, 28, 45, 57, 204, 219 (n. 26)

Gay people, 9, 102, 214 (n. 8); and homophobia, 125

Gee, James Paul, 55

Gender, 3, 5, 7, 8, 14, 64, 77, 81, 83, 104, 185; in deaf commonwealth debate, 157, 161; and hearing line, 14, 118, 134, 135, 161, 167, 172; and passing, 189, 196

Gibson, Nigel C., 142

Ginsberg, Elaine K., 171, 176

Girard, René, 104

Gitter, Elisabeth, 116, 213 (n. 4)

Glyndon, Howard. *See* Searing, Laura Redden

Gramsci, Antonio, 40

Greeley, Horace, 4, 139

Griffiths, Gareth, 25, 45

Groce, Nora Ellen, 29

Harris, Joel Chandler, 172, 193–94

Hawthorne, Nathaniel, 65, 96, 116

Hearing line, 2, 5–6, 35, 69, 129, 132, 151, 199, 203, 208, 210; and Bell, 205; and blackface minstrelsy, 191–92; and Chamberlain, 187–88; and class, 14, 189; and color line, 8, 13, 15–16, 18, 24, 83, 104, 118, 161, 189, 191–92, 216 (n. 4); and Cooper, 79, 88; and deaf presence, 64; efforts to demarcate, 182; efforts to eradicate, 16, 205, 211; and Flournoy, 153, 157; and gender, 14, 104, 118, 135, 161, 189; and Harris, 193; and Jewel, 147; and Melville, 125, 129;

and Native Americans, 222 (n. 9); and passing, 16, 18, 172, 175, 176, 186–88, 189, 199; and power, 15–16, 34, 199, 210; and race, 161; and reality, 6–8, 147; and schools, 39; sentimental depictions of, 106, 116; significance of, 2–3, 18, 211; and Swett, 187, 188, 198; and Twain, 129, 182, 183, 185–86, 194–95, 198, 199; and writing, 16–18, 22, 24, 107, 165, 204

Hearingness, 2, 5, 17, 18, 175; ambivalence toward, 82, 88; and biology, 7, 176; and Cooper, 78–88 passim; and deaf presence, 66; dependency on deafness, 13, 15, 68, 69, 76, 83, 96, 97, 104, 106, 108, 118; as ideology of superiority, 66, 78, 88, 94, 97, 107, 111, 113, 136–37, 173, 177, 199, 232 (n. 3); as invisible norm, 6, 66; as limiting, 81, 94, 97; and Melville, 94, 96, 122, 125; and passing, 176; as shunning deafness, 15, 119, 125; and Sigourney, 112, 113, 225 (n. 9); and Twain, 183; and whiteness, 66, 79, 81, 82, 83, 86, 232 (n. 3); and writing, 3, 17, 18, 22, 31, 132, 203

Hegel, G. W. F., 24

Hill, Barton, 116, 120

Hobbes, Thomas, 177

Howard University, 12, 215 (n. 12)

Howe, Samuel Gridley, 4, 244 (n. 7)

Humphries, Tom, 22, 37, 40, 216 (n. 2), 225–26 (n. 12)

Hybridity, 14, 25, 48; and Clerc, 28, 32

Irving, Washington, 3, 64, 67, 69, 78, 88, 94, 203, 221 (n. 5); "The Legend of Sleepy Hollow," 69, 70–73, 81, 112; "Rip Van Winkle," 69–71, 73–74, 75, 77–78, 112, 122

Isajiw, Wsevolod W., 15, 210

Jameson, Frederic, 17, 128

Jankowski, Katherine A., 10

Jaworski, Adam, 68

Jewel, Adele M., 135, 143–44, 169, 226 (nn. 4–5), 227 (n. 11); *A Brief Narrative of the Life*, 135, 146–48, 165, 167

Johnson, James Weldon, 182

Jordan, I. King, 209

Kawash, Samira, 176

Keller, Helen, 4, 179–81, 184, 220 (n. 33), 230 (nn. 5–6)

Kentucky school, 33, 188

Key, Francis Scott, 110–11, 116, 117

Kristeva, Julia, 17, 100, 104–6, 111, 112, 124, 128, 223–24 (n. 3)

Lane, Harlan, 115, 204, 216 (n. 7), 217–18 (n. 14), 218 (n. 20)

Lazarus, Emma, 95

Lepore, Jill, 23, 213 (n. 4)

Levine, Lawrence, 43

Lincoln, Abraham, 4, 164

Lipsitz, George, 66

Loring, George, 149

Lott, Eric, 172, 191, 192, 231 (n. 13)

Mairs, Nancy, 6

Manifest Destiny, 85

(((INDEX)))

Ong, Walter J., 55
Oralism, 6, 13, 42, 82, 173, 175, 188, 204–5, 209, 231–32 (n. 1)

Padden, Carol, 22, 37, 40, 216 (n. 2)
Passing, 3, 13, 18, 171–78, 181–82; deaf-as-hearing, 177, 178, 182–86, 187–88, 199, 200–201; gender, 189, 196; hearing-as-deaf, 177, 178, 188–98, 199; racial, 172, 176, 182, 189, 191–92
Peale, Charles Willson, 4, 27, 116
Pennsylvania Institution for the Deaf and Dumb, 33, 37; and Carlin, 139
Peters, Cynthia L., 56
Philbrick, Thomas, 82, 222 (n. 8)
Pity, 32, 34, 43, 52, 61, 108, 111, 187; Bergson's theory of, 111, 113
Plato, 9
Porter, Samuel, 163–64, 229 (n. 21)
Postcolonialism, 14, 25, 45, 158, 217–18 (n. 14)

Race, 2, 3, 5, 7, 8, 13, 14, 23, 47, 64, 65, 96, 118, 121, 134, 136, 175, 232 (n. 3); and hearing line, 161; in *The Last of the Mohicans*, 81, 83, 87; and miscegenation, 119, 125; and passing, 172, 176, 182, 189, 191–92
Racism, 13, 47, 125, 135, 214 (nn. 6–7)
Rae, Luzerne, 152
Ranger, Terence, 163
Redden, Laura. *See* Searing, Laura Redden
Religion, 3, 10–11, 30, 32, 43, 50, 65, 85, 87–88, 100, 101–3, 106, 146, 150, 217–18 (n. 14), 225 (n. 10); and

deaf education, 217 (n. 11); and Gallaudet, 37, 217 (n. 12), 231–32 (n. 1); and sentimental poetry, 108, 110–11, 112, 114–15, 116, 120
Resistance literature, 23, 154, 163
Reynolds, David S., 108, 176
Roediger, David, 191
Rogin, Michael, 96
Roscius, 188
Rousseau, Jean-Jacques, 82

Said, Edward W., 3, 37, 48, 129, 138–39, 157, 226 (n. 14)
Scheler, Max, 153, 155
Schools for deaf students, 33, 61, 95, 153, 164, 173, 216–17 (n. 8), 219 (n. 25), 227–28 (n. 14); as coloni-zation, 14, 37, 39, 48, 138–39; and deaf African Americans, 214 (n. 6); and deaf commonwealth debate, 156, 157, 161; and deaf empowerment, 32, 39, 60, 139; deaf people's gratitude for, 39, 146; and deaf women, 135; in Europe, 10, 11, 205; hearing people as co-founders of, 132, 150, 151; as home for deaf people, 137, 156; impact of, 12, 35, 39, 43, 47, 139; and oral-ism, 173, 204–5. *See also* American Asylum for the Deaf and Dumb; Education, deaf; Michigan school; New York Institution for the Deaf and Dumb; Pennsylvania Institu-tion for the Deaf and Dumb
Scott, Moses Y., 67, 103, 107–8, 117, 141, 203–4, 224 (n. 4)
Searing, Laura Redden, 4, 135, 167–69,

Slavery, 8, 10, 11, 12, 43, 96, 126, 230–31
(n. 10); and Booth, 160–61; Crafts'
escape from, 5, 177, 189–90; and
Douglass, 23, 24, 30, 47, 219–20
(n. 28); and Flournoy, 153, 160–61,
229 (n. 19); as metaphor for deaf
·people's condition, 37, 160–61;
and Wheatley, 30
Social Darwinism, 160
Sontag, Susan, 68
Speech, 4, 8, 14, 18, 24, 57, 103–4, 176,
193, 198, 204, 208; as arbitrary, 41;
and Cooper, 78, 79, 81–82, 87; and
deaf presence, 65, 66, 67; hearing
author's anxieties about, 101, 129;
and Irving, 70, 71, 76; as mark
of adulthood, 105; as mark of
humanity, 23, 24, 105, 225–26
(n. 12); and Melville, 88, 89, 93, 94,
123, 124, 125; and Native Americans, 222 (n. 10), 223 (n. 12); sign
as substitute for, 228 (n. 15); and
Sigourney, 112–13, 114–15, 225
(n. 9); and subalterns, 25; as superior, 23, 216 (n. 3); and Twain, 179,
182, 186, 195; versus sign, 13, 18,
208, 218 (n. 18), 218–19 (n. 22);
writing as substitute for, 17, 23, 43,
48, 203. See also English language—spoken; Oralism; Voice
Spivak, Gayatri, 25, 28
Spofford, Fisher Ames, 149
Stallybrass, Peter, 99, 128
Stanford, Raney, 92
Steiner, George, 23, 68
Steiner, Stan, 150
Stowe, Harriet Beecher, 95, 224 (n. 5)

Swett, William B., 134, 135, 186–87,
188, 198, 230–31 (n. 10)
Szwed, John F., 192

Thomson, Rosemarie Garland. See
Garland-Thomson, Rosemarie
Thoreau, Henry David, 68, 74–75
Tiffin, Helen, 25, 45
Todorov, Tzvetan, 37
Trachtenberg, Alan, 175
Turner, Frederick, 153
Twain, Mark (Samuel Langhorne
Clemens), 2, 3, 4, 64, 65, 100, 117–
18, 127, 129, 172, 178–86, 187, 188,
191, 192, 194–201, 229–30 (nn. 4–
6); Adventures of Huckleberry
Finn, 5, 117–18, 171, 179, 194, 195–
98; The Adventures of Tom Sawyer,
194–95, 231 (n. 14); Autobiography,
172, 179, 192, 200–201, 230 (n. 6);
Following the Equator, 230 (n. 5);
"How the Author was Sold in
Newark," 184–85; Life on the Mis-
sissippi, 178–79, 183–84; "A Little
Note to M. Paul Bourget," 185, 192;
"A Murder, a Mystery, and a Marriage," 186; Roughing It, 107, 188;
Speeches, 179, 181

Voice, 19, 21, 25, 204, 208, 211; and
Burnet, 50, 59, 61; and Carlin,
141; and Clerc, 22, 28, 29, 31, 32, 33,
34, 39–40, 47, 48–49, 61; and
Cooper, 79, 82, 87; of deaf people
in public discourse, 17, 35, 135, 161,
164; of deaf people speaking
vocally, 6, 143–44; of deaf shouter

(((INDEX)))

figures, 172, 182–83, 185, 187; dual meaning of, 22, 216 (n. 2); of hearing-as-deaf passers, 190, 194–95, 200; of hearing narrators, 94, 116, 127; and Irving, 71, 73, 77; and Nack, 50, 52, 53, 61; and Sigourney, 114; through writing, 22, 23, 62, 165, 203. *See also* English language—spoken; Oralism; Speech

Webster, Daniel, 96
Weld, Lewis, 83
Wheatley, Phillis, 30, 50, 52
White, Allon, 99, 128

Whiteness, 9, 65, 66, 75, 221 (n. 3), 232 (n. 3); and Cooper, 79, 83, 86; dependency on blackness, 13, 15, 104
Whitman, Walt, 64, 100, 106
Wiggin, Kate Douglas, 190
Women, 14, 43, 45, 54, 64, 66, 79, 87, 102, 105, 115–16, 118, 119, 125, 129, 135, 172, 175, 224 (n. 5), 227 (n. 6); and commonwealth debate, 156, 158, 161; and Fuller, 23, 163, 219–20 (n. 28); male fantasies of speechlessness of, 122, 225 (n. 11). *See also* Gender
Wrigley, Owen, 37, 39, 48